KU-391-958

The Encyclopedia of Desserts

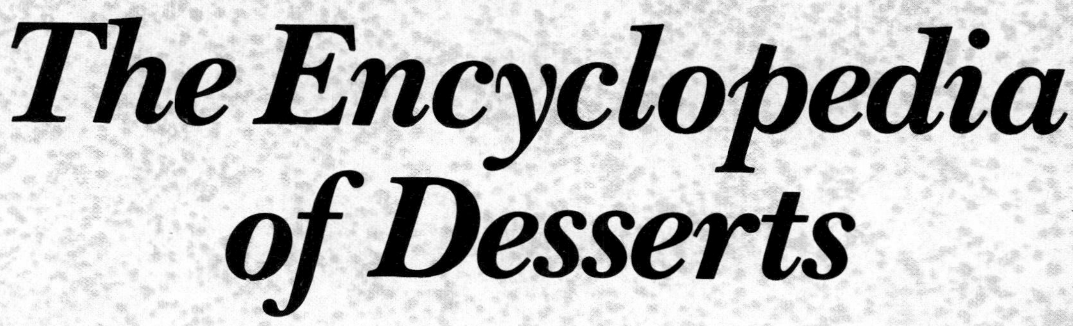

The Encyclopedia of Desserts

Emma Codrington
Michael Raffael

First published in 1983
by Octopus Books Limited
59 Grosvenor Street
London W1

ISBN 0 86273 085 6

Printed in England by
Severn Valley Press Limited

NOTES

1. All recipes serve 4 unless otherwise stated.
2. All spoon measurements are level.
3. All eggs are size 3 and 4 unless otherwise stated.
4. All sugar is granulated unless otherwise stated.
5. Preparation times given are an averate calculated during recipe testing.
6. Metric and imperial measurements have been calculated separately. Use one set of measurements only as they are not exact equivalents.
7. Cooking times may vary slightly depending on the individual oven. Dishes should be placed in the centre of the oven unless otherwise specified.
8. Always preheat the oven or grill to the specified temperature.

CONTENTS

General Introduction

Boxed recipes which feature in many of the chapters either provide the method for making up a standard ingredient of subsequent recipes, for example, Shortcrust pastry in the chapter of Perfect Pies, Flans and Pastries, or give the basic recipe for a particular type of dessert, on which other recipes in that chapter elaborate. For example, the basic Vanilla ice cream in the Ice creams and Frozen Desserts chapter.

The information given here on equipment, raw ingredients, special skills and professional techniques will help you get the most out of cooking, presenting and enjoying the wealth of recipes which follow.

Equipment

When baking desserts, it is important to know your own oven as the performance of it will affect all baked results. Keep it clean for reasons of hygiene.

When purchasing equipment, it is better to buy the best quality you can afford. The type of tin you use, particularly when baking pastries, will affect the cooked results. A coated aluminium baking sheet will slightly accelerate cooking times and encourage even browning as compared to a shiny tin surface.

A bain-marie is used in several recipes. It is a large roasting tin which is filled with hot water in which a smaller pan containing the food is placed for cooking. The water acts as a bath to cook the food gently and evenly.

The information on specific chapters details any special equipment needed.

Recipes

The notes copy on the inside front cover gives details of relevance to all recipes. It is worth stressing, however, that the metric and imperial measurements have been calculated separately and may vary in individual recipes. Use one set of measurements as they are not exact equivalents.

Certain raw ingredients are used time and time again in all varieties of desserts. They are common storecupboard items. The following details concern the different types available and any specialist uses.

Flours and Starches

Plain and self-raising white flour are the most common general purpose flours which are suitable for baking. They are known as soft flours. It is possible to buy special cake flours which have an even lower gluten (protein) content which will give a lighter and softer textured cake. To make plain or self-raising flour a little softer, reduce the flour in a recipe by one tablespoon and replace it with cornflour. Sift the two flours together before use. Self-raising flour has baking powder added by the manufacturer (about 2%). To make your own, baking powder can be purchased and sifted with plain flour in the proportions recommended on the label. However, it is hard to improve on the ready-mixed self-raising flour, which is thoroughly mixed to give an even texture. In an emergency you can also make your own baking powder by combining 2 parts cream of tartar with one part bicarbonate of soda. Strong white bread flour has a higher gluten content more suitable for puff pastry and brioche recipes. Wholemeal and 100% wholewheat flour can be used to make pastries, and gives an interesting change in flavour and texture. It also adds fibre to the diet. Both flours are used in the same way as white flour, but may need a little more liquid to bind.

Other flours and thickeners:
Cornflour is a useful thickening agent for custards. As a guide, 2 tablespoons of cornflour will thicken 600 ml (1 pint) of liquid. To use, the cornflour must be blended to a paste with a little of the cold liquid and stirred into the remaining boiled liquid. Return to the boil and stir constantly for 2–3 minutes.
Arrowroot, when mixed with boiling liquid, forms a clear jelly and can be used to thicken fruit sauces, glaze cheesecake toppings and fruit flans in particular. The resulting sauce or glaze is glossy and appealing. As a guide, 1 tablespoon of arrowroot will thicken 600 ml (1 pint) of liquid to make a glaze. Make as for cornflour custard. If using fruit juice, strain to remove any fibres. Use while still hot.
Rice flour is sometimes used in place of a little plain flour in biscuit recipes (e.g. shortbread) to make the texture extra short and "nutty".

Sugars

Sugar comes from sugar cane or beet, and only serves as a sweetener; some of the less refined sugars also add flavour.
Granulated sugar is the cheapest general purpose sugar on the market. Use it for making caramel and syrups.
Caster sugar is most commonly used in desserts because it dissolves quickly and aerates a mixture better when whipped with

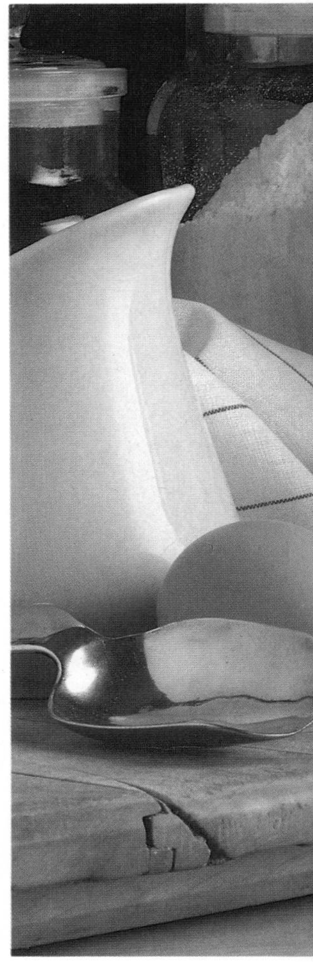

Sifting cornflour and self-raising flour together to make a softer cake flour

fat or eggs. Caster sugar can be made by grinding granulated sugar for a few seconds in a food processor or liquidizer. Caster sugar can be flavoured with a vanilla pod to make vanilla sugar. To make vanilla sugar, place a vanilla pod in a screw-top jar and fill with caster sugar. Leave to stand for 1–2 weeks. Top up with caster sugar as the flavoured sugar is used and shake thoroughly to ensure even flavouring.

Cube sugar is refined and crystallized sugar which is moistened and compressed into cubes. It is recommended for sugar boiling and caramel because of its purity.

Icing sugar is refined sugar ground to a powder. If stored in damp conditions it forms lumps. Keep in an airtight container and sift before use.

Demerara sugar is partly-refined sugar which is hard to dissolve and has less flavour than other soft brown sugars. It is ideal for sprinkling over baked desserts for a crunchy topping. Some demerara-type sugars are refined white sugars with added colour and have less flavour than the authentic.

Light and dark soft brown sugars are partially refined sugars and have more flavour than white sugar. They can replace white sugar except for sugar boiling and icing. The colour and flavour of the dessert will be altered.

Raw cane sugars have a distinctive treacle-like flavour and may be used in place of white sugar in recipes which do not require baking, for sugar boiling and for icings.

Other Sweeteners

Golden Syrup is a light-coloured syrup containing a variety of sugars with flavourings and colourings.

Treacle is the sticky fluid remaining after sugar cane has been processed. It has a pronounced flavour.

Maple Syrup has a distinctive but delicate flavour and is made from sugar derived from the sap of the maple tree. Flavoured syrups are available but are not as good.

Honey is available clear or solid. Flavour varies according to the type of honey and can be used for sweetening sauces and sorbets in particular.

Sugar Boiling

Sugar can be heated to much higher temperatures than water and will not start to burn until it reaches above 180°C (356°F). When sugar is boiled its character changes. First it becomes syrupy, then as the temperature rises, it gets thicker and sets to a soft consistency. The boiled sugar continues to change until it becomes a rich brown caramel which is hard and crisp when set.

Because each change happens at certain temperatures, it is possible to get good results even without a sugar thermometer.

Utensils

Choice of pan It is essential when boiling sugar to use a pan with a heavy base; thin ones will distort with the extreme heat. Aluminium, enamelled cast iron and stainless steel are good, or you may be lucky enough to own a copper sugar boiling pan. Copper pans are ideal for sugar boiling because copper will tolerate very high temperatures and transfers heat to the syrup evenly, particularly important when dissolving sugar and making caramel. The syrup or caramel will also keep its clear and pure appearance when boiled in a copper pan. Copper pans used for sugar boiling should not be tinned. Tin is the protective metal coating given to copper saucepans for general use. Copper is affected by general foods, fruits and vegetables and should always be cooked in tin lined pans. Sugar syrup does not harm copper but the high temperatures may affect the tin lining. Untinned copper pans, therefore, are used for sugar boiling and should always be reserved for this purpose only. Thin enamel pans and non-stick pans are not suitable because the high temperatures may blister and damage the surfaces.

Spoons Always use wooden spoons or spatulas. Metal spoons will scratch the pan and if the handles are metal, they can became very hot and cause burns. Plastic ones will melt.

Use and Care of a Sugar Thermometer Always keep a pan of boiling water on top of the cooker and place the thermometer in this before and after it is used in the syrup.

Make certain that the syrup always covers the bulb of mercury.

Stand the thermometer upright in the pan and ensure that the reading is taken at eye level.

After use, replace the thermometer in the pan of boiling water until it is clean, then rinse carefully in hot water and dry well. To store safely when not in use, keep it in a box in a drawer.

To clean the pan afterwards Allow the pan to cool, then fill with warm water. Cover with a lid and boil until all the sugar has dissolved. Empty the pan, then rinse in clear hot water. Dry thoroughly.

For successful sugar boiling

1. Use a perfectly clean pan.
2. Use a sugar thermometer.
3. Allow the sugar to dissolve slowly, stirring gently if necessary.
4. Make certain that all the sugar has dissolved before the syrup comes to the boil.
5. Never stir a boiling syrup unless a recipe states otherwise.
6. Wash any sugar crystals from the side of the pan with a clean pastry brush dipped into water.
7. Remove any scum which forms on the top of the syrup with a metal spoon.
8. Cook over a moderate heat unless told to cook gently.
9. Have patience. Sugar sometimes takes a long time to rise from one temperature to another and will then rise very rapidly indeed. When the correct temperature is reached, remove the pan from the heat immediately.
10. To keep sugar clear when boiling, add a small pinch of cream of tartar or a small squeeze of lemon juice.

Stages of sugar boiling

Sorbet syrup: 103°C, 215°F. About 1–2 minutes after the sugar reaches boiling point the bubbles in the boiling sugar reduce in size. Used in sorbets.

Thread: 107°C, 225°F. The sugar looks syrupy. Using a small spoon remove a little of the syrup and allow it to fall from the spoon on to a dish. The syrup should form a fine thin thread when the correct stage has been reached. Used in Brown bread ice cream.

Soft Ball: 113–118°C, 235–245°F. Drop a small amount of the syrup into cold water then mould into a soft ball with the fingers. Used for praline and hazelnut clusters.

Hard Ball: 119°–127°C, 246–260°F. Drop a little syrup into cold water, then using the fingers, mould into a ball which is firm but pliable. Used for butter cream and Italian meringue.

Caramel: 154–170°C, 310–335°F. The syrup becomes a light golden brown. As the temperature rises it gets darker in colour. If it becomes too dark, the flavour is bitter.

To prevent caramel from darkening, plunge the pan base containing caramel into iced water. Golden caramel can be poured onto a clean, heatproof surface and cooked until solid, then chipped into pieces for decoration and flavouring. After use, cool and fill the pan with warm water.

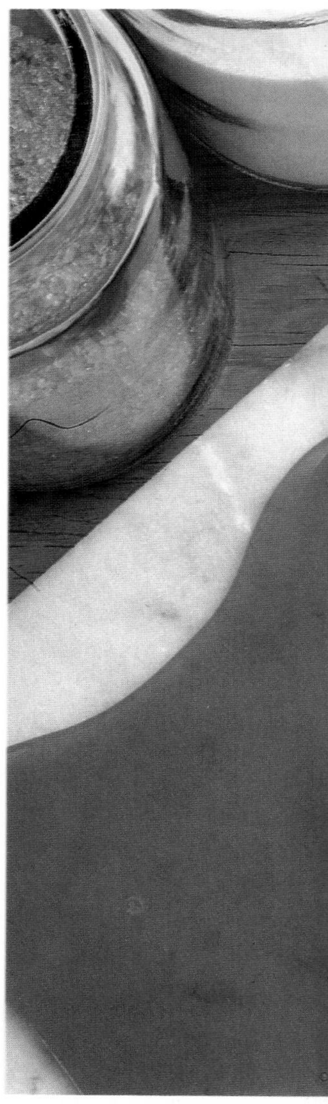

Dairy Products

Nearly all fresh milk has been pasteurized. Dried or evaporated milks are made from whole milk or skimmed milk. UHT (ultra heat treated) milk has been heated to a temperature above boiling point to give it a longer shelf-life. Sterilized, UHT and dried powder milks are useful storecupboard standbys but will affect the flavour of the dessert. For best results, always use fresh pasteurized milk.

Cream: Cream is an essential part of many desserts and the variety of creams available have different butterfat contents which affect the quality of the cream and its ability to be whipped. Double cream and whipping cream have higher fat contents than single, half or top of the milk creams. The former two will whip successfully. The latter can be used for pouring only.

Double cream is the most versatile cream. It adds richness and texture to the dish, will blend with other ingredients well, and can be whipped and piped onto gâteaux and cold desserts. You can make double cream go further by adding an equal amount of single cream or by folding in a whipped egg white in the proportion of 1 egg white to 600 ml (1 pint) of double cream. Extended double cream will not pipe successfully.

Home-made whipping cream can be made by cutting up 100 g (4 oz) of unsalted butter and adding it to 100 ml (3 fl oz) of full cream milk. Heat very gently until the butter has melted. Pour the mixture into a liquidizer. Give the mixture three 10 second bursts. Transfer to a bowl, cover and chill. Use when required.

Butter: For baking use the best quality and freshest unsalted butter you can find. Buy it in small quantities and use it up quickly, as it deteriorates in a short time even when stored in the refrigerator. Unsalted butter

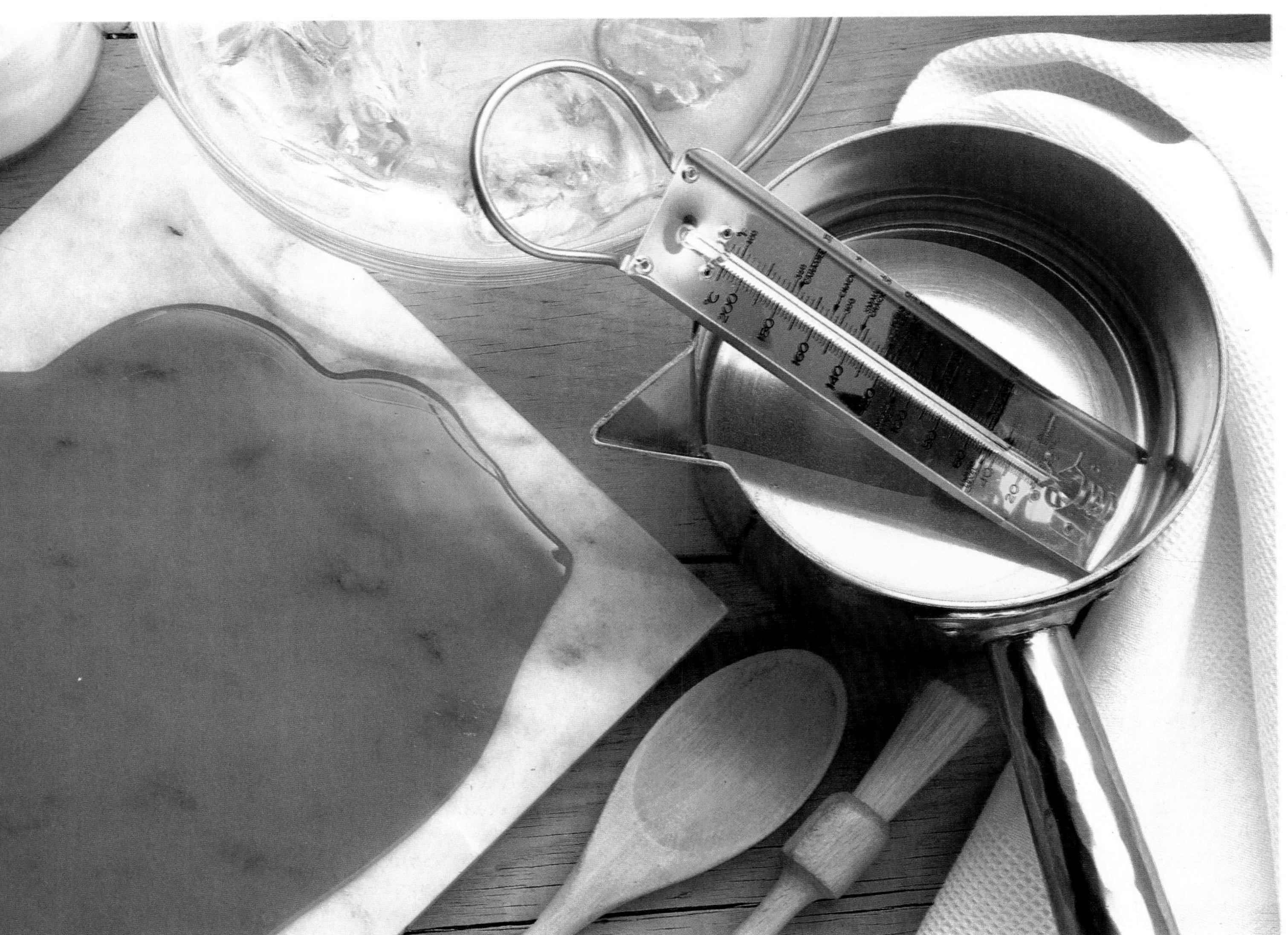

can be frozen for up to 6 months and salted butter for up to 3 months.

It is better but not essential to use clarified butter when greasing cake tins and flan rings in order that the food can be released from the tin more easily. Heat the butter gently in a small pan, skim the froth which rises to the surface and strain into a bowl, leaving the milky deposit in the bottom of the pan. Always keep a little clarified butter in the refrigerator for this purpose. Clarified butter is also good for making pancakes since it does not burn at as low a temperature as unclarified butter.

When making pastry, remove the butter from the refrigerator just before you need it.

When making cakes by a creamed method, the butter should be removed from the refrigerator and left to stand in a warm place to soften and creamed in a warmed mixing bowl.

Cheeses: See Cheesecakes (page 18)

Yogurt: is a milk by-product. It is homogenized, cooled and a special yogurt culture is added. It can be used as a substitute for cream where the latter does not have to be whipped, piped or used in baking. The results will be noticeably tart and less rich, but less fattening.

Eggs

When buying eggs from a supermarket check the date code to ensure they are fresh. At home you can judge how fresh an egg is by breaking it onto a plate: the yolk should sit up like an island surrounded by a sea of transparent white. As the egg ages, the yolk and white spread and the yolk is no longer in the centre of the white. When a recipe states "eggs, separated", make sure that the white is free from any trace of yolk or blood. These, even in minute quantities, will make it impossible to whisk the whites properly.

When separating eggs, ensure that the yolks are covered with clingfilm until used to prevent a skin forming.

Other Fats and Oils

Lard is used in pastry as an alternative to butter. It lacks the special flavour of the latter. Many grades of lard exist so take care to choose one which states on the packet that it is suitable for pastry. It is best used in partnership with butter to make very short pastry.

Suet: shredded suet can be bought in packets for use in steamed puddings. Fresh suet is preferable to the ready shredded variety for flavour. The best kind to buy from the butcher is beef suet found around the kidney area. When purchased fresh, it should be white and crumbly. Remove any skin, gristle or membranes before grating.

Hard Margarines are made either from vegetable oils or from animal fats and can be used in place of butter. The flavour of the dessert will be affected.

Soft margarines may be used in place of butter or hard margarines. They contain a high percentage of polyunsaturated fats and cream easily.

Oils: for deep-frying fritters, etc., choose a groundnut or sunflower oil both of which can be heated to high temperatures and are odourless and flavourless.

Gelatine

Gelatine is a setting agent. Follow a few basic rules for success every time. Powdered gelatine has been used throughout this book. Alternatively, if you prefer using leaf gelatine, 4 leaves soaked in water is the equivalent of one 15 g (½ oz) sachet of the powdered variety. 15 g (½ oz) of gelatine will set 600 ml (1 pint) of liquid.

To dissolve powdered gelatine:

1. Sprinkle the gelatine over about 50 ml (2 fl oz) of liquid in a small heatproof bowl.

2. Stand the bowl in a pan of hot water and heat gently, without boiling and stir until the gelatine has dissolved and has become clear. Hot gelatine can be added directly to any liquid, hot or cold and will not start to set until well below body temperature. Once cooled, 3–4 hours in the refrigerator will be sufficient to set most jellies, bavarois and cheesecakes.

Gelatine sets quite suddenly, therefore if a recipe requires cream and whisked whites to be added after the gelatine, a lighter texture will be obtained if these ingredients are folded in carefully and thoroughly, just as the gelatine starts to set.

Jellies do not freeze.

A selection of chocolate decorations. *From the left:* scrolls; rose leaves; bay leaves; curls

Flavourings, Colourings and Decorations

Chocolate

The amount of cocoa butter added to chocolate liquor during the manufacturing process depends on how the chocolate will be used.

Couverture chocolate has a high proportion of cocoa butter, a rich flavour and a brittle texture which needs repeated heating and cooling to melt it successfully, and is used mainly by professional confectioners.

Plain eating chocolate is made with chocolate liquor, cocoa butter, vegetable fats, sugar and flavour. It is recommended for flavouring desserts and making decorations, such as chocolate leaves.

Bitter chocolate may be used in place of plain chocolate, and has a strong, and slightly bitter chocolate flavour.

Milk chocolate contains similar ingredients to plain chocolate but some of the chocolate liquor is replaced with milk. It has a less strong 'chocolate' flavour and is less commonly used for flavouring desserts.

Dipping cooking chocolate contains an even higher proportion of vegetable fats than eating chocolate, and is used for making chocolate scrolls and curls.

To melt chocolate: break the bar into small pieces and place in a bowl. Stand the bowl over a pan of simmering water. Leave the chocolate to melt for a few minutes without stirring. When melted, remove from the heat. Chocolate thickens and tastes bitter if it becomes overheated.

Chocolate leaves: melt 50 g (2 oz) of plain dark chocolate in a bowl set over a pan of simmering water. Wash and dry a few rose leaves or small bay leaves. Dip the shiny side of the leaves in the chocolate and leave to dry on a sheet of non-stick silicone paper. When the chocolate is firm, peel off the rose or bay leaves carefully. Store in rigid boxes with soft tissue paper between each layer. Keep in a cool, dry place.

Chocolate curls: Hold a bar of chocolate over a board or plate and draw the blade of a vegetable peeler along the thin edge of the bar, allowing the curls to fall. Use to decorate desserts and gâteaux.

Chocolate scrolls: melt 100 g (4 oz) of cooking chocolate. Pour the chocolate onto a cool, clean surface, preferably marble, and spread it thinly over the surface. Cool until set. Using a large palette knife, shave the chocolate holding the knife at a 45° angle to the surface. The chocolate should roll up into scrolls.

Cocoa

If recipes specify cocoa powder always buy it unsweetened.

Coffee

Instant coffee can be dissolved in a little hot water for many recipes. A continental blend will taste stronger and better. However, if you make freshly ground coffee it will give a better result with a bavarois or a granité.

Spirits

When flavouring desserts with spirits, bear in mind that you need more spirit if you are going to cook it than if you are adding it as a flavouring at the last minute, as alcohol evaporates when heated. In ice creams 2 teaspoons added to the Vanilla ice cream recipe (page 88) will be enough to flavour it.

Good quality pays in the long run, for example, you can buy many brands of brown rum, but a 100° proof will have a better flavour and you will use less.

Spices
Cinnamon, ginger, nutmeg and vanilla pods are the spices most often used in dessert making, but the list can be extended to dozens. Just as you can give a personal touch to savoury cooking, so you can add a favourite spice to give character to a gâteau, a sorbet, a fruit salad or a pudding, for example, a bay leaf cooked with a rice pudding or 2–3 lightly crushed cardamom pods added to a sugar syrup. Discard the leaf or pods before serving. Buy ground spices in small quantities and store in airtight containers. Use sparingly.

Nuts

Almonds: are one of the most common nuts used in dessert cookery. Buy them fresh in their shells, whole with their skins on, skinned, nibbed (small pieces of blanched nut), flaked or ground. Slivered almonds are made from blanched almonds cut into narrow strips, lengthways. As a rule the more a nut has been processed the less flavour it has.

To blanch almonds, drop the almonds into boiling water for 15 seconds, drain and then squeeze the nuts out of their skins. Toasted flaked, chopped, slivered or nibbed almonds make an attractive decoration. Take great care when toasting nuts as they burn easily.

Chestnuts: need to have both the shell and the skin removed before poaching or eating. Slit the pointed end of the chestnuts, then place them on a baking sheet in an oven preheated to 190°C, 375°F, Gas Mark 5. Bake for 20–25 minutes. Take out of the oven, hold in oven gloves and peel with a sharp knife.

Coconuts: choose whole coconuts which contain some milk (test by shaking) and grate your own rather than buying desiccated coconut.

To prepare: drill three holes in the coconut, drain the milk and break the shell with a hammer. Toasted grated or shredded coconut makes an attractive decoration.

Pistachios: these nuts are very expensive. Buy them either in their shells or ready shelled. For dessert making ensure they are not salted. They should be crunchy and strongly flavoured.

Walnuts and pecans: are available fresh in their shells and ready shelled. On older walnuts the brown skin has a bitter taste.

Selection of shelled and unshelled nuts. *From the top:* walnuts; pistachios; almonds; chestnuts; coconut; hazelnuts; pecans

Buy whole fresh new-season walnuts, shell them, drop them in to boiling water for a few seconds, drain and remove the skins. Pecans are similar to walnuts in appearance, but have a more oily texture. To decorate, use walnuts or pecans halved or chopped.

Hazelnuts: are available fresh in their shells, ready shelled, with skins and skinned. To skin hazelnuts, bake them in an oven preheated to 200°C, 400°F, Gas Mark 6 for 10 minutes. Remove from the oven, tip them into a clean teatowel and rub off the skin. To decorate, use hazelnuts whole or chopped. Toast if preferred.

Decorating Desserts

The following information lists the various ingredients which can be added to desserts as decoration.

Basic mixtures suitable for decoration: Whipped cream, Crème Chantilly (page 189), Butter cream (page 188), Meringue (pages 41–49)

For most dessert and gâteau decorations a large nylon piping bag and large star nozzle is the most versatile. Use a plain nozzle for meringues, choux pastry and filling. Use small nozzles for butter cream.

Piping:

To fill a piping bag

1. Select the appropriate size and shaped nozzle. Drop the nozzle into the bag so that it protrudes beyond the bag opening.

2. Place the prepared bag, nozzle down into an empty jam jar or jug. Fold the top edge of the bag over the rim.

3. Spoon the mixture to be piped into the bag and push down well towards the nozzle. Half fill the bag. If you overfill a piping bag the contents are likely to squeeze out of the top once you start to pipe.

4. Squeeze the mixture downwards until a little comes through the nozzle.

5. Twist the remaining icing bag 2 or 3 times and hold securely while piping.

Piping Basic Designs:

Star: Hold the filled bag vertically just above the dessert surface. Apply pressure. Once the star is formed, stop squeezing and lift the icing bag cleanly away. Repeat.

Rosettes: Hold the piping bag as for stars, apply pressure and swirl the mixture in a spiral to form a mound, finishing in the centre. Stop squeezing and lift the bag.

A selection of decorative ingredients. *From the top:* angelica; strawberries; candied coffee beans; glacé cherries; piped cream

Shells: With a star or shell nozzle, hold the piping bag at an angle, and a little above the surface. Apply pressure, and begin by moving the nozzle away from you, keeping an even pressure, then back towards you with a little more pressure for the 'fat' part of the shell. Release pressure and pull off sharply to form a point. To make a shell edging, repeat the shells, linking them in a border by beginning the next shell over the tail of the previous one.
Scrolls: With a star or shell nozzle hold the piping bag as for shells with the nozzle just above the surface. Work a question mark shape, beginning with a fairly thick head and gradually releasing the pressure while finishing off the long pointed tail. Scrolls can be used as a border, piped in the same direction or as alternating scrolls.
Coils: With a star nozzle hold the piping bag just above the cake surface. Apply pressure and continue making circular movements in an anti-clockwise direction.
Rope: With a star nozzle hold the piping bag above the cake surface. Apply pressure and make small zig-zag movements.
Flavourings: For flavouring mixtures and creams, use only those that will dissolve, for example coffee dissolved in a little hot water, spirits or essences but not nuts which will block the nozzles.
Colourings: When using vegetable food colourings never pour the colour straight from the bottle. Place a skewer into the bottle and add a drop at a time. If the colouring bottle has a squeezing nozzle, squeeze the colour onto a teaspoon and transfer to the mixture. Mix well.
Glacé cherries are a colourful and useful decoration either halved or quartered. Use especially on children's desserts.
Angelica combines well with glacé cherries, and can be cut into attractive diamond shapes to look like leaves.
Candied coffee beans can be bought from delicatessens or food specialist shops and are a novel decoration for coffee desserts.
Fresh fruit It is always worth buying a little extra fresh fruit for decoration when making elaborate desserts or gâteaux.
Dredging Some desserts such as a chocolate gâteau can look very effective dredged with a little icing sugar, rubbed through a sieve or clean tea strainer.

For a really impressive result, try cutting out a template of a design, such as a bell, and place it on the gâteau. Dredge with icing sugar, then remove the template to leave an attractive and unusual effect.

Trifles, Jellies and Creams

When serving cold desserts, never serve them directly from the refrigerator. The cold will dull the flavour so leave them to stand in a cool place for at least ½ hour before serving.

A jelly-based dessert should never set too firm as it will be unpalatable. It should be clear and should just shiver—barely set. Again do not serve directly from the refrigerator.

Cream, milk and eggs give the creams and bavarois their silky smooth texture. When making a custard base, it is essential that it should be absolutely smooth. Custards should be thickened very gently with continuous stirring.

When folding delicate whipped egg whites and partially whipped cream, use a metal spoon or rubber spatula and fold in a figure of 8 motion to ensure complete mixing and avoid knocking air out.
To unmould a jelly or a bavarois, prepare a bowl of hot water. Lower the mould into the water until it nearly reaches the top. Dry the mould then free the edges from the mould with a knife or light finger touch. Invert the serving dish over the mould, then turn both the plate and mould upside down. Give a sharp shake to release and lift off the mould.

Piped and coloured decorations should be kept simple and are most effective.

Magical Meringues

Meringue is a mixture of egg white and sugar, and is thought to have been invented in the early 18th century by Gaspanni, a Swiss pastrycook, in the town of Mehninyghen.

Meringues are not difficult to make and are ideal for party meals. By adding nuts, coffee essence, cocoa, lemon zest and colouring one can change the basic merginue into many different desserts. The cooking method substantially alters the texture of meringues so that baked meringues are crisp, whereas poached meringues are soft and fluffy.

There are 3 basic types of meringue: Swiss meringue, meringue cuite (cooked meringue) and Italian meringue.
Swiss meringue is the simplest to prepare. The whites are whisked until very stiff, using a hand balloon, or rotary whisk. An electric whisk will take a great deal of time and effort out of whisking. Half the sugar is then whisked in until the mixture is thick and glossy. The remaining sugar is then

A selection of jelly moulds. *In the foreground:* Strawberry cream jelly (page 178)

folded in taking care not to knock out the air. Use this meringue to pipe meringue "shells' and fill with whipped cream, see Meringue Chantilly on page 45.

Avoid overwhisking egg whites and over-folding the sugar or else the meringue will dissolve into a syrup and will not hold its shape while cooking.

Meringue cuite (cooked meringue) is not strictly cooked as it is not cooked in the making. It is firmer than Swiss meringue and is used for baskets and shells.

The egg white and icing sugar are whisked together in a bowl set over a pan of simmering water until thick and glossy.

Italian meringue is similar to meringue cuite but is a lighter and finer mixture. It requires skill in making as a sugar syrup has to be made and cooked to the hard ball stage (page 8) then poured on to stiffly whisked egg whites, whilst whisking continuously until thick and glossy.

The nut meringues are basically Swiss meringue, however all the sugar is beaten into the whisked egg whites gradually and not folded in. Nut meringue is cooked at a higher temperature and makes a delicious dessert sandwiched with fruit and cream.

When making meringues, the use of non-stick silicone paper is a fool-proof guard against meringues sticking. Alternatively, use thoroughly greased greaseproof paper, which has been dusted with flour.

Leftover meringue can be piped or spooned into small shells and baked alongside the main meringue. When completely dried out and cooled they can be stored in an airtight tin for 4–6 weeks.

Collapsed meringue: if meringue does not turn out as planned; it can break or can be too soft, try crushing the meringue and mixing it with lightly whipped cream and chopped fresh or drained canned fruit, turning it into a whipped cream pudding.

All Manner of Mousses

Most cooked soufflés are based on a roux based sauce such as crème pâtissière, or on an arrowroot or cornflour sauce, or may be entirely starch-free.

The skill of soufflé making lies in the way you handle the whisked egg whites (sometimes with the addition of caster sugar which helps them to retain the air). In most recipes they are whipped to stiff peaks.

Egg whites are best folded into the basic mixture with a rubber spatula or a metal spoon. Do not press or squash the whites but cut through and fold until blended.

Butter the mould with clarified butter. To give a hot soufflé a crisp edge, line the moulds with sugar. Chilling the mould before filling and baking makes the top rise more evenly.

When filling a soufflé mould, fill to just below the rim and smooth the surface. It can be left to stand for about 1 hour before baking. Once baked, cooked soufflés cannot wait, because the unsupported mixture which has risen above the rim of the dish slowly collapses. It takes about 3 minutes between taking the soufflé from the oven and serving it before it starts to collapse. A perfectly cooked soufflé should be a little moist at the bottom.

Uncooked soufflés or mousses are made to look like cooked soufflés as the mixture stands above the rim of the dish. A greaseproof or non-stick silicone paper collar is wrapped around the rim of the dish and should be wide enough to stand about 5 cm (2 inches) above the rim of an individual ramekin and about 7.5 cm (3 inches) above

Right: Uncooked soufflé mixture being poured into the soufflé dish prepared with a collar of greaseproof paper. *Left:* Once set, the paper collar can be removed to reveal the soufflé standing above the rim of the dish.

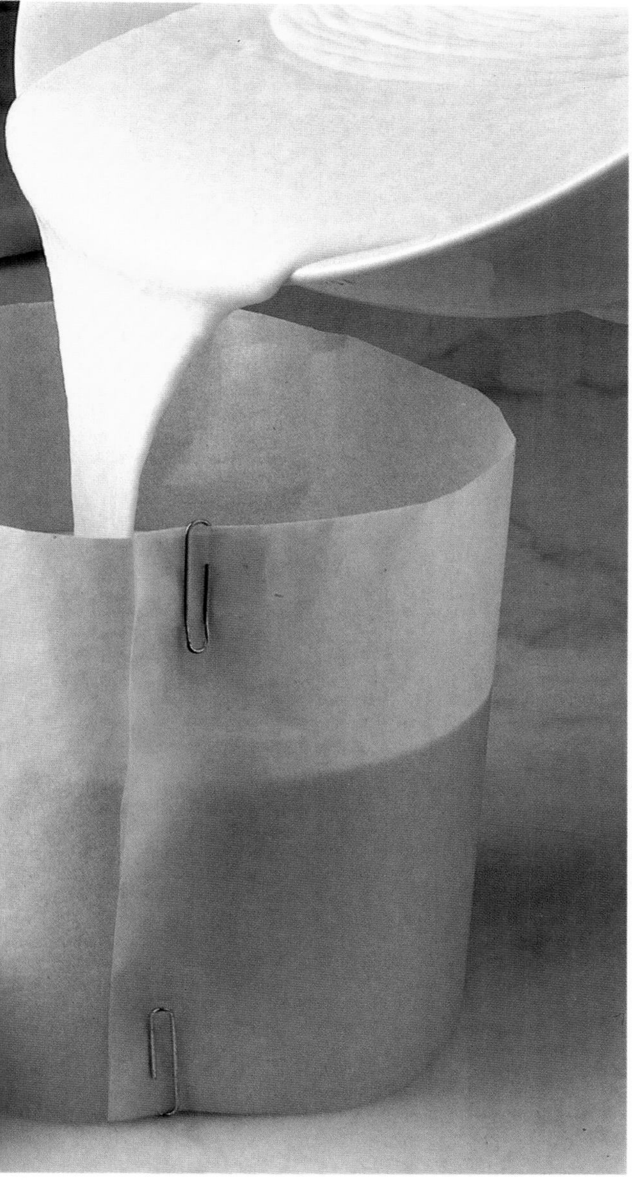

a larger dish. The collar supports the gelatine mixture until it has set.

To remove the collar, run a warm palette knife between the mixture and the mousse taking care not to drag the mixture and spoil the clean edge of the mousse. Peel the paper off without damage.

Fruit snows are very light and use egg whites only. For perfect soufflés, mousses and snows the egg whites should be beaten by hand with a balloon or coil whisk. Rotary whisks or electric whisks do not achieve as great or as light a volume.

When adding cream, this should also be lightly beaten. This helps to give the sweet its light texture. Cold mousses and snows are best eaten on the day they are made. Mousses in particular lose their lightness and tend to become stiffer.

Fresh Fruit Desserts

When choosing fruit always make sure that the fruit is fully ripe or the flavour and appearance of the dessert will be poor. As a guide, look for a good bloom and rich colour on the skin, and a good fresh, fruity smell. Avoid choosing fruit with shrivelled skins, with the exception of passion fruit, when the wrinkled skin is actually an indication that it is ripe and ready to eat.

Remember that bananas, avocados, apples and pears discolour once they have been peeled or cut. A little lemon juice squeezed over them retards discoloration but they are best used as soon as possible.

Black and redcurrants can be removed from their stems with a fork. The stems of the bunches are placed between the prongs and currants pulled gently into a bowl.

Citrus fruit: oranges, lemons, grapefruit, etc. The rind of most citrus fruit has been chemically treated. If a recipe calls for its use, scrub the rind hard under running cold water before grating or zesting.

Grapes are much nicer if they have been peeled, halved and seeded. The seedless varieties make life much easier and need not be skinned.

The Kiwi fruit (or Chinese gooseberry) has a hairy brown skin which is peeled. Trim both ends and slice the bright green flesh. They have a refreshing, tangy flavour.

Kumquats are very small orange fruits shaped like a large olive. They are eaten whole and have a strong, acquired taste.

Lychees have a delicate flavour and are ripe when the skin is a reddish colour. To peel them, pinch the outer skin to crack it and peel it off. Remove the black stone and serve chilled. When in season substitute fresh for canned lychees if desired.

Mangoes have a tough skin which must be peeled. An unripe mango is bright green and as it ripens it becomes yellow then orange. African varieties turn red when fully ripe. It has a sweet delicate flavour. Once peeled, the flesh is cut lengthways along its large stone.

Minneolas are a cross between a variety of grapefruit and tangerine. They are sweet and sharp with a strong aromatic flavour. They have a bell-like shape and are peeled easily.

Passionfruit is sliced in half and the pulp scooped out with a teaspoon. This aromatic fruit is a wonderful addition to a fruit salad or fruit purée.

To remove the outer skins of peaches, nectarines or apricots, plunge into boiling water and blanch for about 30 seconds before peeling. Once peeled, place in cold water with a generous squeeze of lemon juice to prevent discoloration.

Unless absolutely necessary, avoid washing raspberries or strawberries as this impairs the appearance and flavour.

Peeling and segmenting fresh grapefruit or oranges

To peel

1. Hold the fruit firmly with the tips of the fingers on a board.

2. Cut a thin slice from both ends of the fruit until the flesh just shows.

3. Place the fruit, cut side down on a plate. With a sawing action cut the pith and peel off in strips to reveal the flesh.

4. Trim any remaining pith.

To segment

1. Insert a knife between each segment, close to the membrane, and cut through to the centre.

2. Work the knife under the segment and up against the next membrane to release it.

3. Continue separating each segment in the same way.

Julienne of Orange, Lemon or Grapefruit for decoration

1. With a vegetable peeler, peel off strips of the fruit rind, ensuring that no pith is removed.

2. Cut the rind into very fine matchstick strips with a very sharp knife.

3. Place the strips in a small pan of cold water. Bring to the boil, and simmer for 2 minutes then plunge into ice cold water.

4. Drain, then dry on paper towels.

Lemon, orange and lime twists

Thinly slice a lemon. Cut each slice to the centre, then twist each cut edge in opposite directions.

Dried fruit: many fruits are dried. For desserts the most commonly used are apricots and prunes. Turkish or Californian apricots are often of good quality; they should be brightly coloured and without blemishes. Prunes (Californian or French *pruneaux d'Agen* are good) should be soft and glossy-skinned.

Choice Cheesecakes

Cheesecakes can be made with curd cheese, full fat soft cheese, low fat soft cheese or sieved and blended cottage cheese. The difference in texture between these cheeses and the final result is slight but noticeable. Cottage cheese and low fat cheesecakes will be lighter and curd and full fat soft cheese will give richer results. When making cheesecakes use springform tins or deep loose-bottomed cake tins.

Cooked cheesecakes

Before putting the cheesecake base into the tin, brush the base and sides with an odourless, flavourless oil such as sunflower or groundnut oil. Spread the mixture making up the base evenly, pressing it well into the angle of the tin so that the filling will not leak during cooking.

To make a cooked cheesecake as light as possible beat or whisk the basic cheese,

On board, bottom row, left: peeled zest from an orange; julienne strips; lemon twists; lemon slices; lemon
Centre row, from the left: an orange with zest peeled; an orange with pith and zest removed ready for segmenting; orange segments
Top left: blanched juliennes in ice-cold water to curl
Left: Oranges in Grapefruit and Caramel (page 65)

sugar and egg yolk mixture for about 5 minutes before adding the cream and egg whites. The cream should be lightly whipped and the egg whites whisked to stiff peaks to obtain the maximum volume. Fold into the mixture and incorporate them with a metal spoon or rubber spatula.

When cooked the cheesecake can be cooled in the oven which has been turned off and the door left ajar. Cheesecakes rise a little like a sponge cake but sink on cooling.

Uncooked cheesecakes are cheese-based mousses and the technique of adding the gelatine, cream and eggwhite is the same as for a mousse. The base is the same as for the cooked cheesecake, but does not need cooking.

To unmould, free the cheesecake from the edges of the tin with a thin bladed knife or unclip the springform mould. If using a loose-bottomed cake tin, place the cheesecake over a wide-necked jar and push the sides of the tin downwards leaving the cheesecake freestanding on top of the jar. Push a metal spatula or cake slice between the base of the tin and the cheesecake and slide it onto a serving dish.

An uncooked cheesecake can be prepared in a porcelain tart dish and served direct from the tart without moulding.

Ice Creams and Frozen Desserts

Maybe we hesitate to make ice creams and sorbets because we do not own a special machine? Perfectly good ices can be made without electric equipment and it is actually questionable whether domestic machines give a better result than hand-made ice cream.

Equipment Ice cream and sorbets need to be beaten during freezing, so choose a mixing bowl with a rounded edge. This prevents ice crystals forming in the corners.

Most freezer compartments are set at − 18°C. This is cold enough to freeze any ice cream or sorbet. If you are using the ice box of a refrigerator, turn the refrigerator to its coldest setting.

Ices take different lengths of time to freeze. A granité or a sorbet made with fruit purée freezes quite quickly, maybe in a couple of hours at − 18°C. If, however, you add alcohol, freezing may take much longer. An extra sweet ice also takes considerably longer to freeze to the firm stage.

Ice creams

Most ice creams are made with a custard and cream base. Always let hot custard cool before adding extra flavouring or whipped cream. Never place in the freezer until completely cold. Leave the freezing custard in the freezer until it has almost set hard. Take it out of the freezer then scrape the ice cream from the edges towards the softer centre of the bowl. Beat it thoroughly until the crystals have broken down. Ice cream expands during freezing and beating as air is incorporated into the mixture. Refreeze until fully set. When making ice creams for the first time, beat the ice cream 2 or 3 times during the setting period in order to obtain the smooth texture you are looking for. In this case beat it once when the edges start to freeze and thereafter at one hour intervals, probably twice more before it is fully set.

Fill the ice cream scoop with the mixture before releasing the ball.

Sorbets and granités
These are a mixture of fruit purée and syrup or wine and syrup or alcohol and syrup. Sorbets are only as good as the raw materials. Liquidized tinned peaches and turned into a sorbet will still taste of tinned peaches. For fruit sorbets, clear honey is a good alternative to the standard sugar syrup (page 95). It brings out the flavour of the fruit very well.

Several sorbet recipes include the addition of egg whites, which lighten the mixture. Beat sorbets hard before they freeze to disperse and smooth the ice crystals.

Granités are different from sorbets in that the resulting larger ice crystals are intentional. It is best to freeze granités in a shallow tray. Check the mixture after an hour, scrape the crystals around the edges into the centre but do not beat. Return the tray to the freezer and repeat the process every 30 minutes until the granité has set. Then carefully fork through the frozen crystals so that they do not form a hard lump of frozen ice.

Parfaits and frozen soufflés and mousses
These richer versions of ice cream are not made with a cooked custard but with whipped double cream. When a recipe indicates that you should whisk the yolks and sugar until thick and creamy, this may take almost 10 minutes in an electric machine and longer by hand.

To serve frozen desserts:
Transfer the ice cream or sorbet from the freezer to the refrigerator 15–30 minutes before serving so it can be scooped.

An ice cream scoop is a worthwhile investment. To serve, have a jug of cold water ready. Dip the scoop into the water then into the ice cream. When the scoop is full, level the surface with a knife. Release the ice cream into a serving dish or coupe (an individual stainless steel bowl traditionally used for serving ice cream) then dip the scoop back into the water and repeat.

Home-made ice cream can be stored for several weeks but is best eaten within a few days of making when its aroma and flavour are best.

Do not refreeze ice cream once it has melted as there is a danger of food poisoning.

Sorbets containing alcohol take longer to freeze and will melt quickly when exposed to room temperature. Keep all serving utensils and serving dishes chilled and serve immediately once portioned.

Pancakes, Waffles and Sweet Omelettes

The basic pancake, waffle and fritter batter is made with eggs, flour and milk.

The batter must be completely smooth. This is achieved by gradually incorporating the flour, eggs and a little of the milk and beating until thoroughly blended. The remaining milk is then stirred in. If any lumps form, strain through a sieve or make the batter in a liquidizer.

The pancake pan: The pancake pan should be small, with a base of 15 cm (6 inches) in diameter. The characteristic shallow sides of the pan about 2 cm (¾ inch) makes tossing easier. A small omelette pan can be used as an alternative.

Proving: A new pancake pan will need proving before using. Wash and dry the pan, pour in a generous amount of oil and heat it until it begins to darken and smoke. Remove the pan from the heat and allow to cool. Pour away the oil and wipe the pan dry with paper towels. It is now ready for use. After proving, never wash a pancake or omelette pan. If any mixture sticks to the pan rub it off with salt and oil with a dry cloth and paper towels.

To cook pancakes: Oil the pancake pan and place over a moderate heat. When hot, pour in enough batter to cover the base.

Thin pancakes need to be handled with care. Have a palette knife at the ready to free the edges. Brown on the second side.

Once cooked, stack the pancakes on a warmed plate until required.

Stored in an airtight container, they will keep in the refrigerator for about 3 days or several months in a freezer interleaved with greaseproof paper.

Waffle Irons: There are two types of waffle iron. The cast-iron type which is heated over a cooker, or the electric waffle iron which cooks both sides of the waffle.

In each case the waffle iron is brushed with melted butter, and the batter is ladled onto the bottom grid to barely fill it. The iron is closed, excess batter that oozes out is discarded and it is cooked until golden.

Batters are cooked in other ways such as the traditional French batter pudding clafoutis (page 109).

Sweet Omelettes do not contain flour. The eggs are separated and the yolks and whites are whisked independently to create an omelette similar in lightness to a soufflé. Sweetening and flavouring with liqueur makes a delicious dessert ready in minutes.

Perfect Pies, Flans and Pastries

Five types of pastry are included in the recipes of this chapter: shortcrust, puff, choux, pâte brisée and pâte sablée. As well as describing these variations, the following information will give you some helpful general guidelines for whatever type of pastry you are making.

It is essential to work in a cool kitchen, hence the marble topped work surface found in old kitchens and now often introduced into modern fitted kitchens. Marble stays cold and is a useful surface for rolling out pastry and, in some cases, for mixing the dough on. If the fat becomes too hot, it will melt into the flour and spoil the result.

When warm, the pastry readily sticks to the work surface when rolled. To prevent this extra flour is sprinkled on to the work surface which the pastry then absorbs and which may alter the character of the pastry.

In hot conditions, chill all mixing utensils. Keep rinsing your hands and wrists under running cold water before handling pastry. Iced water is not essential for good pastry, unless the weather is hot and the tap water tepid.

Resting: Flour contains protein (gluten) which toughens and becomes elastic the more it is kneaded. A flan ring lined with freshly rolled pastry and baked immediately will shrink. Resting the pastry in a cool place for about 30 minutes before baking will allow the pastry to relax and it will be less likely to shrink.

Rolling: Pastry will harden if refrigerated for too long. Before rolling it should be cool but supple. Sprinkle the work surface lightly with flour. Give the pastry a couple of rolls, turn it through 90° and reroll. Continue rolling and turning until the pastry is about 4–5 mm (¼ inch) thick. When rolling do not stretch the pastry by rolling too hard. A good heavy rolling pin will do most of the work without you having to press too hard. Roll in one direction only.

To line a flan ring

1. Butter a 20 cm (8 inch) flan ring if liked, and place on a buttered baking sheet.

2. On a floured work surface, roll the pastry into a circle which will extend at least 4 cm (1½ inches) beyond the ring all round.

3. Lift the pastry into the ring rolled over the rolling pin and ease into the angle at the base of the ring and press the pastry onto the sides with a floured finger. Roll the rolling pin across the top of the flan ring to trim the extra pastry.

Pricking the base of a tart When pastry bakes any air trapped under the pastry base will swell and force up the pastry like a blister. Pricking the pastry all over with a fork allows any air to escape and the base remains flat.

Baking blind

Oven: 200°,C, 400°F, Gas Mark 6

1. Cut out a circle of buttered greaseproof paper 8 cm (3 inches) larger than the flan ring diameter.

2. Line the inside of the pastry with the paper and fill with haricot beans, rice or ceramic beads.

3. Bake according to the recipe or in a preheated oven for 15–20 minutes.

4. In some recipes it will be necessary to remove the paper and beans then complete the baking. Cool and store the beans. They can be used repeatedly.

Removing pastry from a flan ring Pastry shrinks during baking however well it has been made. In most cases it will be simple to lift the flan ring from the cooked pastry. Sticking may occur if the filling has bubbled over the edges. Free the pastry from the ring with a sharp, thin-bladed knife.

Pie lids Always make a hole in the middle of the pie lid to let the steam escape. Use a pie funnel which is placed in the centre of the pie dish and sticks up through the hole. This gives the pastry a good shape. Alternatively shape a double-thickness of foil round a finger, then fit it, like a chimney through the hole in the centre of the pastry.

Crimping the edges Special crimping tweezers can be purchased to seal two pastry edges together. However, the simpler technique of sealing and decorating the edges of a pie is as follows:

1. Brush one of the two pastry edges with water.

2. Press to seal the edges together.

3. Knock the edges with the blunt side of a knife dipped in flour, to give a flaked appearance to the pastry.

4. Flute the edges by pressing down with the thumb on the edge of the pastry and drawing the blunt edge of the knife upwards at 2.5 cm (1 inch) intervals around the flaked edge of the pie.

Lattice patterns

1. Roll out the pastry trimmings a little longer than the tart's diameter.

2. Cut them into 1 cm (½ inch) strips. Lay half the strips parallel over the tart.

3. Lay more parallel strips at right angles to the former.

Glazing pastry The most attractive and

Roll pastry on a floured surface with a floured rolling pin. Press the pastry into the angle of the ring without stretching. Prick the base with a fork. Line the case with greased greaseproof paper and fill with beans before baking blind.

golden glaze on pastry is egg yolk lightly beaten with a teaspoon of water. Whole egg, beaten, or milk and a little sugar can also be used. Make sure the pastry surface is moist before applying lattice decoration otherwise the strips will not stay in place during cooking. If the top of the pastry is well coloured before the baking time is completed, place a sheet of foil over the pastry to prevent the glaze from burning.

Pâte brisée is a crisp, crunchy pastry, which has a biscuit-like quality. The pastry becomes golden brown when baked. This pastry is suitable for continental fruit tarts. The traditional French way to make this pastry is on a board.

Shortcrust pastry is the traditional English pastry. It should melt in the mouth and have a delicately tinted colour. As it is quick to make and easy to shape and bake, it is frequently made into pies, tarts, pastries and tartlets.

Puff pastry is the lightest and richest of all the pastries and rises in a dramatic way. Home-made puff pastry is unrivalled for taste and texture, but ready-made puff pastry can be purchased as a short cut. The weight of pastry given in the recipe refers to the prepared total weight, and not the weight of the raw ingredients. Puff pastry is best made with strong white flour. The amount of water which the flour will absorb varies from brand to brand, so it is advisable to reserve 65 g (2½ oz) of the flour in the recipe and then add it to the flour and water base if it seems to be too wet. Use puff pastry for pies, turnovers and tarts.

Pâte sablée is a sweet, rich, biscuity pastry used almost exclusively for flans. Trimmings can be rolled out, cut into triangles or circles, brushed with milk and dusted with sugar and then baked in a hot oven preheated to 200°C, 400°F, Gas Mark 6 for about 10 minutes and you will have a ration of tea biscuits.

Choux pastry: For best results, weigh and measure the ingredients accurately. Ensure the butter has melted before the water starts to boil. The water must boil before the flour is added.

Traditional Steamed and Baked Puddings

Steamed puddings are part of the English dessert tradition dating as far back as the medieval times, when they were a rich mixture of meat, fruit and spices bound together and wrapped in cloth.

Now these great desserts are all made of sweet ingredients apart from the beef suet which is added to such desserts as Christmas pudding and Spotted Dick.

When steaming, the pudding does not actually come into contact with the boiling water but only with its vapour. A steamer is normally used, a container with perforations at the bottom and a close fitting lid. Some steamers have a graduated ridged base so that they will fit onto a variety of saucepans.

Alternatively, the pudding basin can be lowered directly into a saucepan two-thirds filled with boiling water.

A pudding can also be boiled, such as Christmas pudding and jam roly poly. The pudding is wrapped in floured greaseproof paper then in a large piece of cotton or muslin which has been washed and boiled, and secured into a ball or roll shape and immersed and cooked in boiling water. Boiled puddings tend to be heavier than steamed, and cook for a shorter time.

The lightest steamed sponge puddings are those where the butter and sugar are creamed together.

Suet puddings should be rich and light. To obtain a really light texture, try adding 25–50 g (1–2 oz) of fresh white breadcrumbs in place of some of the flour.

General method to cook steamed puddings:

1. Grease a boilable pudding basin with melted butter.

2. Cut and grease a disc of greaseproof paper to fit the base.

3. Fill the basin to about two-thirds full with the pudding mixture.

4. Grease a piece of greaseproof paper and pleat it to allow for expansion.

5. Cover with a piece of boilable cloth or aluminium foil. Secure around the rim of the basin with string.

6. Make a handle with the loose ends of the cloth, with a piece of string or place a strip of foil of several thicknesses under the basin so the pudding can be lifted out of the pan.

To steam:

1. Place the pudding in a large pan, two-thirds full of boiling water.

2. Cover and steam over a low heat for the

A selection of ingredients used in a Christmas Pudding. *On the board from the left, clockwise:* glacé cherries; candied papaya; fresh grapefruit; grated grapefruit rind; dried dates *From the back, clockwise:* raisins; dark brown sugar; sultanas

cooking time given in the recipe.
3. Top up with hot water if necessary during the cooking time.

When the pudding has cooked, it will have risen to the top of the basin and will feel firm to the touch.

Foil pudding basins can be used and reduce the cooking time by about 10–15 minutes. Choose the specially treated foil basins for Christmas Puddings which are to be stored for long periods.

To serve:
Remove the string, foil and paper.
Invert a warmed serving dish over the pudding. With oven gloves, turn the pudding upsidedown with the plate.
Shake to release the pudding, then lift off the basin. Remove the disc of greaseproof paper. Serve with custard, cream, syrup, fruit or flavoured sauces.

A pressure cooker and microwave cooker can be used to reduce cooking times of puddings. To cook, follow the manufacturer's instructions. Remember that foil or metal rimmed pudding basins cannot be used in the microwave cooker.

Baked puddings
To test when baked
Puddings where the butter and sugar in the ingredients are creamed should be golden brown, well risen, and springy to touch.

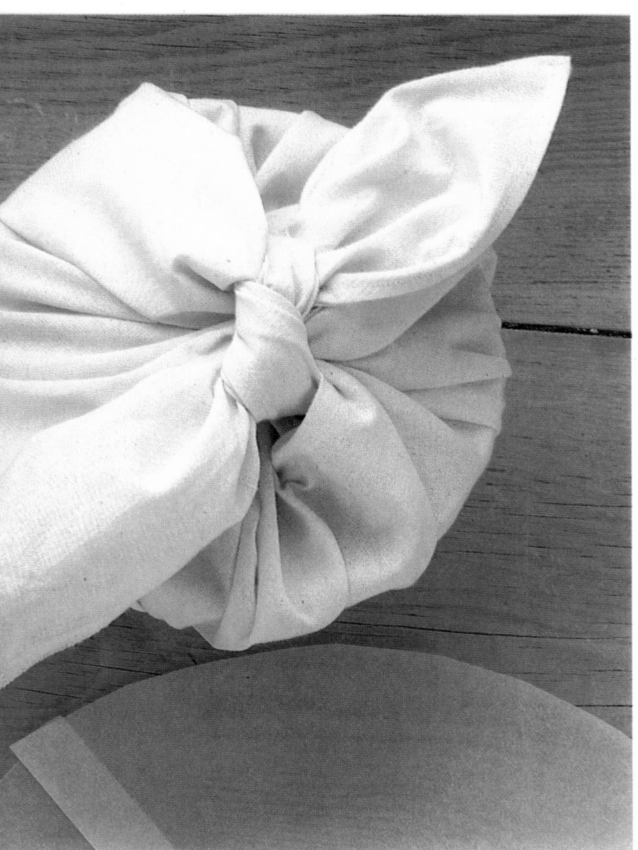

Milk-based puddings should have a light golden skin, and have a firm jelly-like consistency when shaken slightly.

Charlottes, Apricot Brown Betty and crumbles can be tested by inserting a skewer into the pudding. The skewer should penetrate with ease and when removed the skewer should be completely hot and clean.

Glorious Gâteaux

Whisked sponges and Victoria sandwiches are popular bases used for gâteaux. Whisked sponges are light and airy when freshly baked. However, as no fat is incorporated into the mixture, they should be eaten on the day they are made. These cakes are filled with fresh cream and fruit, which again are best eaten on the day of making.

A Victoria sandwich is made with butter and will keep moist for several days when stored in a tin, a point worth remembering when planning a special occasion.

The yeasted doughs, such as the rum babas and savarin are perhaps best described as batters because they are liquid. However, the batter rises to form a large or several individual light airy cakes which are saturated in a liqueur syrup and filled with fresh fruit and cream.

Children's Favourites

Children love colourful, sweet and appealing desserts. Chocolate is a great favourite and recognizable shapes, such as ducks, rabbits, faces, and hedgehogs are popular.

Vegetable colourings make cakes more appetizing and spectacular, for example Multi-coloured marble cake and strawberry meringues.

Decorating puddings with sweets, glacé cherries, angelica, multi-coloured or chocolate vermicelli adds to the attraction.

Desserts Around the World

All the recipes in this chapter reflect a tradition or particular ingredient renowned in a single country. They use a variety of skills and techniques.

Finishing Touches

The chapter on Finishing Touches provides a host of ideas for decorating desserts and many of the home-made biscuits are particularly suitable for combining with fresh fruit desserts, jellies and creams, soufflés, mousses, parfaits, ice creams and frozen desserts.

Trifles, Jellies & Creams

Ogen Jelly

1 ogen melon, weighing at least 300 g (11 oz)
juice of 1 lemon
100 g (4 oz) sugar
100 ml (4 fl oz) hot water
15 g (½ oz) powdered gelatine
To decorate:
220 g (8 oz) strawberries, sliced
caster sugar

Preparation time: *20 minutes, plus setting*

Jelly moulds are designed to shape food, by pouring it into a mould and turning it out when set. They are not essential but create a lavish dessert out of simple ingredients. When left to set, it is essential that the moulds stand absolutely level and are not subject to vibration. Moulds can be made of copper and tin lined, porcelain, toughened glass, aluminium and plastic. In all cases, they should be thoroughly clean and free from grease before pouring in the jelly mixture.

1. Halve the melon. Discard the seeds then scoop out the flesh and blend to a purée with the lemon juice.
2. Dissolve the sugar in half the hot water. Sprinkle the gelatine over the remaining water in a heatproof bowl. Stand the bowl in a pan of hot water and heat gently, without boiling and stir until the gelatine has dissolved. Remove from the heat. Add the sugar and the gelatine to the melon purée.
3. Pour the jelly mixture into a 600 ml (1 pint) ring mould and chill until set.
4. Dip the mould into hot water for a few seconds to loosen the jelly from the sides. Turn onto a serving dish. To decorate, pile strawberries into the centre of the ring.

Grape and Moselle Jelly

120 g (generous 4½ oz) sugar
150 ml (5 fl oz) water, plus 3 tablespoons
15 g (½ oz) powdered gelatine
350 ml (12 fl oz) Moselle wine, e.g. Piesporter
about 20 grapes, peeled and seeded
grapes, peeled and seeded, to decorate

Preparation time: *30 minutes, plus setting*

1. Dissolve 30 g (generous 1 oz) of the sugar in the 3 tablespoons of water, then boil for about 1 minute. Pour into a 600 ml (1 pint) jelly mould and coat the sides with the syrup. Chill the mould in the freezer.
2. Dissolve the remaining sugar in a pan with half of the water.
3. Sprinkle the gelatine over the remaining water in a small heatproof bowl. Stand the bowl in a pan of hot water and heat gently, without boiling and stir until the gelatine has dissolved. Remove from the heat.
4. Combine the gelatine and water with the sugar and water and add the Moselle. Remove the mould from the freezer. Quarter fill with the liquid jelly, then return to the freezer to set for about 15 minutes.
5. Remove from the freezer, then arrange the grapes neatly on the surface of the jelly. Chill in the refrigerator.
6. When the remaining jelly is on the point of setting, spoon it carefully into the mould, taking care not to disturb the grapes.
7. Return to the refrigerator until completely set. Dip the mould in hot water for a few seconds to loosen the jelly from the sides, then turn out on to a serving dish.
8. Serve surrounded by peeled and seeded grapes.

From the top: Grape and moselle jelly; Ogen jelly

Port Jelly

90 g (3½ oz) sugar
150 ml (5 fl oz) hot water
15 g (½ oz) powdered gelatine
300 ml (½ pint) ruby port
2 teaspoons brandy

Serves 6
Preparation time: *20 minutes, plus setting*

1. Dissolve the sugar in half the water in a pan over a gentle heat.
2. Sprinkle the gelatine over the remaining water in a small heatproof bowl. Stand the bowl in a pan of hot water and heat gently, without boiling and stir until the gelatine has dissolved. Remove from the heat.
3. Combine the gelatine and water with the sugar and water, then add the port and brandy. Pour into 6 wineglasses and chill until set.

Crème Caramel

250 ml (8 fl oz) full cream milk
1 egg
2 egg yolks
100 g (4 oz) vanilla sugar
100 g (4 oz) sugar
pinch of cream of tartar

Preparation time: *20 minutes, plus cooling*
Cooking time: *40 minutes*
Oven: *160°C, 325°F, Gas Mark 5*

1. Heat the milk to simmering point. Whisk the egg, yolks and vanilla sugar together then beat in the hot milk.
2. Place the sugar, cream of tartar and a little water in a separate pan and boil to a mid-amber caramel. Pour into 4 dariole moulds, or one 600 ml (1 pint) mould.
3. Pour the custard into the mould, then stand them in a bain marie. Bake in a preheated oven for 40 minutes. Remove from the oven and cool in the bain marie.
4. Turn on to a plate and serve with a Fruit coulis (page 188).

From the left: Port jelly; Crème caramel

From the left: Coconut jelly; Orange brûlée

Coconut Jelly

1 fresh coconut
200 ml (⅓ pint) milk
100 ml (3½ fl oz) double cream
15 g (½ oz) powdered gelatine
50 ml (2 fl oz) hot water

Preparation time: *25 minutes, plus setting*

1. Make 2 holes in the coconut shell and drain the milk into a measuring jug. Add sufficient water to make the milk up to 200 ml (⅓ pint).
2. Split open the coconut and grate 225 g (8 oz) of the flesh.
3. Place the coconut 'milk', milk and grated coconut in a liquidizer and blend for 30 seconds. Leave to stand for 5 minutes. Strain the milk through a muslin cloth to obtain about 400 ml (⅔ pint), then stir in the cream.
4. Sprinkle the gelatine over the water in a small heatproof bowl. Stand the bowl in a pan of hot water and heat gently, without boiling, stirring constantly until the gelatine has dissolved. Remove from the heat. Add to the milk and stir well. Pour into 4 individual moulds and chill until set.
5. Dip the mould in hot water for a few seconds to loosen the jelly from the sides. Turn out.

Variations:
This jelly can be served with a Fruit Coulis (page 188) an ice cream or a Sorbet (pages 86–101).

Orange Brûlée

1 egg
4 egg yolks
50 g (2 oz) vanilla sugar
400 ml (⅔ pint) double cream
2 tablespoons Grand Marnier
50 g (2 oz) sugar
rind of 1 orange, cut into fine matchstick strips
65 g (2½ oz) caster sugar

Serves 6
Preparation time: *25 minutes, plus cooling*
Cooking time: *40 minutes*
Oven: *160°C, 325°F, Gas Mark 3*

1. Beat the egg, yolks and the vanilla sugar until light and creamy. Add the double cream and mix well. Then add the Grand Marnier. Pour into six 150 ml (¼ pint) ramekin dishes.
2. Stand the ramekins in a bain marie and bake in a preheated oven for 40 minutes. Remove from the oven and cool.
3. Place the sugar in a pan with a little water and boil until a mid-amber caramel. Stir in the orange rind and cook for 2 minutes, taking care that the caramel does not burn.
4. Using a pair of tweezers, lift the rind on to a sheet of non-stick silicone paper.
5. Sprinkle caster sugar over the cooked *crèmes*, then place under a preheated grill until glazed. Cool until the sugar hardens.
6. Arrange caramelized orange on the top of each ramekin. Serve within 1 hour or the caramel will lose its brittleness.

Cream Crowdie

120 g (4½ oz) porridge oats
100 g (4 oz) unsalted butter, melted
90 g (3½ oz) demarara sugar
250 ml (8 fl oz) double cream
1 tablespoon whisky
1 tablespoon clear honey
175 g (6 oz) raspberries

Preparation time: *20 minutes, plus cooling*
Cooking time: *20 minutes*
Oven: *180°C, 350°F, Gas Mark 4*

1. Mix the oats, butter and sugar and spread over the base of a baking or roasting tin. Bake in a preheated oven for 20 minutes. Cool, then crumble the mixture with a fork.
2. Whip the double cream until it starts to thicken. Add the whisky and honey and whip until the cream holds its shape on the whisk.
3. Reserve 1 tablespoon of the oat mixture for decoration and fold the remainder into the cream.
4. Reserve a few raspberries for decoration.
5. Spoon enough of the mixture to one third fill 4 wine glasses. Arrange half the remaining raspberries on top. Repeat these 2 layers once more, then spoon the remaining mixture over the raspberries.
6. Decorate with the reserved oat mixture and a little cluster of raspberries.

Chocobaya

75 g (3 oz) plain chocolate
1 teaspoon instant coffee dissolved in a little boiling water
150 g (5 oz) ripe banana
1 tablespoon light golden soft brown sugar
300 ml (½ pint) plain unsweetened yogurt
100 ml (3½ fl oz) double cream
20 g (¾ oz) plain chocolate, grated, to decorate

Preparation: *20 minutes, plus chilling*

1. Melt the chocolate in a bowl over a pan of simmering water. Add the coffee and mix well.
2. Blend the banana to a smooth purée, then add to the chocolate mixture together with the sugar and yogurt.
3. Whip the cream until it begins to hold its shape on the whisk then fold into the mixture. Pour into 4 glasses or glass dishes and chill.
4. Decorate with the grated chocolate.

Victoria Syllabub

300 ml (1/2 pint) double cream
65 g (2 1/2 oz) caster sugar
1 lemon
50 ml (2 fl oz) Madeira
julienne of lemon rind, to decorate

Preparation time: *10 minutes*

1. Whip the double cream and sugar until it holds its shape on the whisk.
2. Grate the rind of half the lemon then squeeze the juice from the whole fruit. Combine with the Madeira.
3. Whisk the rind, juice and Madeira into the cream, a little at a time, until the syllabub holds its shape on the whisk. Spoon into 4 wine glasses. Decorate with the julienne and serve accompanied by Brandysnaps (page 183).

Rhubarb Fool

200 g (7 oz) rhubarb, chopped into 2.5 cm (1 inch) lengths
40 g (1 1/2 oz) caster sugar
40 g (1 1/2 oz) clear honey
300 ml (1/2 pint) double cream

Preparation time: *20 minutes, plus cooling and chilling*

Try making this fool replacing the rhubarb with another fruit or combination of fruits. Firm fruits such as apricots, plums, peaches and nectarines would need to be liquidized after stewing. Fruits such as raspberries, loganberries or blackberries can be strained through a sieve after stewing, if liked, to remove the seeds.

1. Place the rhubarb in a pan with a tablespoon of water. Cover and stew till tender. Add the sugar and honey, then leave to cool.
2. Whip the cream until it holds its shape on the whisk. Beat the rhubarb and juice into the cream a little at a time, then spoon into 4 wine glasses and chill.

Variation:
The fool can be flavoured with a teaspoon of Pernod or any other aniseed-flavoured liqueur.

Almond and Apricot Charlotte

225 g (8 oz) dried apricots, soaked overnight and drained
250 ml (8 fl oz) Dubonnet
300 ml (1/2 pint) double cream
3 drops almond essence
100 g (4 oz) caster sugar
75 g (3 oz) ground almonds
24 Chocolate Fairy Fingers (page 185)

Preparation time: *40 minutes, plus marinating and chilling*

1. Put the apricots in a saucepan with the Dubonnet and enough water to cover. Bring to the boil and simmer for 5 minutes. Leave the apricots to cool completely in the Dubonnet.
2. Whisk the double cream, almond essence and caster sugar together until stiff. Fold in the ground almonds.
3. Strain the apricots and pour the Dubonnet and water into a shallow dish.
4. Dip the fairy fingers into the Dubonnet one at a time. Line a 1.2 litre (2 pint) charlotte mould with fairy fingers.
5. Spread one third of the almond cream over the bottom of the charlotte mould. Arrange half the apricots on top. Cover them with a second layer of cream, arrange the remaining apricots on top and cover with the remaining cream.
6. Trim the ends of the fingers if they are uneven. Cover the cream with the fairy finger trimmings. Put a sheet of aluminium foil over the mould. Chill in a refrigerator for 4 hours.
7. To serve, turn out the charlotte on to a flat dish. Pipe a border of cream, if liked and sprinkle with toasted chopped almonds. Serve with a Fruit coulis (page 188) or a chilled Crème anglaise (page 189).

Passionfruit Syllabub and Minneolas

8 passionfruit
90 g (3 1/2 oz) caster sugar
250 ml (8 fl oz) double cream, chilled
2 egg whites
4 minneolas, peeled and divided into segments

Preparation time: *15 minutes*

Passionfruits are tropical and similar in size and shape to a large plum. The tough, purple skin is wrinkled when ripe. The pulp is sweet, juicy, aromatic and contains small black seeds. The seeds are eaten with the flesh. Minneolas look similar to small oranges but have a deep orange, aromatic skin.

1. Scoop out the passionfruit pulp. Pass it through a sieve over a mixing bowl to collect the juice.
2. Add the sugar and double cream. Whisk until the mixture starts to hold its shape on the whisk.
3. Add the egg whites and continue whisking until the mixture holds its shape again.
4. Half-fill 4 glasses or desserts bowls with syllabub. Arrange half the minneola segments on top and cover them with the remaining syllabub. Decorate with the remaining minneola segments. Serve immediately.

Dean's Creams

120 g (4 1/2 oz) sponge cake
40 g (1 1/2 oz) tawny marmalade
40 g (1 1/2 oz) raspberry jam
16 ratafias
150 ml (1/4 pint) Amontillado sherry
300 ml (1/2 pint) double cream
65 g (2 1/2 oz) caster sugar
3 tablespoons Madeira
3 tablespoons brandy
rind and juice of 1/2 lemon
20 g (3/4 oz) redcurrant jelly, to decorate

Preparation time: *30 minutes*

1. Divide the sponge into 8 pieces. Spread marmalade on 4 of them and raspberry jam on the remainder.
2. Arrange a piece of jam-coated sponge and a piece of marmalade-coated sponge in each of 6 glass coupes. Place 4 ratafias on each one. Spoon the sherry on top.
3. Whisk the double cream with the sugar until it holds its shape on the whisk.
4. Combine the Madeira, brandy, lemon rind and juice. Whisk into the cream until the cream is stiff.
5. Spoon the cream over the 4 coupes. It should just reach the top of the bowls. Smooth the surface with the back of a knife.
6. Stir the redcurrant jelly into a teaspoon of hot water until dissolved. Using a piping bag and a writing nozzle, pipe a design with the melted jelly on the top of each cream.

From the top, clockwise: Almond and apricot charlotte; Dean's creams; Passionfruit syllabub and minneolas

From the left: Coffee bavarois; Chocolate marquise

Coffee Bavarois

200 ml (7 fl oz) milk
3 egg yolks
75 g (3 oz) sugar
15 g (½ oz) powdered gelatine
50 ml (2 fl oz) hot water
100 ml (4 fl oz) strong black coffee
100 ml (4 fl oz) double cream, whipped

Preparation time: *1 hour, plus setting*

1. Heat the milk to simmering point. Whisk the yolks and sugar until light then pour the milk into the yolks. Mix well.
2. Return the custard to the rinsed pan and heat without boiling until it coats the back of a wooden spoon. Remove from the heat and pour into a deep baking tin.
3. Sprinkle the gelatine over the hot water in a small heatproof bowl. Stand the bowl in a pan of hot water and heat gently, without boiling, and stir until the gelatine has dissolved. Remove from the heat and stir into the custard. Add the black coffee, then chill until on the point of setting.
4. Fold the cream into the custard. Pour the bavarois into a 900 ml (1½ pint) mould. Chill until set.
5. Dip the mould in hot water for a few seconds then turn on to a serving dish. An attractive way of decorating a coffee bavarois is to pipe rosettes of cream on top. Decorate with confectionery coffee beans.

Chocolate Marquise

165 g (5½ oz) plain chocolate
1 tablespoon water
2 tablespoons of whisky, armagnac or rum (optional)
90 g (3½ oz) unsalted butter, softened
50 g (2 oz) icing sugar
2 eggs, separated
20 g (½ oz) caster sugar

Preparation time: *25 minutes, plus setting*

1. Break the chocolate into pieces and place in a bowl with the water and alcohol, if using. Stand over a pan of simmering water until the chocolate melts. Remove the bowl from the pan. Stir well and allow 5 minutes to cool.
2. Cream the softened butter and icing sugar. Beat in the yolks, then fold in the melted chocolate.
3. Whisk the egg whites and caster sugar until very stiff and fold into the chocolate mixture. Pour into a 600 ml (1 pint) mould or 4 individual moulds lined with foil, and chill until set.
4. To serve dip the mould or individual moulds in hot water for a few seconds to loosen the marquise from the sides, then turn out on to a dish. Peel off the foil and serve with orange segments and Vanillekipferl (page 183).

Exotic Fruit Terrine

500 ml (18 fl oz) milk
6 egg yolks
150 g (5 oz) vanilla sugar
25 g (1 oz) powdered gelatine
120 ml (4 fl oz) water
200 ml (8 fl oz) double cream
300 g (11 oz) chopped lychees
100 g (4 oz) ripe mango, chopped
To decorate:
½ mango, reserve a few slices to finish
vanilla sugar, to taste

Serves 6
Preparation time: *1 hour, plus setting*

If canned lychees are used, the lychees syrup may be substituted for the orange juice. This dessert is best eaten on the day it is made.

1. Heat the milk to simmering point.
2. Whisk the yolks and sugar until light and creamy. Pour over the milk and mix thoroughly.
3. Return the milk, sugar and eggs to the rinsed pan and heat without boiling until the custard coats the back of a wooden spoon. Remove from the heat and pour into a deep baking tin.
4. Sprinkle the gelatine over the water in a small heatproof bowl. Stand the bowl in a pan of hot water and heat gently without boiling and stir until the gelatine has dissolved. Remove from the heat and stir into the custard. Chill until on the point of setting.
5. Whip the cream until it holds its shape on the whisk and fold into the custard. Fold in the lychees and mango. Pour the mixture into a rectangular loaf tin cover with cling film and chill until set, for about 4 hours.
6. To serve, dip the tin in hot water for a few seconds to loosen the terrine from the sides. Turn out.
7. Blend the mango to a smooth purée and sweeten to taste. Coat 4 or 6 chilled plates with the purée. Cut the terrine into slices and arrange some in the centre of each plate and decorate with the reserved slices of mango.

Variation:
Replace the exotic fruits with soft fruit, such as strawberries, raspberries, kiwi fruits, peaches and nectarines.

Exotic fruit terrine

Raspberry Trifle

65 g (2½ oz) sugar
50 ml (2 fl oz) water
25 ml (1 fl oz) raspberry liqueur or Kirsch
½ quantity Biscuits à la Cuiller (page 186)
4 ratafias
4 heaped teaspoons raspberry jam
½ quantity hot Crème Anglaise (page 189)
1 quantity Crème Chantilly (page 189)
12 raspberries, to decorate

Preparation time: *50 minutes, plus standing and chilling.*

1. Boil the sugar and water until the sugar dissolves. Cool, then add the raspberry liqueur or Kirsch.
2. Break the biscuits into several pieces and arrange in a bowl with the ratafias. Pour over the syrup.
3. Spoon half the biscuits into the bottoms of 4 glass dishes. Spoon the raspberry jam over the top and cover with the remaining biscuits and ratafias. Pour over the hot crème anglaise. Stand for 15 minutes to cool, then chill for 15 minutes.
4. Fit a piping bag with a large star nozzle and fill with the crème chantilly. Decorate the top edge of the 4 trifles with cream, leaving the centre free. Place 3 raspberries into the centre of each and chill for a few minutes before serving.

Trifle With a Syllabub on the Top

65 g (2½ oz) sugar
100 ml (4 fl oz) water
75 ml (3 fl oz) Maderia
½ quantity Biscuits à la Cuiller (page 186)
½ quantity hot Crème Anglaise (page 189)
150 ml (¼ pint) double cream
30 g (generous 1 oz) caster sugar
grated rind and juice of ½ lemon

Preparation time: *45 minutes, plus chilling*

This dessert is best eaten on the day it is made. Stand in a cool place.

1. Boil the sugar and water until the sugar dissolves. Cool and add 50 ml (2 fl oz) of the Madeira.
2. Break the biscuits into several pieces and place in a bowl and pour over the syrup. Spoon the biscuits in to a glass trifle dish. Pour over the hot crème anglaise. Stand until cool, then chill.
3. Whip the double cream and caster sugar until it holds its shape. Combine the lemon juice and remaining Madeira and gradually whisk into the cream. Continue to whisk until the cream holds its shape.
4. Pile the syllabub on the trifle and sprinkle with the grated lemon rind.

Strawberry Charlotte

200 ml (7 fl oz) milk
3 egg yolks
75 g (3 oz) caster sugar
15 g (½ oz) powdered gelatine
50 ml (2 fl oz) hot water
200 g (7 oz) strawberries
100 ml (4 fl oz) double cream
16 Biscuits à la Cuiller (page 186)

Serves 6–8
Preparation time: *1 hour, plus setting*

1. Heat the milk to simmering point. Whisk the yolks and sugar until light, then pour over the milk and mix well.
2. Return the custard to the rinsed pan and heat without boiling until it coats the back of a wooden spoon. Remove from the heat and pour into a deep baking tin.
3. Sprinkle the gelatine over the water in a small heatproof bowl. Stand the bowl in a pan of hot water and heat gently, without boiling and stir until the gelatine has dissolved. Stir the gelatine into the custard.
4. Blend the strawberries to a purée and chop the remainder. Add the purée and chopped fruit to the custard. Chill until on the point of setting.
5. Whip the cream until it holds its shape and fold into the custard. Line a charlotte mould or brioche tin (without a funnel) with foil. Arrange the biscuits on the bottom and round the sides of the tin and fill with the charlotte mixture. Chill for 4 hours.
6. To serve, unmould the charlotte then carefully remove the foil. Decorate with cream and sliced strawberries, if liked.

From the left, anticlockwise:
Raspberry trifle; Trifle with a syllabub on the top; Strawberry charlotte

Tipsy Cake

250 ml (8 fl oz) sweet sherry
50 ml (2 fl oz) brandy
30 Biscuits à la Cuiller (page 186)
65 g (2½ oz) sugar
50 ml (2 fl oz) water
100 g (4 oz) nibbed almonds
Custard:
3 egg yolks
150 g (5 oz) vanilla sugar
150 ml (5 fl oz) double cream
150 ml (5 fl oz) milk

Preparation time: *45 minutes, plus cooling*

1. Mix the sherry and brandy together and thoroughly soak the biscuits in the mixture. Carefully arrange the biscuits in a neat pile, about 6 storeys high in the middle of a serving dish.
2. Boil the sugar and water in a pan for 4 minutes, then add the nibbed almonds. Continue to boil, until they are well coated in the syrup. Pour on to non-stick silicone paper and spread them using a palette knife so that they do not stick together. Cool. Stick the almonds into the cake.
3. To make the custard, whisk the yolks and sugar until creamy. Combine the cream and milk. Heat to simmering point, then pour over the yolks. Mix well.
4. Pour the custard into a clean pan and heat without boiling until the mixture thickens. Cool.
5. To serve, pour a little of the custard round the tipsy cake and serve the rest separately.

Ginger Wine Trifle

120 g (4½ oz) sponge cake, cut into cubes
120 ml (4 fl oz) ginger wine
65 g (2½ oz) strawberry jam
150 ml (¼ pint) milk
300 ml (½ pint) double cream
4 egg yolks, beaten
50 g (2 oz) caster sugar
1 teaspoon cornflour
grated rind of ½ lemon
1 pinch cinnamon
To decorate:
12 ratafias
1 piece crystallized stem ginger, finely chopped

Preparation time: *40 minutes, plus cooling*

For extra ginger flavour, sprinkle finely chopped stem ginger over the sponge.

1. Arrange the sponge cake in the base of a trifle dish. Moisten with ginger wine. Spread the strawberry jam on top.
2. In a small heavy pan, scald the milk and 65 ml (2½ fl oz) of the double cream. Mix the egg yolks with 25 g (1 oz) of the sugar and the cornflour in a mixing bowl. Add the hot milk and cream to the sweetened egg yolks, stirring all the time. Return the mixture to a clean pan. Heat gently until thickened, stirring constantly. Pour the hot custard over the jam. Leave to cool, and chill in the refrigerator.
3. Whip the remaining cream with the grated lemon rind, cinnamon and remaining sugar. Pile on top of the custard.
4. Decorate with ratafias and ginger.

From the top, left: Tipsy cake; Ginger wine trifle
From the bottom, left: Blackcurrant diplomat; Whim-Whams

Blackcurrant Diplomat

250 g (9 oz) blackcurrants
200 g (7 oz) caster sugar
275 ml (9 fl oz) water
50 ml (2 fl oz) Crème de Cassis
15 ratafias
16–20 Biscuits à la Cuiller (page 186)
1 teaspoon arrowroot

Preparation time: *30 minutes, plus setting*
Cooking time: *15 minutes*

1. Place the blackcurrants, caster sugar and water in a pan and poach for 15 minutes. Drain and reserve the juice. Add the crème de cassis to the syrup.
2. Line a charlotte mould with foil. Dip the ratafias and biscuits à la cuiller in the syrup, a few at a time, and arrange a layer of the biscuits in the base of the mould. Sprinkle some blackcurrants on top, then crumble 3 ratafias over them. Repeat the 3 layers and end with a layer of biscuits à la cuiller. Chill for at least 2 hours until set.
3. Dissolve the arrowoot in a little water. Heat the remaining blackcurrant syrup and whisk in the arrowroot. Stirring constantly, heat until thickened. Cool.
4. To serve, turn out the diplomat on to a serving dish. Pour over a little of the thickened syrup and serve the rest from a sauce boat. Serve with Crème chantilly (page 189) or Crème anglaise (page 189).

Variation:
If fresh blackcurrants are not obtainable use 1 × 450 g (16 oz) can of blackcurrants and omit step 1.

Whim-Whams

450 ml (¾ pint) double cream
65 g (2½ oz) caster sugar
90 ml (3½ fl oz) sweet white wine
20 ratafias
150 ml (¼ pint) made up blackberry jelly, set

Preparation time: *20 minutes*

1. Whip the double cream and sugar until it holds its shape on the whisk. Whisk in the white wine. Take care not to overbeat or the cream will separate.
2. Divide a third of the cream between four 150 ml (¼ pint) stemmed wine glasses.
3. Arrange 2 ratafias on top. Spread with half the blackberry jelly.
4. Cover with half the remaining cream. Arrange 3 ratafias on top. Spread the remaining jelly on them.
5. Top with the rest of the cream.

Magical Meringues

Meringue Shells Filled With Kiwi Fruit

1 quantity Meringue Cuite (page 42)
Filling:
150 ml (¼ pint) double cream, whipped
4 kiwi fruits, peeled and sliced
2 tablespoons apricot jam, warmed

Serves 8
Preparation time: *30 minutes*
Cooking time: *1 hour*
Oven: *140°C, 275°F, Gas Mark 1*

Kiwi fruit gives this dessert a refreshing, tangy flavour which combines well with the meringue.

1. Line a baking sheet with non-stick silicone or lightly greased greaseproof paper and draw eight 7.5 cm (3 inch) circles.
2. Spoon the meringue cuite into a piping bag fitted with a large star nozzle.
3. Using the drawn circles as a guide, pipe concentric circles to form the base of the meringue shell, then pipe another circle around the edge to form the wall.
4. Bake in a preheated oven for about 1 hour or until the meringue is crisp. Cool and remove from the paper.
5. Spoon a little cream into the bottom of each shell. Arrange the sliced kiwi fruit on top and glaze with a little warmed apricot jam.

Variation

Use 100 g (4 oz) white grapes and 100 g 4 oz) black grapes, seeded in place of the kiwi fruit. Arrange the grapes in a pattern alternating the colours. Omit the apricot jam.

From the top: Strawberry meringue basket; Meringue shells filled with kiwi fruit

Strawberry Meringue Basket

2 quantities Meringue Cuite (page 42)
600 ml (1 pint) double cream, whipped
450 g (1 lb) strawberries

Serves 10
Preparation time: *1 hour, plus cooling*
Cooking time: *2–3 hours*
Oven: *140°C, 275°F, Gas Mark 1*

1. Line 2 baking sheets with non-stick silicone or lightly greased greaseproof paper and draw a 20 cm (8 inch) circle on each.
2. Make up the meringue cuite in 2 separate batches. Beginning with the first batch, spoon the mixture into a piping bag fitted with a large 1 cm (½ inch) plain nozzle. Following the drawn circle, pipe the meringue mixture working inwards to the centre in concentric circles, to form the base.
3. On the second baking sheet just pipe a ring following the circle. Keep the remaining mixture covered with a damp cloth.
4. Bake both in a preheated oven for approximately 1 hour or until the meringue is crisp. Allow to cool.
5. When the first batch of meringues are cooked, pipe out another 2 rings and bake as before, until crisp. Allow to cool.
6. Make up the second batch of meringue mixture.
7. Place the cooled base on a baking sheet lined with a new piece of non-stick silicone or greaseproof paper. Using a little of the new mixture, stick the rings on top of one another over the base.
8. Fit a large rose nozzle into a piping bag and fill with the remaining mixture.
9. Working from the base of the meringue basket upwards, pipe vertical lines or meringue all around the basket, then pipe stars or rosettes around the base and rim.
10. Return the basket to the oven and bake for 45 minutes, or until crisp. Allow to cool.
11. To serve, fill with whipped cream and strawberries.

Praline Surprise

1 quantity Nut Meringue (see below)
100 g (4 oz) sugar
85 ml (3 fl oz) water
2 egg whites
100 g (4 oz) butter, softened
3 quantities Praline (page 188)

Serves 8
Preparation time: *45 minutes*
Cooking time: *30 minutes*
Oven: *180°C, 350°F, Gas Mark 4*

1. Line 2 baking sheets with non-stick silicone or lightly greased greaseproof paper and draw sixteen 7.5 cm (3 inch) circles.
2. Spoon the nut meringue into a piping bag fitted with a plain 5 mm (¼ inch) nozzle.
3. Pipe concentric circles to form a disc of meringue following the drawn line as a guide. Bake in a preheated oven for about 1 hour or until crisp and lightly coloured.
4. Meanwhile prepare the butter cream. With the sugar, water and egg whites make up some Italian Meringue as for the Coffee Meringues (page 49). Cream the butter until soft and gradually beat in the meringue mixture.
5. Once the meringue discs are completely cool sandwich pairs together with the butter cream and spread more over the sides, reserving some for decoration.
6. Roll the sides of each surprise into the praline, gently pressing it on to the surface.
7. Spoon the remaining butter cream in to a piping bag fitted with a small star nozzle. Pipe small stars on the top of each.

Meringue Cuite or Cooked Meringue

4 egg whites
225 g (8 oz) icing sugar
few drops of vanilla essence

1. Place the egg whites and icing sugar in a large heatproof bowl and stand over a pan a third full of simmering water. Using an electric or rotary beater whisk until very thick and glossy.
2. Add the vanilla essence and any other flavouring ingredients.

Nut Meringue

4 egg whites
250 g (9 oz) caster sugar
few drops of vanilla essence
½ teaspoon lemon juice
100 g (4 oz) almonds, blanched, toasted and ground.

1. Whisk the egg whites until stiff, then add the sugar 1 tablespoon at a time, whisking continuously until the mixture is thick and holds its shape.
2. Gently fold in the vanilla essence, lemon juice and nuts.

Vacherin Mont Blanc

1 quantity Meringue Cuite (see opposite)
Filling:
300 ml (½ pint) double cream
150 ml (¼ pint) fromage blanc or yogurt
1 × 225 g (8 oz) can sweetened chestnut purée
2–3 tablespoons brandy

Serves 6–8
Preparation time: *30 minutes*
Cooking time: *1½–2 hours*
Oven: *140°C, 275°F, Gas Mark 1*

1. Line a baking sheet with non-stick silicone or lightly greased greaseproof paper and draw a 20 cm (8 inch) circle.
2. Spoon the meringue cuite into a piping bag fitted with a large star nozzle.
3. Using the circle as a guide, pipe a continuous circle spiral working from the outside in, to form the base.
4. Pipe another circle around the edge to form a wall and with any mixture left over pipe rosettes on top to form a decorative wall. Bake in a preheated oven for 1½–2 hours or until crisp. Cool and remove the paper.
5. To make the filling, whip the cream until thick, fold in the fromage blanc or yogurt, reserving 2 tablespoons. Add the chestnut purée to the cream mixture and flavour with the brandy.
6. Spoon the filling into the meringue, piling it up into a mound. Spoon the reserved cream over the peak for a snow-capped effect.

From the left: Praline surprise; Vacherin Mont Blanc

From the left: Almond meringue cake; Meringue chantilly

Almond Meringue Cake

1 quantity Nut Meringue (page 42)
100 g (4 oz) dried apricots, soaked overnight
25 g (1 oz) caster sugar
300 ml (½ pint) double cream, whipped
To decorate:
8 hazelnuts, toasted
1 × 300 g (11 oz) can apricot halves

Serves 6
Preparation time: *40 minutes, plus soaking*
Cooking time: *40–45 minutes*
Oven: *180°C, 350°F, Gas Mark 4*

1. Draw two 20 cm (8 inch) circles on non-stick silicone or lightly greased greaseproof paper and place on 2 baking sheets.
2. Spoon or pipe the nut meringue on to the prepared baking sheets, following the marked circles.
3. Bake in a preheated oven for 40–45 minutes until crisp and lightly coloured, and like marshmallow inside.
4. To make the filling, simmer the soaked apricots in their liquid until they are tender and have reduced to a thick purée. Cool and sweeten to taste.
5. Reserve half the cream and mix the remainder with the apricot purée.
6. Sandwich the meringues with the apricot cream and decorate the top with piped cream rosettes, hazelnuts and apricots.

Strawberry Meringue Heart

1 quantity Nut Meringue (page 42) using 100 g (4 oz) hazelnuts, toasted and ground
450 ml (¾ pint) double cream, whipped
225 g (8 oz) fresh strawberries

Serves 6
Preparation time: *40 minutes, plus cooling*
Cooking time: *40–45 minutes*
Oven: *180°C, 350°F, Gas Mark 4*

1. Line 2 baking sheets with non-stick silicone or lightly greased greaseproof paper and draw a 23 cm (9 inch) wide heart on each.
2. Spoon the nut meringue into a piping bag fitted with a large star nozzle.
3. Pipe a heart shape on 1 sheet, following the line as a guide. Working inwards, pipe smaller and smaller hearts until you have a solid base of concentric hearts; do the same for the other heart.
4. Bake in a preheated oven for about 40–45 minutes or until they are crisp and lightly coloured, then cool.
5. Reserve about one third of the cream and 8–10 strawberries for decoration. Sandwich the 2 hearts together with the remaining cream and strawberries.
6. Pipe cream rosettes around the edge of the heart and decorate with strawberries.

Meringue Chantilly

1 quantity Swiss Meringue (page 46)
few drops of vanilla essence
300 ml (½ pint) double cream
vanilla sugar, to taste
50 g (2 oz) flaked almonds, toasted, to decorate

Serves 6
Preparation time: *30 minutes*
Cooking time: *1 hour*
Oven: *140°C, 275°F, Gas Mark 1*

1. Line 2 baking sheets with lightly greased and floured greaseproof paper, or use non-stick silicone paper.
2. Carefully fold the vanilla essence into the Swiss meringue.
3. Spoon the meringue into a large piping bag fitted with a large star nozzle, and pipe 12 even-size swirls on to the prepared baking sheets.
4. Bake in a preheated oven for about 1 hour or until crisp and lightly coloured.
5. Cool on a wire tray and peel off the paper.
6. To make the filling, whip the cream until thick, add sugar to taste and sandwich pairs of meringues together. Decorate with the toasted almonds.

Strawberry meringue heart

Chocolate Meringue Cake

1 quantity Swiss Meringue (see right)
2 teaspoons cocoa powder, sieved

Filling:

50 ml (2 fl oz) strong black coffee
2 tablespoons brandy
225 g (8 oz) plain dark chocolate, broken into small pieces
600 ml (1 pint) double cream
100 g (4 oz) plain cooking chocolate, to decorate

Serves 6–8
Preparation time: *1 hour, plus cooling*
Cooking time: *1 hour*
Oven: *140°C, 275°F, Gas Mark 1*

1. Line 3 baking sheets with non-stick silicone or lightly greased greaseproof paper.
2. Carefully fold the cocoa powder into the Swiss meringue.
3. Divide the mixture between the 3 baking sheets and spread out into thin 20–23 cm (8–9 inch) rounds. Bake in a preheated oven for about 1 hour or until crisp.
4. To make the filling, gently heat the coffee and brandy in a small pan. Away from the heat, add the chocolate and stir until melted. Cool.
5. Whip the cream until slightly thickened, then add the chocolate and continue whipping until thick.
6. When the meringues are cool, sandwich each layer together with the chocolate cream. Spread more filling on top and on the sides of the meringue.
7. To decorate, melt the cooking chocolate in a bowl set over a pan of hot water. Pour the melted chocolate on to a cool, clean surface, preferably marble, and spread it thinly over the surface. Cool until set.
8. Using a large palette knife, start to shave the chocolate, holding the knife at a 45° angle to the surface. The chocolate should roll up into scrolls.
9. Cover the top and the sides of the meringue with these scrolls, then leave the cake for several hours for the meringue to soften before serving.

From the left: Lemon meringues with lemon curd filling; Chocolate meringue cake

Swiss Meringue

4 egg whites
250 g (9 oz) caster sugar

1. Whisk the egg whites until stiff.
2. Gradually whisk in half the sugar until the mixture is thick and glossy.
3. Carefully fold in the remaining sugar.

Lemon Meringues With Lemon Curd Filling

½ quantity Swiss Meringue (see opposite)
1 teaspoon finely grated lemon or lime rind
Filling:
300 ml (½ pint) double cream
5 tablespoons lemon curd
lemon or lime peel, to decorate

Serves 6
Preparation time: *30 minutes*
Cooking time: *1 hour*
Oven: *140°C, 275°F, Gas Mark 1*

These meringues are delicious served with home-made lemon curd.

1. Line 2 baking sheets with lightly greased and floured greaseproof paper, or use non-stick silicone paper.
2. Carefully fold the grated lemon or lime rind into the Swiss meringue.
3. Spoon the meringue into a large piping bag fitted with a large star nozzle, and pipe 12 even-size swirls on to the prepared baking sheets.
4. Bake in a preheated oven for about 1 hour or until crisp and lightly coloured.
5. Cool on a wire tray and peel off the paper.
6. To make the filling, whip the cream until stiff, fold in the lemon curd and use to sandwich together pairs of the meringues.
7. To decorate, prepare fine juliennes of lemon or lime peel and place a few juliennes on top of each meringue.

From the left: Floating islands with raspberry and redcurrant sauce; Coffee meringues

Floating Islands With Raspberry and Redcurrant Sauce

300 ml (1/2 pint) milk
40 g (1 1/2 oz) vanilla sugar
Meringue Islands:
4 egg whites
225 g (8 oz) caster sugar
Custard:
4 egg yolks
2 oz caster sugar
Sauce:
225 g (8 oz) fresh or frozen raspberries
225 g (8 oz) fresh or frozen redcurrants
sugar, to taste

Preparation time: *50 minutes*
Cooking time: *30 minutes*

1. Simmer the milk and sugar together.
2. Whisk the egg whites until they stand in firm peaks. Add half the sugar, 1 tablespoon at a time, whisking between each addition until stiff and glossy. Fold in the remaining sugar.
3. Scoop tablespoons of the meringue mixture and slide them on to the milk and simmer. Cook for about 3 minutes, turning them over once.
4. Using a slotted draining spoon, lift them out and drain them on a paper towels. Continue poaching a few at a time until all the meringue mixture has been cooked.
5. Strain the milk and prepare the custard. Whisk the egg yolks with the caster sugar until thick. Pour the strained milk into the egg mixture, stirring constantly.
6. Return the mixture to the pan and stir continuously over a low heat, without boiling, until it thickens and coats the back of the spoon. Cool and pour into a serving dish. Place the poached meringues on the surface of the custard in a mound.
7. To make the sauce, simmer the fruits together until they have reduced to a thick purée and sweeten to taste. Serve the cooled fruit sauce with the floating islands.

Meringues Croquembouches

150 g (5 oz) Swiss Meringue mixture (page 46)
150 ml (¼ pint) double cream
40 g (1½ oz) caster sugar
225 g (8 oz) fresh fruit in season, chopped

Preparation time: *15 minutes, plus cooling*
Cooking time: *50 minutes*
Oven: *150°C, 300°F, Gas Mark 2*

1. Line a baking sheet with non-stick silicone or lightly greased greaseproof paper.
2. Fill a piping bag fitted with a 1 cm (½ inch) nozzle with the meringue. Pipe twelve 7.5 cm (3 inch) rings on the paper. Bake for 50 minutes in a preheated oven and cool.
3. Whip the double cream with the sugar until it holds its shape on the whisk.
4. Spread a little whipped cream on 4 of the meringue rings. Arrange half of the mixed fruit on top. Put some cream on 4 more meringues. Put them cream side down on the fruit sandwich-fashion. Spread each one with more cream and put the rest of the fruit on top. Spread the rest of the cream on the 4 remaining meringues and put them cream side down on the fruit. Top with fruit.

Meringues croquembouches

Coffee Meringues

Italian Meringue:
225 g (8 oz) sugar
150 ml (¼ pint) water
4 egg whites
1 teaspoon coffee essence

Serves 4–6
Preparation time: *30 minutes*
Cooking time: *1–1½ hours*
Oven: *140°C, 275°F, Gas Mark 1*

Italian meringue is extremely versatile. Not only can it be cooked to form a crisp shell, but it can also be used as a filling, as in this recipe. It can also be mixed with equal parts of whipped cream and fruit purée to make a delicious cake filling.

1. Line a baking sheet with non-stick silicone or lightly greased greaseproof paper.
2. Dissolve the sugar and the water over a low heat without boiling.
3. Once dissolved, bring to the boil without stirring until it reaches hard ball stage, 121°C, 250°F on a sugar thermometer.
4. Meanwhile, whisk the egg whites until stiff. When the syrup is ready, pour the syrup in a slow steady stream on to the stiff egg whites, beating continuously until the meringue is cool. Beat in the coffee essence.
5. Reserve a quarter of the mixture and pipe the remainder into 8–12 swirls with a star nozzle on to the prepared baking sheet and bake in a preheated oven for about 1–1½ hours or until crisp. Cool, then remove the paper.
6. Place the reserved mixture into the piping bag. When the meringues are cold, pipe the uncooked meringue on to one half and sandwich the pairs together.

All Manner of Mousses

Lemon Mousse

3 eggs, separated
100 g (4 oz) caster sugar
grated rind and juice of 1 lemon
2 teaspoons powdered gelatine
50 ml (2 fl oz) water
150 ml (5 fl oz) double cream
To decorate:
65 ml (2½ fl oz) double cream
1 tablespoon orange juice
10 g (¼ oz) caster sugar
crystallized lemon segments

Preparation time: *30 minutes, plus setting*

1. Cut out a sheet of non-stick silicone paper 55 × 15 cm (22 × 6 inches). Fasten the paper around a 15 cm (6 inch) soufflé dish to form a collar 7.5 cm (3 inches) above the rim of the dish. Use either string or an elastic band to secure the paper.
2. Place the yolks in a bowl with the sugar. Stand the bowl over a basin of simmering water. Whisk until thick and creamy. Add the grated lemon rind and juice.
3. Sprinkle the gelatine over the water in a small heatproof bowl. Stand the bowl in a pan of hot water and stir until the gelatine has dissolved. Remove from the heat. Whisk the gelatine into the yolks and sugar mixture and cool.
4. Whisk the double cream until it holds its shape on the whisk. Using a clean whisk, whisk the egg whites until stiff. Fold the cream into the yolks and sugar base, then carefully fold in the egg white. Pour the mixture into the soufflé dish and chill.
5. To decorate, whisk the double cream until it holds its shape on the whisk. Add the juice and sugar. Continue whisking until it returns to the same consistency. Fit a piping bag with a large star nozzle and fill with the cream. Remove the paper collar from the mousse. Pipe rosettes of cream on top of the mousse and decorate with the lemon segments.

From the top: Lemon mousse; Pink grapefruit and maraschino mousse

Pink Grapefruit and Maraschino Mousse

2 pink grapefruit
3 eggs, separated
100 g (4 oz) caster sugar
15 g (½ oz) powdered gelatine
1 tablespoon maraschino cherry syrup
300 ml (½ pint) double cream
To decorate:
50 g (2 oz) chopped almonds, toasted
1 quantity Crème Chantilly (page 189)
12 maraschino cherries

Preparation time: *35 minutes, plus setting*

1. Halve the grapefruit and trim the rounded bases so they will stand firm. Cut out the flesh without damaging the peel. Liquidize the segments to obtain the juice and strain into a small heatproof bowl.
2. Cut out 4 sheets of non-stick silicone paper, long enough to wrap around the outside of the grapefruit halves and at least 15 cm (6 inches) wide. Fasten the paper around the halves to form a collar 7.5 cm (3 inches) above the rim of the grapefruit half. Use either string or an elastic band to secure the paper.
3. Place the egg yolks in a bowl with the sugar. Stand the bowl over a basin of simmering water and whisk until thick.
4. Sprinkle the gelatine over the grapefruit juice. Stand the bowl in a pan of hot water and stir until dissolved. Remove from the heat. Whisk the gelatine and the maraschino syrup into the yolks and sugar mixture and cool.
5. Whisk the double cream until it holds its shape on the whisk. Using a clean whisk, whisk the egg whites until stiff. Fold the cream into the yolks and sugar mixture, then carefully fold in the egg whites. Pour into the grapefruit halves and chill until set.
6. To serve, remove the paper, press the nuts on to the edge of the mousses and decorate with whirls of chantilly cream and maraschino cherries.

Liqueur Mousse

3 eggs, separated
100 g (4 oz) caster sugar
grated rind and juice of 1 lemon
1 tablespoon Grand Marnier
2 tablespoons Kirsch
1 tablespoon rum
2 teaspoons powdered gelatine
50 ml (2 fl oz) water
150 ml (5 fl oz) double cream
To decorate:
double cream, whipped
6 liqueur chocolates

Preparation time: *25 minutes, plus setting*

1. Cut out a sheet of non-stick silicone paper 55 × 15 cm (22 × 6 inches). Fasten the paper around a 15 cm (6 inch) soufflé dish to form a collar 7.5 cm (3 inches) above the rim of the dish. Secure the paper.
2. Place the egg yolks and sugar in a bowl and stand over a pan of simmering water. Whisk until thick and creamy. Add the lemon rind, juice, liqueurs and rum.
3. Sprinkle the gelatine over the water in a small heatproof bowl. Stand the bowl in a pan of hot water and stir until the gelatine has dissolved. Remove from the heat. Whisk the gelatine into the yolk and sugar mixture and cool.
4. Whisk the double cream until it holds its shape on the whisk. Using a clean whisk, whisk the egg whites until stiff.
5. Fold the cream into the yolk and sugar mixture, then carefully fold in the egg whites. Pour the mixture into the soufflé dish and chill until set.
6. To serve, remove the paper collar and pipe rosettes of cream. Decorate with liqueur chocolates.

Iced Chocolate and Orange Mousse

125 g (4½ oz) plain chocolate
75 g (3 oz) soft brown sugar
4 eggs, separated
2 tablespoons Curaçao
grated rind of 1 orange
150 ml (5 fl oz) double cream
50 g (2 oz) plain chocolate, to decorate

Preparation time: *25 minutes, plus setting and freezing overnight*

1. Cut out a sheet of non-stick silicone paper 55 × 15 cm (22 × 6 inches). Fasten the paper around a 15 cm (6 inch) soufflé dish to form a collar 7.5 cm (3 inches) above the rim of the dish. Use either string or an elastic band to secure the paper.
2. Break the chocolate into small pieces and place in a bowl over a pan of simmering water. When melted, beat in the sugar, egg yolks, orange curaçao and orange rind. Cool slightly.
3. Whisk the cream until it holds its shape on the whisk. Using a clean whisk, whisk the egg whites until stiff. Fold the cream into the chocolate mixture then lightly fold in the egg whites. Pour into the prepared soufflé dish and place in the freezer overnight.
4. Fifteen minutes before serving, remove the paper collar and transfer to the refrigerator.
5. To decorate, melt the chocolate. Spread it on a cool, clean work surface. Leave until almost set. Make chocolate shavings by pulling a sharp, rigid knife through the chocolate. Arrange the shavings on top of the mousse and serve.

From the top left, clockwise: Liqueur mousse; Chocolate and whisky pots; Hazelnut mousse; Iced chocolate and orange mousse

Chocolate and Whisky Pots

175 g (6 oz) plain chocolate
25 g (1 oz) unsalted butter
3 eggs, separated
2 tablespoons whisky
1 egg white
4–6 chocolate Fairy Fingers (page 185), to decorate

Preparation time: *25 minutes, plus setting*

1. Break the chocolate into small pieces and place in a bowl with the butter. Stand the bowl over a pan of simmering water until melted.
2. Beat the egg yolks and whisky into the chocolate and chill until cool, but do not allow the mixture to set.
3. Whisk all 4 egg whites until stiff and fold into the chocolate mixture.
4. Pour into four 150 ml (¼ pint) ramekin dishes or six 100 ml (4 fl oz) chocolate pots. Chill for at least 6 hours until set.
5. Before serving, if liked, stick a fairy finger into each pot. Alternatively serve with Langues de Chats (page 185).

Hazelnut Mousse

100 g (4 oz) hazelnuts
4 eggs, separated
100 g (4 oz) caster sugar plus 1 tablespoon
1 teaspoon cornflour
300 ml (½ pint) milk
15 g (½ oz) powdered gelatine
50 ml (2 fl oz) water
4–6 Hazelnut Clusters (page 187), to decorate

Preparation time: *35 minutes, plus setting*
Cooking time: *15 minutes*
Oven: *200°C, 400°F, Gas Mark 6*

1. Spread the hazelnuts on a baking sheet and roast in the oven for 15 minutes. Remove from the oven, cool slightly, then rub off the skins. Grind to a powder.
2. Place the egg yolks, 100 g (4 oz) caster sugar and flour in a bowl and whisk until creamy.
3. Heat the milk then pour over the yolk and sugar mixture. Blend thoroughly. Pour into a clean pan and heat gently, stirring constantly, until the custard coats the back of a wooden spoon.
4. Sprinkle the gelatine over the water in a small heatproof bowl. Stand the bowl in a pan of hot water and stir until the gelatine has dissolved. Remove from the heat. Whisk into the custard then pour the custard into a bowl. Add the ground nuts and cool until on the point of setting.
5. Cut out a sheet of non-stick silicone paper 55 × 15 cm (22 × 6 inches). Fasten it around a 15 cm (6 inch) soufflé dish to form a collar 7.5 cm (3 inches) above the rim of the dish. Secure the paper.
6. Whisk the egg whites and remaining caster sugar until very stiff. Fold into the hazelnut flavoured custard and pour into the mould. Chill until set.
7. Remove the paper collar and decorate with the hazelnut clusters.

Soufflé Rothschild

75 g (3 oz) crystallized fruit
25 ml (1 fl oz) Curaçao
25 g (1 oz) unsalted butter
40 g (1½ oz) caster sugar plus 1 teaspoon
2 eggs, separated
1 egg white
20 g (¾ oz) cornflour
125 ml (4½ fl oz) milk
icing sugar, to decorate

Serves 2
Preparation time: *25 minutes*
Cooking time: *20 minutes*
Oven: *200°C, 400°F, Gas Mark 6*

Soufflé Rothschild

1. Finely chop the crystallized fruit and mix with the orange curaçao. Reserve.
2. Melt 10 g (¼ oz) of the butter and use to brush the inside of a 15 cm (6 inch) soufflé dish. Coat with 1 teaspoon of the caster sugar and chill.
3. Beat the egg yolks, remaining caster sugar and cornflour in a mixing bowl. Heat the milk and pour over the yolks, flour and sugar. Mix well. Pour into the rinsed pan and heat until the custard thickens. Beat in the remaining butter.
4. Fold in the curaçao and crystallized fruit mixture.
5. Whisk the egg whites until stiff and fold into the custard mixture.
6. Pour into the prepared soufflé dish. Smooth the top with a palette knife. Bake in a preheated oven for 20 minutes. Dust with icing sugar and serve immediately.

Basic Vanilla Soufflé

35 g (1¼ oz) unsalted butter
1 tablespoon caster sugar
4 eggs, separated
75 g (3 oz) vanilla sugar
40 g (1½ oz) cornflour
250 ml (8 fl oz) milk

Preparation time: *25 minutes*
Cooking time: *25–30 minutes*
Oven: *190°C, 375°F, Gas Mark 5*

1. Melt 10 g (¼ oz) of the butter and use to brush the inside of a 1.25 litre (2 pint) soufflé dish. Coat the dish with caster sugar and place in the freezer.
2. Place the yolks, vanilla sugar and cornflour in a mixing bowl. Whisk until creamy. Heat the milk and pour over the yolks, sugar and flour and mix well. Pour into the rinsed pan and heat until the custard thickens. Beat in the remaining butter.
3. Whisk the egg whites until stiff, then fold into the custard mixture. Pour into the prepared soufflé dish and smooth the top with a palette knife. Bake in a preheated oven for 35 to 30 minutes. Serve immediately.

Variations:
Flavour the basic soufflé with 25 ml (1 fl oz) of any liqueur, or candied violets crushed to a powder, or coffee.

Honey Soufflé Pudding, With a Rum Sabayon

60 g (2¼ oz) unsalted butter
2 tablespoons caster sugar
50 g (2 oz) honey
50 g (2 oz) flour
grated rind of 1 lemon
150 ml (¼ pint) milk
2 eggs, separated
Sabayon:
2 egg yolks
20 g (¾ oz) caster sugar
20 g (¾ oz) honey
1 tablespoon rum
4 tablespoons milk

Preparation time: *35 minutes*
Cooking time: *30–35 minutes*
Oven: *190°C, 375°F, Gas Mark 5*

1. Melt 10 g (¼ oz) of the butter and use to brush the insides of four 150 ml (¼ pint) soufflé dishes. Dust with the sugar.
2. Cream the remaining butter, honey, flour and lemon rind. Heat the milk and pour over the butter, honey, flour and lemon mixture and blend well. Pour into the rinsed pan and heat until thickened. Beat in the egg yolks.
3. Whisk the egg whites until stiff and fold into the mixture. Pour into the prepared soufflé dishes and smooth the top with a palette knife.
4. Stand the dishes in a roasting tin containing sufficient simmering water to come half way up the sides of the dishes. Bake in a preheated oven for 30–35 minutes. Cover with a piece of buttered foil after 20 minutes.
5. Meanwhile, make the Sabayon sauce. Whisk the egg yolks, sugar and honey until creamy. Add the rum and milk, then stand the bowl containing the mixture over a pan of simmering water. Whisk until the sabayon has increased its volume and is fluffy.
6. Remove the puddings from the oven, loosen the edges with a knife and immediately turn out on to 4 dessert plates. Pour a generous amount of the sabayon over them. Serve any remaining sabayon in a sauce boat with a ladle.

Honey soufflé pudding with a rum sabayon

From the left:
Chocolate soufflé;
Tangerine soufflé

Chocolate Soufflé

35 g (1¼ oz) unsalted butter
175 g (6 oz) plain chocolate
1 tablespoon water
3 eggs, separated
1 egg white
icing sugar, to dredge

Preparation time: *25 minutes, plus chilling*
Cooking time: *10 minutes*
Oven: *230°C, 450°F, Gas Mark 8*

1. Melt 10 g (¼ oz) of the butter and use to brush the inside of four 150 ml (¼ pint) soufflé dishes.
2. Break the chocolate into small pieces and place in a bowl with the water and remaining butter. Stand over a pan of simmering water until melted. Beat in the egg yolks, then chill the mixture until cool but not set.
3. Whisk all 4 egg whites until stiff and fold into the chocolate mixture.
4. Pour the mixture into the prepared soufflé dishes and bake in a preheated oven for 10 minutes. Dredge with icing sugar and serve immediately.

Tangerine Soufflé

10 g (¼ oz) unsalted butter, melted
65 g (2½ oz) caster sugar
plus 2 tablespoons
grated rind of 2 tangerines
250 ml (8 fl oz) tangerine juice
(about 12 tangerines)
25 g (1 oz) arrowroot
25 ml (1 fl oz) water
3 eggs, separated

Preparation time: *25 minutes*
Cooking time: *10 minutes*
Oven: *230°C, 450°F, Gas Mark 8*

1. Brush four 150 ml (¼ pint) soufflé dishes with the melted butter. Dust with 1 tablespoon of the caster sugar and place in the freezer.
2. Heat the rind, tangerine juice and 65 g (2½ oz) of the caster sugar to simmering point. Blend the arrowroot and water together and whisk into the hot juice, stirring until it thickens. Cool slightly, then beat in the egg yolks.
3. Whisk the egg whites with the remaining 1 tablespoon of caster sugar until stiff and fold the whites into the tangerine mixture.
4. Pour into the prepared soufflé dishes and smooth the tops with a palette knife.
5. Bake in a preheated oven for 10 minutes. Serve immediately.

Banana and Rum Soufflé

25 g (1 oz) unsalted butter
60 g (2¼ oz) caster sugar, plus 1 tablespoon
4 eggs, separated
20 g (¾ oz) flour
150 ml (¼ pint) milk
2 bananas
50 ml (2 fl oz) rum

Sauce:

3 egg yolks
50 g (2 oz) caster sugar
40 ml (1½ fl oz) rum
1 tablespoon orange juice
icing sugar, to dredge

Preparation time: *30 minutes*
Cooking time: *30 minutes*
Oven: *190°C, 375°F, Gas Mark 5*

1. Melt 10 g (¼ oz) of the butter and use to brush the inside of a 1.25 litre (2¼ pint) soufflé dish. Coat with 1 tablespoon of the caster sugar and chill.
2. Whisk the egg yolks, 40 g (1½ oz) of the caster sugar and the flour in a mixing bowl. Heat the milk and pour over the mixture. Blend thoroughly. Pour into a clean pan and heat gently without boiling, stirring constantly, until the custard thickens. Beat in the remaining butter.
3. Slice 1 banana and leave to marinate in the rum. Blend the second banana to a purée and add to the custard.
4. Whisk the egg whites and remaining caster sugar until stiff. Fold the rum and banana slices into the custard, then fold in the egg whites.
5. Pour into a soufflé dish. Smooth the top with a palette knife, then bake in a preheated oven for 30 minutes.
6. Meanwhile, make the sauce. Whisk the yolks and sugar until creamy. Add the rum and orange juice. Stand the bowl containing the yolks and sugar mixture over a pan of simmering water. Whisk until the sauce becomes light and fluffy.
7. Dredge with icing sugar then serve the soufflé immediately, accompanied by the sauce.

Banana and rum soufflé

Lemon Soufflé

10 g (¼ oz) unsalted butter, melted
200 g (7 oz) caster sugar plus 1 tablespoon
2 eggs, separated
75 ml (3 fl oz) lemon juice
1 egg white
40 g (1½ oz) unsalted butter
peel of ¼ lemon, cut into fine matchstick strips
juice of ½ lemon

Preparation time: *35 minutes*
Cooking time: *10 minutes*
Oven: *230°C, 450°F, Gas Mark 8*

1. Brush four 150 ml (5 fl oz) soufflé dishes with melted butter and dust with 1 tablespoon of the sugar. Place in the freezer.
2. Put the yolks, lemon juice and 100 g (4 oz) of the sugar into a mixing bowl. Whisk over a pan of hot water until thick.
3. Whisk all the egg whites until stiff and fold into the lemon mixture. Pour into the prepared soufflé dishes and bake in a preheated oven for 10 minutes.
4. To make the sauce place all the remaining ingredients into a pan and boil until the sauce is syrupy.
5. To serve, remove the soufflés from the oven. Make a small hole in the centre of the soufflés. Pour the sauce into the holes.

Lemon soufflé

Apple Snow

4 large cooking apples
100 g (4 oz) sugar
4 egg whites
25 g (1 oz) caster sugar
To decorate:
8 orange segments
8 grapefruit segments

Preparation time: *25 minutes, plus cooling*
Cooking time: *45 minutes*
Oven: *200°C, 400°F, Gas Mark 6*

1. Using a sharp knife, cut the skin around the top of the apples. Place them in a roasting tin and bake in a preheated oven for 45 minutes.
2. Remove the apples from the oven and scrape the pulp out of the skin. Sieve the pulp and mix with the sugar and cool.
3. Whisk the egg whites and caster sugar until stiff and fold into the apple pulp. Spoon into a glass bowl or individual glasses and chill.
4. Decorate with the fruit segments.

From the left: Apple snow; Kiwi snow; Brown snow

Kiwi Snow

5 kiwi fruit, peeled
40 g (1½ oz) vanilla sugar
75 g (3 oz) caster sugar
3 egg whites

Preparation time: *15 minutes*

This light, refreshing dessert is perfect after a rich main course.

1. Slice 1½ of the kiwi fruits in to rings and sprinkle with 25 g (1 oz) of the vanilla sugar. Reserve.
2. Blend the remaining fruit and the caster sugar to a smooth purée.
3. Whisk the egg whites with the remaining vanilla sugar and fold the fruit purée into the egg whites.
4. Pour half the snow into 4 glasses and cover with a few kiwi slices. Spoon the rest of the snow on top. Decorate the top with the remaining kiwi slices. Serve within 1 hour, because the mixture starts to separate and cannot be mixed again.

Brown Snow

250 g (8 oz) canned or stewed prunes, drained and stoned
65 g (2½ oz) caster sugar
juice of ½ lemon
juice of ½ orange
50 ml (2 fl oz) Curaçao
3 egg whites

Preparation time: *15 minutes, plus freezing*

1. Blend the prunes, 50 g (2 oz) of the caster sugar, the lemon juice, orange juice and curaçao to a smooth purée. Pour into a mixing bowl.
2. Whisk the egg whites and remaining caster sugar until stiff. Fold the egg whites into the prune mixture.
3. Spoon into 4 glass coupes and place in the freezer until just beginning to firm.
4. Decorate with a quartered slice of orange just before serving, if liked.

Fresh Fruit Desserts

Watermelon Basket With 5 Fresh Fruits in Season

1 large, ripe watermelon
450 g–750 g (1–1½ lb) mixed fruit (choose 5 from strawberries, raspberries, mango, kiwi fruit, peaches, passion fruit, oranges, pineapple
juice of 1 lime
sugar, to taste

Serves 6–8
Preparation time: *45 minutes*

1. To make the watermelon basket, tie a piece of string horizontally around the centre of the melon to give a guideline.
2. With a sharp knife score 2 arcs on the top of the melon, 2.5 cm (1 inch) apart, either side of the stalk and down to the string to form the handle.
3. Cut around the melon, following the string, being careful not to cut through the marked out handle. Then follow and cut the score lines of the handle.
4. Remove the 2 wedges of melon on either side of the handle and reserve them.
5. Remove the centre section of flesh underneath the handle. Ease out the flesh gently, discarding the seeds as you work.
6. Scoop out the remaining flesh with a spoon to form a cavity.
7. Cut up half the flesh into bite-sized pieces. The remainder can be stored and used on another occasion.
8. Prepare the other chosen fruits. Leave strawberries and raspberries whole, peel and slice the mango, kiwi fruit and peaches, remove the seeds from the passion fruit, peel the grapes, peel and segment the oranges and skin and dice the pineapple. Place them in a bowl with the melon pieces. Sprinkle with lime juice and sugar to taste.
9. Mix the fruit gently and arrange it in the basket. If desired, place the basket in a large bowl and surround it with crushed ice.

From the top: Watermelon basket with 5 fresh fruits in season; Chartreuse salad

Chartreuse Salad

100 g (4 oz) sugar
150 ml (¼ pint) water
juice of ½ lemon
2 tablespoons Chartreuse
1 small Ogen melon
2 passion fruit
225 g (8 oz) green, seedless grapes, peeled
2 kiwi fruit, sliced

Serves 6
Preparation time: *40 minutes, plus chilling*

To make melon balls it is worthwhile purchasing a food baller to make perfectly round shapes. A melon baller normally has a handle with a cup on one or both ends and comes in different sizes. The baller may have a hole at the bottom of the cup so that the melon ball will release easily once made.

To make melon balls, cut the melon in half and scrape out all the seeds. Push the baller, cup shape downwards into the flesh. Rotate the cup in the flesh to make a complete ball. Lift out and transfer to a dish. Pieces of leftover melon flesh can be chopped or puréed and used for another dish.

1. Dissolve the sugar in the water in a heavy saucepan. Bring to the boil for 2–3 minutes.
2. Let the syrup cool, add the lemon juice and Chartreuse and pour into a serving bowl.
3. Cut the melon in half, discard the pips, and scoop out melon balls.
4. Cut the passion fruit in half and spoon out the flesh.
5. Mix the grapes, melon balls, slices of kiwi fruit and the passion fruit together carefully in the syrup and chill.
6. Serve with Almond and Ginger Tuiles (page 186).

Winter Fruit Salad

450 g (1 lb) mixed dried fruits (apricots, prunes, pears, figs, apples, peaches), soaked overnight in 1.2 litres (2 pints) water
175 g (6 oz) sugar
1 cinnamon stick
a few cloves
rind and juice of 1 lemon or orange
50 g (2 oz) flaked almonds, toasted

Serves 6
Preparation time: *20 minutes, plus soaking*

Buy dried fruit in small quantities so it is as fresh and as full of flavour as possible. Purchase dried fruits separately so you can add more of the fruits you particularly like.

1. Pour 600 ml (1 pint) of the dried fruit liquor into a pan with the sugar, cinnamon stick, cloves and rind and juice of the lemon or orange. Boil briskly for 5 minutes.
2. Add the fruit and simmer for 15 minutes until the fruit is plump and tender.
3. Serve hot or cold. Sprinkle with the almonds just before serving.

Peaches in Red Wine

4 peaches
juice of 1 lemon
300 ml (1/2 pint) red wine
100 g (4 oz) caster sugar
1 cinnamon stick

Preparation time: *45 minutes, plus cooling*

1. Dip the peaches into boiling water for a few seconds, then put them into a bowl of iced water to stop them cooking.
2. Carefully peel the peaches and rub a little lemon juice over them to prevent discoloration.
3. Put the wine, sugar and cinnamon stick in a saucepan and bring to the boil, stirring until the sugar has dissolved.
4. Lower the heat and place the peaches in the wine syrup. Poach for about 30 minutes until they are tender.
5. Remove the peaches from the syrup with a slotted spoon and place in a serving dish.
6. Boil the syrup fiercely until it is thick enough to coat the peaches. Spoon the syrup over the peaches and leave to cool.

From the left: Peaches in red wine; Winter fruit salad

From the left:
Pineapple flambé;
Baked stuffed nectarines

Pineapple Flambé

90g (3½oz) caster sugar
grated rind and juice of 1 orange
juice of ½ lemon
40g (1½oz) unsalted butter
4 thick slices fresh pineapple
2 tablespoons Kirsch (or rum)

Preparation time: *15 minutes*

1. Put the sugar, grated rind and juices in a frying pan. Bring to the boil, stirring, until the sugar dissolves and the mixture thickens to a syrup.
2. Lower the heat and add the butter. Swirl it around the pan until melted.
3. Add the pineapple slices and cook them gently until heated through, basting them regularly with the syrup. Lift each slice out of the pan with a slotted spoon on to warmed individual serving dishes.
4. Pour the kirsch or rum into the pan. Set alight to the syrup carefully and pour it, still flaming, over the pineapple slices.

Variation:
Banana Flambée: follow the recipe as above. Replace the caster sugar with soft brown sugar and 4 bananas peeled and halved lengthways in place of the pineapple. Use rum in place of kirsch.

Baked Stuffed Nectarines

6 large, ripe nectarines
4 almond macaroons or 8 Chocolate Macaroons (page 184), crushed
50g (2oz) mixed glacé fruits, finely shredded
½ egg, beaten
25g (1oz) butter
150ml (¼ pint) sweet white wine or sweet sherry

Serves 6
Preparation time: *30 minutes*
Cooking time: *20–30 minutes*
Oven: *200°C, 400°F, Gas Mark 6*

1. Wash the nectarines and halve them.
2. Remove the stones. Using a teaspoon, scrape and slightly enlarge the cavity.
3. Put the extra pulp into a bowl and mix together with the crushed macaroons, glacé fruits and the beaten egg.
4. Fill the nectarine cavities with the mixture.
5. Using 15g (½oz) of the butter, lightly grease a shallow dish, large enough to hold the nectarine halves in a single layer.
6. Place the halves stuffing side up. Dot each one with a little of the remaining butter and sprinkle with the wine.
7. Bake in a preheated oven for 20–30 minutes until tender and serve hot with whipped cream.

Praline Pears

4 ripe, even-sized Comice pears
1 quantity light sugar syrup (page 95)
300 ml (½ pint) double cream
100 g (4 oz) Praline (page 188)

Preparation time: *30 minutes, plus cooling*

1. Peel and core the pears, leaving them whole with the stalks still on. Poach the pears in the syrup for 10 minutes, turning occasionally so they cook evenly. Leave them in the syrup until cold.

2. Lift the pears out of the syrup with a slotted spoon and leave to drain completely. Place either in 1 large or 4 individual serving dishes.

3. Whip the double cream until it is stiff and fold in half the praline. Cover the pears completely with the cream.

4. Sprinkle the remaining praline over the pears and serve.

From the top left, clockwise: Praline pears; Oranges dionysus; Pickled pears in spiced vinegar; Orange and grapefruit in caramel

Orange and Grapefruit in Caramel

4 seedless oranges
4 grapefruits
225 g (8 oz) sugar
250 ml (8 fl oz) water
3 tablespoons Grand Marnier

Serves 8
Preparation time: *40 minutes, plus chilling*

1. With a sharp knife or vegetable peeler, pare the rind from 1 orange and half a grapefruit and shred finely.
2. Put the rind in a small pan and cover with boiling water. Bring to the boil and simmer for 2 minutes then drain.
3. Peel the oranges and grapefruits, removing all the pith.
4. Cut the fruit into segments and arrange them in a dish.
5. Put the sugar and 120 ml (4 fl oz) of the water into a heavy saucepan. Heat gently without letting it boil until all the sugar has dissolved.
6. Increase the heat and boil until it is a rich golden caramel.
7. Bring the remaining water to the boil in a saucepan. Remove the caramel from the heat and quickly pour in the hot water. Take great care as the water will splutter over the pan.
8. Stir until the caramel has melted, returning to the heat briefly if necessary. Leave to cool. Add the Grand Marnier.
9. Sprinkle the segments with the prepared peel and pour the syrup over the top.
10. Chill for several hours before serving with Langues de Chats (page 185).

Oranges Dionysus

4 oranges
250 ml (8 fl oz) red wine
100 g (4 oz) caster sugar
1 teaspoon cinnamon
2 tablespoons Curaçao
1 lemon, sliced
100 g (4 oz) sugar
1 tablespoon water

Preparation time: *20 minutes, plus chilling*

When slicing the oranges make sure that all the pips are removed. If the central fibrous core is thick, this should also be removed. When mandarins, tangerines and kumquats (use whole) are in season try using these in place of the oranges.

1. Remove the rind thinly from the oranges. Cut it into very fine strips.
2. Peel away the remaining rind and pith. Thinly slice the oranges and arrange them in a shallow serving dish.
3. Heat the wine to simmering point. Add the caster sugar and cinnamon to the wine, stirring until the sugar has dissolved. Add the Curaçao. Pour the hot wine over the oranges. Leave to cool.
4. Halve the lemon slices and add them to the oranges, then chill.
5. Put the sugar in a small heavy saucepan. Add the water and bring to the boil, stirring constantly, until the sugar starts to caramelize. Remove the pan from the heat, add the strips of orange rind and coat them well with the caramel.
6. Using tweezers, remove the strips of rind from the pan and arrange them on top of the orange slices.

Pickled Pears in Spiced Vinegar

200 g (7 oz) sugar
250 ml (8 fl oz) water
50 ml (2 fl oz) red wine
50 ml (2 fl oz) red wine vinegar
3 cloves
1 blade of mace
5 black peppercorns
4 pears, peeled, halved and cored and sprinkled with lemon juice

Preparation time: *15 minutes, plus chilling*
Cooking time: *about 45 minutes*

1. Put the sugar and water in a saucepan and bring to the boil, stirring, until the sugar dissolves. Add the wine, the wine vinegar, cloves, mace and peppercorns.
2. Lower the heat and place the pears in the syrup. Poach for about 30 minutes, until completely tender.
3. Lift the pears out of the pan with a slotted spoon and arrange them in a glass serving dish.
4. Bring the syrup back to the boil until it is reduced to a thick syrup. Pour it over the pears. Leave to cool, then chill. Serve with whipped double cream to which a little of the cold syrup has been added and Shortbread (page 184).

Exotic Fruit Salad

1 large pineapple
2 passion fruit
2 kiwi fruit, peeled and sliced
1 mango, peeled and sliced, stone removed
3 tablespoons Kirsch

Serves 6–8
Preparation time: *30 minutes, plus cooling*

1. Cut off the top of the pineapple. Carefully pull away 2 or 3 leaves for decoration.
2. Cut out the flesh of the pineapple by cutting round it with a long, sharp knife and scooping out the flesh with a spoon.
3. Slice the flesh into bite-sized pieces, discarding the core.
4. Halve the passion fruit and spoon out the flesh.
5. Mix all the fruits together in a bowl with the Kirsch. Spoon them into the pineapple shell and chill.
6. Just before serving, decorate with the pineapple leaves. Serve with plain unsweetened yogurt or a pouring cream.

Lychee and Orange Salad
in a handmade ice bowl

6 oranges
1 × 300 g (11 oz) can lychees

Preparation time: *30–40 minutes, plus freezing overnight*

1. Take 2 plastic bowls, about 15 cm (6 inch) and 20 cm (8 inch) in diameter.
2. Fill the large bowl half full with water and place the smaller bowl inside, weighted to prevent it bobbing about. Adjust the weight, so that the ice bowl will be about 2.5 cm (1 inch) thick at the bottom and 1 cm (½ inch) below the rim of the large bowl.
3. Secure the rims with tape to keep the small bowl centred. Freeze overnight.
4. Peel away the skin and the pith of the oranges and divide into segments.
5. Mix the oranges in a bowl with the lychees and their syrup. Keep cool.
6. Remove the ice bowl from the freezer and let it stand for 10–15 minutes at room temperature. Do not place under hot or cold water or the ice bowl will crack.
7. Remove the bowls (they should slip off) and place the ice bowl on a serving dish.
8. Transfer the fruit salad to the ice bowl and serve immediately.

Above: Kumquats in Grenadine; *Left, from the top:* Lychee and orange salad; Exotic fruit salad

Kumquats in Grenadine

750 g (1½ lb) kumquats
25 g (1 oz) caster sugar
150 ml (¼ pint) Grenadine

Serves 4–6
Preparation time: *10 minutes*

Kumquats are of Chinese origin and are no bigger than a large olive. The skins, which are usually eaten, are sweet and the inside is tart.

1. Wash the kumquats, and cut each one into about 4 slices. Arrange the slices in individual dishes.
2. Sprinkle with sugar and pour over the Grenadine.
3. Chill and serve with Brandysnaps (page 183) filled with cream.

Summer Pudding

750g (1½lb) mixed fruit
(loganberries, blackcurrants, redcurrants, blackberries, strawberries, raspberries)
150ml (¼ pint) water
100g (4oz) caster sugar
8 slices slightly stale white bread, crusts removed

Serves 6
Preparation time: *40 minutes, plus chilling overnight*

This is a classic English pudding which was served as far back as the 18th century to patients who were not allowed rich desserts. It is a beautifully flavoured dessert which uses the best of the English summer fruits. The balance of the fruits can be varied. Make a spring pudding by adding some tender stewed rhubarb with the early soft fruits, or add a higher proportion of stewed blackberries and eating apple to make an autumn pudding.

1. Place the fruit and water in a heavy pan with the sugar. Cook gently for 10 minutes. If using strawberries or raspberries add them after the rest of the fruit has been cooked to avoid them disintegrating.
2. Strain the fruit, reserving the cooking juice until later.
3. Cut a circle from one of the slices of bread to line the base of a 900ml (1½ pint) pudding basin. Cut sufficient wedges of bread to line the sides of the basin. Use scraps of bread to fill any gaps in the bread lining.
4. Dip each piece of this bread into the reserved juice and line the basin. Fill with half the fruit, place another layer of bread on top, then pour in the rest of the fruit and top with another layer of bread.
5. Spoon over any remaining fruit juice.
6. Put a plate that just fits inside the basin's rim on the pudding and put several heavy weights on top. Chill overnight.
7. Turn the pudding on to a serving dish and serve with Crème chantilly (page 189).

Strawberry Romanoff

750 g (1½ lb) strawberries, hulled
100 g (4 oz) caster sugar
50 ml (2 fl oz) Curaçao
25 ml (1 fl oz) port

Preparation time: *10 minutes, plus chilling*

Try using Cointreau or Grand Marnier in place of the Curaçao.

1. Roll the strawberries in sugar. Arrange them in a serving dish or individual glasses and pour over the Curaçao and port.
2. Chill well for 1 hour and serve with cream and Langues de chats (page 185).

Compôte of Redcurrants and Blackcurrants

225 g (8 oz) sugar
300 ml (½ pint) water
450 g (1 lb) redcurrants
450 g (1 lb) blackcurrants
1 tablespoon arrowroot
juice of ½ lemon

Serves 8
Preparation time: *30 minutes, plus cooling*

1. Dissolve the sugar and water in a pan over a gentle heat.
2. Bring to the boil, then add the fruit and simmer gently for 15 minutes.
3. Strain the fruit, reserving the liquor and spoon the fruit into a serving dish.
4. Return the syrup to the pan and bring it to the boil. Blend the arrowroot with the lemon juice. Remove the saucepan from the heat and stir in the arrowroot.
5. Return the pan to the heat, stirring until the syrup is thick and clear. Pour the syrup over the fruit. Cool before serving.

Figs With Lemon Cream

8 fresh, ripe figs
1 teaspoon caster sugar
juice of 1 lemon
175 ml (6 fl oz) double cream
8 sprigs of mint, to decorate

Preparation time: *20 minutes, plus chilling*

1. Peel the figs if preferred, and cut a cross on the top of each one.
2. Press gently to open the cross (as one would do to a baked potato).
3. Arrange the figs on a serving dish and chill for 1 hour.
4. Dissolve the sugar in the lemon juice and slowly stir in the cream. Adding the cream slowly to the sweetened lemon juice will thicken the cream.
5. Spoon the cream into the figs, and decorate with sprigs of mint.

Apples in Cider Syrup With Cracked Caramel

100 g (4 oz) sugar
300 ml (1/2 pint) dry cider
4 large dessert apples, peeled, cored and quartered
Cracked caramel:
50 g (2 oz) sugar
4 tablespoons water

Preparation time: *40 minutes, plus cooling*

1. Place the sugar and cider in a pan and heat gently until dissolved.
2. Bring to the boil and simmer for 5–10 minutes.
3. Place the apples in the syrup and cook for 15 minutes over a gentle heat.
4. Lift the apples from the syrup with a slotted spoon and transfer to a serving dish. Leave to cool.
5. Return the syrup to the heat and boil rapidly until it thickens.
6. Pour the syrup over the apples.
7. To prepare the caramel, place the sugar and water into a heavy pan over a moderate heat. Stir until the sugar has dissolved. Do not allow the syrup to boil.
8. When the sugar has dissolved, boil rapidly until the syrup becomes a golden caramel.
9. Pour the caramel out on to a greased baking sheet and leave to cool. When set, break up the caramel and sprinkle over the apples. Serve immediately.

From the left: Figs with lemon cream; Apples in cider syrup with cracked caramel; Rhubarb and ginger compôte; Elderberry and apple purée

Rhubarb and Ginger Compôte

225 g (8 oz) sugar
300 ml (1/2 pint) water
1 kg (2 lb) rhubarb, washed
75 g (3 oz) stem ginger, finely, chopped

Serves 6
Preparation time: *30 minutes, plus cooling*
Cooking time: *15–20 minutes*

1. Dissolve the sugar and water in a pan over a gentle heat. Bring to the boil.
2. Top and tail the rhubarb. Remove the stringy skin. Cut into 5 cm (2 inch) lengths.
3. Add the rhubarb and the ginger to the syrup, reserving 2 or 3 pieces of ginger for decoration. Simmer gently for 15 minutes.
4. Pour the compôte into a serving dish and leave to cool.
5. Decorate with pieces of stem ginger. Serve with ice cream or whipped cream.

Elderberry and Apple Purée

1 kg (2 lb) cooking apples, peeled and cored
juice of 1 lemon
15 g (½ oz) butter
50 ml (2 fl oz) water
caster sugar, to sweeten
225 g (8 oz) elderberries

Preparation time: *30–40 minutes, plus cooling*

Elderberries grow in many hedgerows in the countryside in August and September and add a wonderful flavour to fruit purées, especially apple.

1. To make the apple purée, slice the apples thinly into a bowl with the lemon juice to prevent discoloration.
2. Grease the bottom of a thick saucepan with the butter and place the apples and water in it.
3. Cover and cook gently until the apple slices are pulpy.
4. Remove the lid and continue to cook, stirring the apple until all the liquid has evaporated. Beat into a thick, smooth purée or blend in a liquidizer for a really smooth result.
5. Add sugar to taste and stir in the elderberries.
6. Spoon into a serving dish and leave to cool.
7. Serve with whipped cream flavoured with a little grated lemon rind and sugar if desired.

Variation
Use blackberries or loganberries in place of the elderberries.

Fruit Brûlée

1 egg
1 egg yolk
25 g (1 oz) caster sugar
1 teaspoon plain flour
200 ml (1/3 pint) double cream
1 dessert apple, peeled, cored and sliced
1 nectarine, stoned and sliced
1 orange, peeled, segmented and pith and skin removed
1 banana, peeled and sliced on the slant
250 g (8 oz) sugar
65 ml (2½ fl oz) water

Preparation time: *30 minutes, plus chilling*
Cooking time: *about 1½ minutes*

1. Put 4 dessert plates in the freezer or the freezing compartment of the refrigerator for 30 minutes.
2. Beat the egg, egg yolk, sugar and flour together in a mixing bowl.
3. Scald the double cream in a small saucepan. Pour it into the mixture, stirring constantly to combine the ingredients thoroughly.
4. Pour the custard into a clean pan. Heat gently, stirring constantly until the custard thickens.
5. Pour the custard on to the cold plates.
6. Divide the slices of fruit equally between the plates, arranging them decoratively on top of the custard.
7. Make a golden caramel with the sugar and water. Spoon over the fruit and custard. Repeat the glazing process with each portion. Cool slightly before serving.

Variation.
Substitute fruits with those in season. Soft fruits are good as an alternative.

From the top: Fruit brûlée; Cox's orange slices

Cox's Orange Slices

200 g (7 oz) unsalted butter
4 small Cox's apples, peeled, cored and cut into 8 segments
65 g (2½ oz) soft dark brown sugar
juice of ¼ lemon
juice of 1 orange
2 cloves
25 g (1 oz) raisins
4 large slices brown bread

Preparation time: *20 minutes*

1. Heat 65 g (2½ oz) of the butter in a pan. Fry the apple segments until they start to brown.
2. Add the sugar, lemon and orange juice, cloves and raisins. Simmer gently until the apple is cooked through.
3. Trim the slices of bread so they are circular or use a plain round cutter.
4. Heat the remaining butter in a large frying pan and fry the bread until crisp.
5. Place the slices of bread on a serving dish. Arrange 8 apple segments on each one in a neat pattern and spoon over the syrup and raisins. Serve hot.

Fruit Fondue

25 g (1 oz) unsalted butter
100 g (4 oz) plain chocolate, broken into squares
25 ml (1 fl oz) double cream
½ quantity Fruit Coulis (page 188) made with raspberries
½ quantity Fruit Coulis (page 188) made with stewed apricots
1 quantity Crème Chantilly (page 189)
120 g (4½ oz) caster sugar
1.5 kg (3 lb) fresh fruit (strawberries, pears, oranges, nectarines, pineapples depending on season). Hull, peel, core and cut the fruit into bite-sized pieces where appropriate.

Serves 6–8
Preparation time: *30 minutes*

Each guest is given a chilled plate, on which a selection of fresh fruits is arranged in bite-sized pieces, and a fondue fork to dip them into chocolate fondue, fruit coulis, crème chantilly or sugar.

1. Put the butter and chocolate into an enamel fondue pan. Melt them together, stirring frequently, over a very low flame.
2. Beat in the double cream. Heat thoroughly without boiling. Transfer the pan to the fondue burner. Keep it warm, but at the lowest possible temperature setting.
3. Put the raspberry and apricot coulis, crème chantilly and sugar into small bowls.
4. Arrange the pieces of fruit neatly on chilled serving plates.
5. To serve, stand the burner and chocolate sauce in the middle of the table, surrounded by the bowls of sauces and sugar.

Fruit fondue

Choice Cheesecakes

Brandysnap Cheesecake

150 g (5 oz) gingersnap biscuits
75 g (3 oz) unsalted butter, melted
Filling:
275 g (10 oz) curd cheese
40 g (1½ oz) caster sugar
6 Brandysnaps (page 183), ground to a powder
3 eggs, separated
grated rind of ½ lemon
½ root of ginger, peeled, chopped and juice extracted
15 g (½ oz) powdered gelatine
50 ml (2 fl oz) water
120 ml (4 fl oz) double cream
To decorate:
1 quantity Crème Chantilly (page 189)
6 Brandysnaps (page 183)
6 slices crystallized stem ginger, chopped

Makes one 20 cm (8 inch) cake
Preparation time: *50 minutes, plus chilling*

1. Crush the biscuits or blend them in a food processor. Combine the biscuit crumbs with the butter.
2. Spread the mixture evenly over the base of a buttered 20 cm (8 inch) springform tin.
3. Put the curd cheese and 50 g (2 oz) of the sugar in a bowl and blend in the crushed brandy snaps. Beat in the egg yolks and grated lemon rind and ginger juice.
4. Sprinkle the gelatine over the water in a small heatproof bowl. Stand the bowl in a pan of hot water and heat gently, stirring until dissolved. Add to the mixture.
5. Beat the double cream until it holds its shape and fold it into the mixture.
6. Whisk the egg whites with the remaining sugar until very stiff. Fold them into the cheese mixture. Pour the filling over the base, then chill.
7. When the cheesecake is set, transfer it to a serving dish. To decorate, pipe crème chantilly into each end of the brandy snaps. Arrange on top of the cheesecake, the ginger slices in between.

From the top: Brandysnap cheesecake; Chocolate cheesecake

Chocolate Cheesecake

120 g (4½ oz) digestive biscuits
50 g (2 oz) unsalted butter, melted
25 g (1 oz) plain chocolate, melted
50 g (2 oz) caster sugar
Filling:
225 g (8 oz) full fat soft cheese or low fat soft cheese
2 eggs, separated
120 g (4½ oz) caster sugar
15 g (½ oz) powdered gelatine
50 ml (2 fl oz) water
150 ml (¼ pint) double cream
150 g (5 oz) plain chocolate
whipped cream, to decorate

Makes one 20 cm (8 inch) cake
Preparation time: *1 hour, plus setting*

1. Butter a 20 cm (8 inch) springform tin.
2. Crush the biscuits or blend them in a food processor. Combine the biscuit crumbs with the butter, chocolate and sugar.
3. Spread the mixture evenly over the base.
4. To make the filling, beat the cheese and egg yolks with 100 g (4 oz) of the sugar in a mixing bowl.
5. Sprinkle the gelatine over the water in a small heatproof bowl. Stand the bowl in a pan of hot water and heat gently stir until dissolved. Add to the mixture.
6. Whip the cream until it holds it shape on the whisk. Fold into the cheese mixture.
7. Whisk the egg whites with the remaining sugar until they are very stiff.
8. Melt 75 g (3 oz) of the chocolate. Trail the chocolate into the mixture and mix it roughly to obtain a ripple effect. Pour the filling into the tin.
9. Chill the cheesecake for about 4 hours to set. Transfer it to a serving dish.
10. To decorate, melt the remaining chocolate and pour on to a cold, clean work surface. Spread as finely as possible. Cool until just set. Using a very sharp knife, cut triangles of chocolate. Pipe rosettes of cream on top of the cheesecake and decorate with the triangles.

Lemon Cheesecake

300 g (11 oz) sugar
500 ml (18 fl oz) water
2 lemons, very thinly sliced, seeds removed

Filling:

200 g (7 oz) low fat curd cheese
90 g (3½ oz) caster sugar
2 eggs, separated
grated rind ½ lemon
1 tablespoon powdered gelatine
50 ml (2 fl oz) water
120 ml (4 fl oz) double cream

Makes one 18 cm (7 inch) cake
Preparation time: *1 hour, plus steeping the lemon slices overnight*

1. Put the sugar and water in a pan. Bring to the boil, stirring, until the sugar has dissolved. Add the lemon slices. Simmer for 2 hours. Let the lemon slices cool in the syrup overnight.
2. Beat together the curd cheese, sugar, egg yolks and grated lemon rind.
3. Sprinkle the gelatine over the water in a small heatproof bowl. Stand the bowl in a pan of hot water and heat gently until dissolved. Add to the cheese mixture.
4. Line the base and sides of an 18 cm (7 inch) cake tin with the lemon slices.
5. Whip the cream until it holds its shape on the whisk. Fold it into the mixture.
6. Whisk the egg whites until they are stiff. Fold them into the mixture.
7. Pour the filling into the tin. Chill until set firm.
8. To serve, turn the cheesecake out carefully on to a serving dish.

From the left: Lemon cheesecake; Pink grapefruit cheesecake

Pink Grapefruit Cheesecake

150 g (5 oz) digestive biscuits
75 g (3 oz) unsalted butter, melted
a pinch of ground cinnamon

Filling:

250 g (9 oz) curd cheese
65 g (2½ oz) caster sugar
2 eggs, separated
1 tablespoon clear honey
1 tablespoon powdered gelatine
100 ml (3½ fl oz) grapefruit juice
grated rind of 1 pink grapefruit
100 ml (3½ fl oz) double cream
1 pink grapefruit, divided in segments, to decorate
julienne strips, to decorate

Makes one 20 cm (8 inch) cake
Preparation time: *40 minutes, plus setting*

1. Crush the biscuits and combine the biscuit crumbs with the butter and spice.
2. Spread the biscuit mixture evenly over the base of a 20 cm (8 inch) springform tin and firm it down.
3. To make the filling, beat the curd cheese with the caster sugar, egg yolks and honey in a mixing bowl.
4. Sprinkle the gelatine over the grapefruit juice in a small heatproof bowl. Stand the bowl in a pan of hot water and heat gently until dissolved. Mix the gelatine and grated rind into the curd cheese mixture.
5. Whip the cream until it holds its shape on the whisk and fold it into the mixture.
6. Whisk the egg whites until they are stiff and fold them into the mixture.
7. Pour the filling over the biscuit base, spreading it evenly. Chill until set.
8. Transfer the cheesecake to a serving dish. Decorate with the segments and strips.

Basic Uncooked Cheesecake

100 g (4 oz) digestive biscuits
40 g (1½ oz) unsalted butter, melted

Filling:

225 g (8 oz) curd cheese
2 eggs, separated
120 g (4½ oz) caster sugar
grated rind and juice of ½ lemon
15 g (½ oz) powdered gelatine
50 ml (2 fl oz) water
150 ml (¼ pint) double cream

Makes one 20 cm (8 inch) cake
Preparation time: *45 minutes, plus setting*

1. Butter a 20 cm (8 inch) springform tin.
2. Crush the biscuits and combine with the melted butter.
3. Spread the mixture evenly over the base of the tin and firm it down at the edges.
4. Beat together the cheese, egg yolks, 100 g (4 oz) of the sugar, the grated lemon rind and juice.
5. Sprinkle the gelatine over the water in a small heatproof bowl. Stand the bowl in a pan of hot water and heat gently until dissolved. Incorporate into the cheese mixture.
6. Whip the cream until it holds its shape on the whisk. Fold it into the cheese mixture.
7. Whisk the egg whites with the remaining caster sugar until they are very stiff. Fold into the cheese mixture and pour the filling into the tin.
8. Cool for about 4 hours to set.

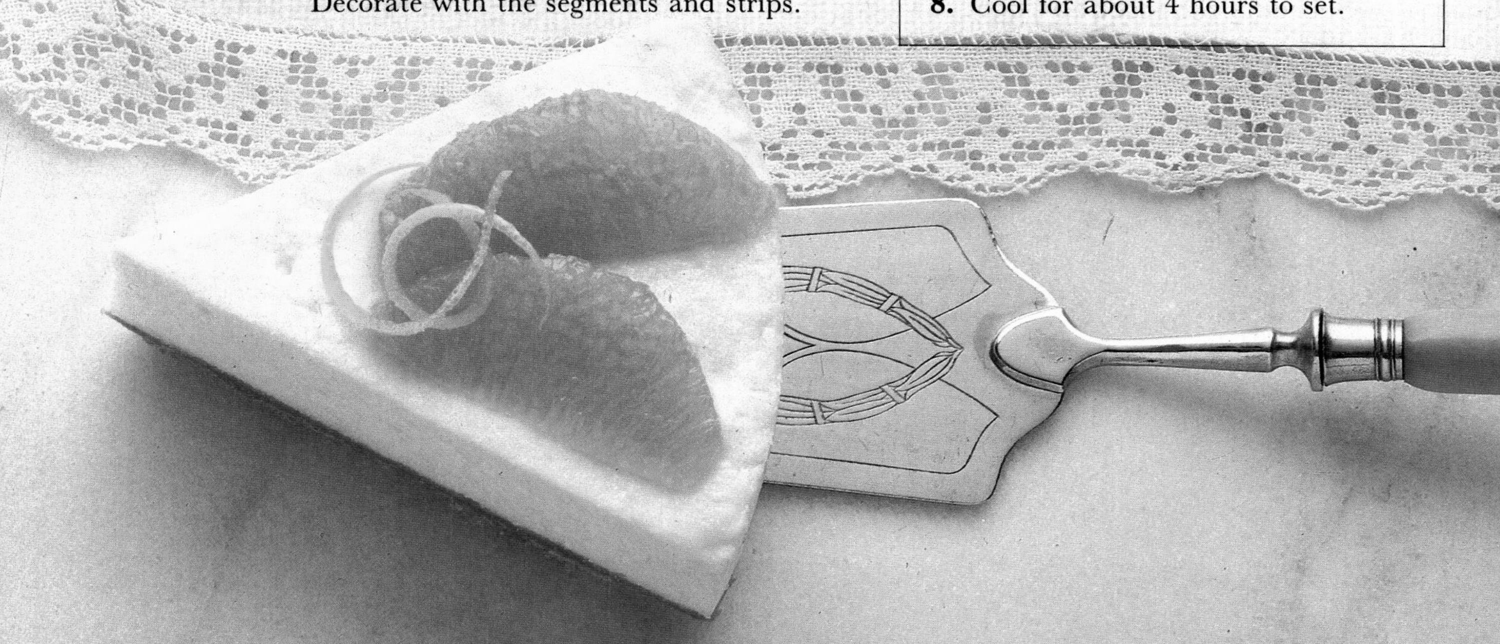

Avocado and Mint Cheesecake

50 g (2 oz) unsalted butter, melted
50 g (2 oz) caster sugar
120 g (4½ oz) Shortbread (page 184), crumbed

Filling:

6–8 fresh mint leaves
1 large ripe avocado pear
juice of 1 lemon
225 g (8 oz) full fat soft cheese
100 g (4 oz) caster sugar
2 eggs, separated
15 g (½ oz) powdered gelatine
50 ml (2 fl oz) water
150 ml (¼ pint) double cream

To decorate:

1 sprig of mint
lime slices

Preparation time: *50 minutes, plus setting*

1. Combine the butter, sugar and shortbread crumbs. Line the base of a 20 cm (8 inch) springform tin with the mixture.
2. Drop the mint leaves in boiling water for 5 seconds. Drain and chop the leaves.
3. Peel and stone the avocado pear and chop the flesh. Beat the mint, avocado, lemon juice, cheese, sugar and egg yolks together thoroughly or blend in a food processor.
4. Sprinkle the gelatine over the water in a small heatproof bowl. Stand the bowl in a pan of hot water and heat gently until dissolved. Add to the filling.
5. Whisk the cream until it holds its shape on the whisk and fold it into the mixture.
6. Whisk the egg whites until they are stiff and fold them in.
7. Pour the mixture over the crumb base. Leave to set in the refrigerator.
8. Transfer the cheesecake to a serving dish. Decorate with a sprig of mint and lime slices.

Avocado and mint cheesecake

Pina colada cheesecake

Pina Colada Cheesecake

150 g (6 oz) coconut biscuits or coconut kisses
75 g (3 oz) butter, melted

Filling:

275 g (10 oz) curd cheese
120 g (4½ oz) caster sugar
75 ml (3 fl oz) Pina colada
1 tablespoon white rum
3 eggs, separated
15 g (½ oz) powdered gelatine
50 ml (2 fl oz) water
120 ml (4 fl oz) double cream

To decorate:

½ fresh pineapple, cored and finely sliced
25 g (1 oz) caster sugar

Makes one 20 cm (8 inch) cake
Preparation time: *50 minutes, plus cooling*

1. Crush the biscuits or blend them in a food processor. Combine the biscuit crumbs with the butter.
2. Spread the mixture over the base of a buttered 20 cm (8 inch) springform tin.
3. To make the filling, beat the curd cheese and 100 g (4 oz) of the sugar in a bowl. Add the Pina colada and rum. Beat in the egg yolks.
4. Sprinkle the gelatine over the water in a small heatproof bowl. Stand the bowl in a pan of hot water and heat gently until dissolved. Add to the cheese mixture.
5. Whisk the double cream until it holds its shape on the whisk. Fold into the mixture.
6. Whisk the egg whites with the remaining sugar until they are very stiff. Fold them into the mixture.
7. Pour the filling over the biscuit base, then chill.
8. When the cheesecake is set, transfer it to a serving dish. Arrange the pineapple slices on top and sprinkle with sugar.

Basic Cooked Cheesecake

175 g (6 oz) digestive biscuits
75 g (3 oz) unsalted butter, melted
Filling:
225 g (8 oz) curd cheese
3 eggs, separated
150 g (5 oz) caster sugar
25 g (1 oz) plain flour
grated rind of 1 lemon
150 ml (1/4 pint) double cream

Makes one 20 cm (8 inch) cake
Preparation time: *45 minutes*
Cooking time: *1½–1¾ hours, plus cooling*
Oven: *160°C, 325°F, Gas Mark 3*

1. Butter a 20 cm (8 inch) springform tin.
2. Crush the biscuits or blend them in a food processor. Combine the biscuit crumbs with the butter and spread the mixture evenly over the base of the tin and firm down.
3. To make the filling, beat the curd cheese, egg yolks, 100 g (4 oz) of the sugar, the flour and grated rind in a mixing bowl for at least 5 minutes or blend in a food processor.
4. Whisk the cream until it starts to thicken. Combine with the curd mixture.
5. Whisk the egg whites and the remaining sugar until they are very stiff. Fold into the curd cheese mixture.
6. Fill the tin with the mixture. Smooth the top so the cheesecake bakes evenly. Bake in a preheated oven for 1½–1¾ hours. Leave to cool in the oven.
7. When the cheesecake is cool, transfer it to a serving dish.

Serving suggestions:
Decorate the cheesecake with icing sugar, fruit or fruit sauces or whipped cream. Serve with cream, soured cream or a syllabub.

Honey and Spice Cheesecake

175 g (6 oz) digestive biscuits
75 g (3 oz) unsalted butter, melted
Filling:
225 g (8 oz) curd cheese
120 g (4½ oz) clear honey
1 teaspoon ground ginger
1 teaspoon mixed spice
40 g (1½ oz) flour
3 eggs, separated
10 g (1/4 oz) caster sugar
150 ml (1/4 pint) double cream
icing sugar, to decorate

Makes one 20 cm (8 inch) cake
Preparation time: *30 minutes, plus cooling*
Cooking time: *1½–1¾ hours*
Oven: *160°C, 325°F, Gas Mark 3*

A spring-form tin with a spring release side clip is a worthwhile investment if you enjoy cheesecakes. They normally have a choice of 2 bases, one flat and one fluted with a tube. Other bases may be available. When the clip is unfastened, the sides expand by about 1 cm (½ inch) freeing the base. The sides are lifted off, thus making the removal of the fragile cheesecake simple.

1. Butter a 20 cm (8 inch) springform tin.
2. Crush the biscuits or blend them in a food processor. Combine the biscuit crumbs with the butter and spread evenly over the base of the tin and firm down.
3. To make the filling, beat the curd cheese, honey, ginger, spice, flour and egg yolks in a mixing bowl for at least 5 minutes or blend in a food processor.
4. Whisk the cream until it starts to thicken. Combine with the curd cheese mixture.
5. Whisk the egg whites with the sugar until they are very stiff. Fold into the curd cheese mixture.
6. Pour the filling into the tin. Spread the top evenly.
7. Bake in a preheated oven for 1½–1¾ hours. Leave to cool in the oven then transfer to a serving dish.
8. Cut 8 strips of paper 1 cm (½ inch) × 20 cm (8 inches) and arrange them in a criss-cross pattern on top of the cake. Dust the top of the cake with icing sugar. Carefully lift off the strips of paper to leave a pattern on top of the cheesecake.

From the left: Honey and spice cheesecake; Old fashioned cheesecake

Old Fashioned Cheesecake

350 g (12 oz) Shortcrust Pastry (page 114)
50 g (2 oz) unsalted butter
100 g (4 oz) soft brown sugar
225 g (8 oz) full fat soft cheese
1 tablespoon clear honey
50 ml (2 fl oz) double cream
1 tablespoon Amaretto di Saronns or brandy
3 egg yolks
50 g (2 oz) ground almonds
25 g (1 oz) flaked almonds
2 egg whites

Topping:

25 g (1 oz) soft brown sugar
½ teaspoon ground cinnamon
25 g (1 oz) flaked almonds

Makes one 20 cm (8 inch) cake
Preparation time: *40 minutes, plus cooling*
Cooking time: *1½–1¾ hours*
Oven: *160°C, 325°F, Gas Mark 3*

1. Line a 20 cm (8 inch) loose bottomed cake tin with the pastry.
2. Cream the butter and sugar. Add the cheese, honey, cream, liqueur, egg yolks and ground almonds. Beat together for about five minutes. Fold in the flaked almonds.
3. Whisk the egg whites until stiff and fold into the cheese mixture. Pour the filling into the cake tin.
4. Bake in a preheated oven for 1 hour. Remove the cheesecake from the oven and sprinkle the top with brown sugar, cinnamon and almonds. Return it to the oven and continue to bake until set, about 30 minutes longer. If the almonds are browning too quickly, cover with a sheet of greased foil and continue baking. Leave to cool in the oven.
5. Transfer from the tin on to a serving dish. Serve with a Fruit coulis (page 188) if desired.

Plum Cheesecakes

10 large plums
250 ml (8 fl oz) water
150 g (5 oz) sugar
2 teaspoons cornflour

Base:

120 g (4½ oz) digestive biscuits
40 g (1½ oz) unsalted butter, melted
40 g (1½ oz) caster sugar

Filling:

120 g (4½ oz) curd cheese
2 eggs, separated
50 g (2 oz) caster sugar

Makes four 7.5 cm (3 inch) cakes
Preparation time: *1 hour, plus cooling*
Cooking time: *1 hour*
Oven: *160°C, 325°F, Gas Mark 3*

1. Slit the plums. Put the water and sugar in a saucepan and bring to the boil, stirring, until the sugar has dissolved.
2. Add the plums. Poach them for 15 minutes or until tender. Lift out the plums with a slotted spoon. Remove the stones and cut the plums in half. Reserve 4 halves.
3. Dissolve the cornflour in a little water. Measure 150 ml (¼ pint) of the syrup into a small saucepan. Whisk in the cornflour and boil until thickened. Set aside.
4. Crush the biscuits and combine with the butter and caster sugar.
5. Divide the biscuit mixture equally between four 7.5 cm (3 inch) tartlet tins. Firm the mixture well into the tins.
6. To make the filling, beat the curd cheese with the egg yolks, reserved 4 halves and sugar until light and creamy.
7. Whisk the egg whites until they are stiff. Fold them into the curd mixture.
8. Pour the filling into the tartlet tins. Bake in a preheated oven for 1 hour. Leave to cool. Remove from the tartlet tins.
9. Arrange 4 plum halves on each tartlet and spoon the syrup on top.

Double Currant Cheesecake

175 g (6 oz) digestive biscuits
75 g (3 oz) unsalted butter, melted
50 g (2 oz) caster sugar

Filling:

225 g (8 oz) curd cheese
3 eggs, separated
150 g (5 oz) caster sugar
25 g (1 oz) plain flour
grated rind of 1 lemon
150 ml (¼ pint) double cream
100 g (4 oz) dried currants, soaked in 50 ml (2 fl oz) dark rum for 30 minutes

Topping:

120 g (4½ oz) blackcurrants
65 g (2½ oz) sugar
50 ml (2 fl oz) water
1 teaspoon cornflour

Makes one 20 cm (8 inch) cake
Preparation time: *1 hour, plus cooling*
Cooking time: *1½–1¾ hours*
Oven: *160°C, 325°F, Gas Mark 3*

1. Butter a 20 cm (8 inch) springform tin.
2. Crush the biscuits and combine the biscuit crumbs with the butter and sugar.
3. Spread the mixture evenly over the base of the tin and firm down.
4. To make the filling, beat the curd cheese, egg yolks, 100 g (4 oz) of the sugar, flour, grated rind in a large mixing bowl for at least 5 minutes.
5. Whisk the cream, currants and rum until the cream starts to thicken. Combine with the curd cheese mixture.
6. Whisk the egg whites and remaining sugar until they are very stiff. Fold into the curd cheese mixture.
7. Fill the tin with the mixture. Smooth the top so the cheesecake cooks evenly. Bake in a preheated oven for 1½–1¾ hours.
8. Cool in the oven, then transfer to a serving dish.
9. To make the topping, stew the blackcurrants with the sugar and water until tender. Blend the cornflour with a little water and whisk it into the blackcurrants. Continue to cook until thickened. Cool slightly, then pour the topping over the cheesecake.

From the left: Plum cheesecakes; Double currant cheesecake; Meringue cheesecakes

Meringue Cheesecakes

2 egg whites
65 g (2½ oz) caster sugar
65 g (2½ oz) icing sugar

Filling:

25 g (1 oz) low fat soft cheese
25 g (1 oz) unsalted butter
25 g (1 oz) caster sugar
1 tablespoon lemon juice
85 ml (3 fl oz) double cream
12 raspberries, to decorate

Preparation time: *30 minutes*
Cooking time: *1¼ hours*
Oven: *120°C, 250°F, Gas Mark ½*

1. Whisk the egg whites and 1 tablespoon of the caster sugar until stiff. Fold the remaining sugars into the egg whites.
2. Line a baking sheet with non-stick silicone paper. Put the meringue into a piping bag fitted with a plain nozzle and pipe 4 meringue nests about 10–13 cm (4–5 inches) wide on to the sheet. Bake in a preheated oven for 1¼ hours until set.
3. Cream the cheese, butter, caster sugar and lemon juice in a mixing bowl. Whisk in the double cream until the texture is stiff.
4. Fill the meringue nests with the cheese and arrange the raspberries on top.

Pecan and Maple Syrup Cheesecake

120 g (4½ oz) digestive biscuits
40 g (1½ oz) unsalted butter, melted
40 g (1½ oz) caster sugar
Filling:
225 g (8 oz) low fat soft cheese
3 eggs, separated
120 g (4½ oz) maple syrup
40 g (1½ oz) flour
65 g (2½ oz) sugar
1 tablespoon water
65 g (2½ oz) shelled pecan nuts
150 ml (¼ pint) double cream, whipped
To decorate:
1 quantity Crème Chantilly (page 189)
8 pecan nuts, shelled

Makes one 25 cm (10 inch) cake
Preparation time: *40 minutes*
Cooking time: *1½–1¾ hours*
Oven: *160°C, 325°F, Gas Mark 3*

1. Crush the digestive biscuits or blend them in a food processor. Combine the crumbs with the melted butter and sugar.
2. Spread the mixture over the base of a buttered 25 cm (10 inch) porcelain flan dish.
3. To make the filling, beat the cheese, egg yolks, maple syrup and flour in a mixing bowl for at least 5 minutes or blend in a food processor.
4. Put the sugar in a pan with the water. Bring to the boil, stirring, until the sugar has dissolved. Boil for 3 minutes. Add the pecan nuts and take the pan off the heat.
5. Stir with a wooden spoon until the nuts are covered in a sugar crust. Return to the heat and continue to cook, stirring constantly, until the sugar caramelizes. Turn the nuts on to a sheet of non-stick silicone paper and leave to cool.
6. Crush the caramel-coated nuts or blend them in the food processor. Fold into the cheese mixture.
7. Whisk the egg whites until stiff and fold them into the mixture.
8. Fold the whipped cream into the mixture.
9. Fill the flan dish with the cheese mixture. Bake in a preheated oven for 1½–1¾ hours. Leave to cool in the oven.
10. Decorate with crème chantilly and whole pecan nuts.

Pecan and maple syrup cheesecake;

Orange Cheese Torte

350 g (12 oz) Pâte Brisée (page 120)
225 g (8 oz) low fat soft cheese
2 eggs, separated
grated rind and juice of 1 orange
100 g (4 oz) caster sugar
25 g (1 oz) plain flour
120 ml (4 fl oz) double cream
To decorate:
1 orange, finely sliced
65 g (2½ oz) caster sugar
120 ml (4 fl oz) water

Serves 6
Preparation time: *45 minutes, plus resting and cooling*
Cooking time: *1 hour*
Oven: *190°C, 375°F, Gas Mark 5; 200°C, 400°F, Gas Mark 6*

1. Line a 20 cm (8 inch) flan ring with the pastry and prick with a fork. Rest for 30 minutes. Bake blind in a preheated oven for 15 minutes.
2. Beat the cheese, egg yolks, orange rind and juice, sugar, flour and cream together.
3. Whisk the egg whites until they form soft peaks. Fold them into the cheese mixture.
4. Pour the mixture into the pastry shell. Reduce the heat and bake for 30 minutes.
5. Put the orange slices unpeeled in a pan. Sprinkle them with the sugar and add the water. Bring the liquid slowly to simmering point and simmer for 15 minutes. Drain the orange slices on paper towels.
6. Arrange the slices in a ring around the top of the torte, pressing them down gently. Return the torte to the oven and bake for a further 15 minutes. Serve hot or cold.

Caramelized Cheesecake

120 g (4½ oz) sugar
225 g (8 oz) low fat soft cheese
3 eggs, separated
100 g (4 oz) caster sugar
grated rind of 1 lemon
50 g (2 oz) plain flour
150 ml (¼ pint) double cream

Preparation time: *30 minutes*
Cooking time: *1½ hours*
Oven: *160°C, 325°F, Gas Mark 3*

1. Place the sugar in a small pan and moisten with a little water. Heat until the sugar turns to a mid amber caramel. Immediately pour the caramel into an oiled 20 cm (8 inch) cake tin with a fixed base.
2. Put the cheese, egg yolks, caster sugar, grated lemon rind and flour in a mixing bowl and beat for at least 5 minutes.
3. Whip the cream until it holds its shape on the whisk. Fold it into the cheese mixture and beat for 2 minutes more.
4. Whisk the egg whites until they are stiff. Fold them into the cheese and cream mixture. Pour into the cake tin and bake in a preheated oven for 1½ hours.
5. Turn the cheesecake out immediately on to a serving dish.

From the top:
Caramelized cheesecake; Orange cheese torte

Ice Cream & Frozen Desserts

Amaretti Ice Box Pudding

18 Amaretti biscuits
2 egg yolks
65 g (2½ oz) caster sugar
200 ml (7 fl oz) double cream
2 egg whites
To decorate:
whipped cream
Amaretti biscuits

Preparation time: *25 minutes, plus freezing*

1. Grind the biscuits to a powder and line the base of a 15 cm (6 inch) soufflé dish with 50 g (2 oz) of the powder.
2. Whisk the yolks until white and creamy, then whisk in the caster sugar and continue whisking until stiff.
3. Whisk the double cream until it holds its shape on the whisk.
4. Using a clean whisk, whisk the egg whites until stiff.
5. Fold the yolks and sugar into the whipped cream. Fold in the remaining powdered Amaretti biscuits and the egg whites. Spoon into the soufflé dish and place in the freezer. Freeze for 2–3 hours or until set.
6. To serve, transfer the pudding to the refrigerator 15 minutes before serving. Free the ice cream from the edges of the dish and turn out onto a serving dish. Pipe rosettes of cream around the base and the top, then decorate with halved Amaretti biscuits on top. Cut the cake into wedge shaped portions and serve immediately.

Pistachio Ice Cream

3 egg yolks
120 g (4½ oz) vanilla sugar
250 ml (8 fl oz) milk
65 g (2½ oz) pistachio nuts, ground to a powder
300 ml (½ pint) double cream

Makes 6–8 portions
Preparation time: *20 minutes, plus cooling and freezing*

The pistachio nut has a small, bright green kernel which is delicate in flavour and is slightly sweet. The kernel is covered with a yellowish-red skin and a bluish husk. They can be bought in their husks or shelled and blanched. They can be chopped or sliced and used to decorate desserts, gâteaux and frozen desserts. They make a particularly delicious flavouring for ice-cream.

1. Whisk the egg yolks and sugar until they whiten. Heat the milk to simmering point, then pour over the yolk and sugar mixture. Blend well.
2. Return the custard to the rinsed pan. Heat until it coats the back of a wooden spoon. Pour into a freezer container. Stir in the ground pistachios and cool.
3. Whisk the double cream until it starts to thicken. Fold into the cold custard.
4. Transfer the custard mixture to a freezer container and place in the freezer. Freeze for 2–3 hours or until just beginning to set.
5. Remove from the freezer and whisk thoroughly to break down the ice crystals. Return to the freezer for 1–2 hours or until firm.
6. If the ice cream has been in the freezer for 24 hours or longer, transfer to the refrigerator 15 minutes before serving to soften slightly.

From the top: Amaretti ice box pudding; Pistachio ice cream

From the left: Vanilla ice cream; Orange and rosemary ice cream; Banana ice cream

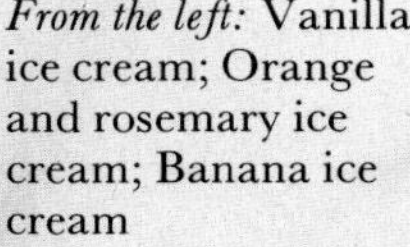

Vanilla Ice Cream

3 egg yolks
100 g (4 oz) vanilla sugar
250 ml (8 fl oz) milk
300 ml (½ pint) double cream

Makes 6–8 portions
Preparation: *20 minutes, plus cooling and freezing*

1. Whisk the yolks and sugar until white and creamy. Heat the milk to simmering point and pour over the yolks and sugar. Blend well.
2. Pour the custard into the rinsed pan and heat until it coats the back of a wooden spoon. Pour into a bowl and cool.
3. Whisk the double cream until it thickens, then fold into the custard.
4. Pour the custard into a freezer container and place in the freezer. Freeze for about 2–3 hours or until it begins to set at the edges.
5. Remove the custard from the freezer and whisk thoroughly to break down the ice crystals. Return to the freezer for 1–2 hours or until firm.
6. If the ice cream has been in the freezer for 24 hours or longer, transfer to the refrigerator 15 minutes before serving, to soften slightly.

Orange and Rosemary Ice Cream

200 ml (8 fl oz) water
150 g (5 oz) sugar
grated rind of 2 oranges
2 × 15 cm (6 inch) sprigs of rosemary
juice of 2 oranges
100 ml (4 fl oz) double cream

Preparation time: *20 minutes, plus cooling and freezing*

1. Place the water and sugar in a pan and bring to the boil. Stir constantly until the sugar is dissolved.
2. Add the orange rind and rosemary and leave to stand for 15 minutes. Remove the rosemary and discard.
3. Stir in the orange juice, then pour the mixture into a freezer container and place in the freezer. Freeze for 2–3 hours or until almost set.
4. Whip the double cream until it holds its shape on the whisk then beat into the orange mixture. Return the mixture to the freezer for 2–3 hours or until firm.
5. If the ice cream has been in the freezer for 24 hours or longer, transfer to the refrigerator 15 minutes before serving to soften slightly.

Banana Ice Cream

2 egg yolks
100 g (4 oz) caster sugar
1 teaspoon flour
200 ml (7 fl oz) milk
1 banana
300 ml (½ pint) double cream

Serves 6–8
Preparation time: *25 minutes, plus cooling and freezing*

1. Whisk the yolks, sugar and flour until white and creamy. Heat the milk to simmering point and pour over the yolks and sugar. Mix well.
2. Pour the custard in to the rinsed pan and heat until it coats the back of a wooden spoon. Pour into a freezer container and cool.
3. Blend the banana to a purée. Whisk the double cream until it starts to thicken. Fold the pureé and then the cream into the cold custard.
4. Place the freezer container in the freezer for 2–3 hours. Remove from the freezer and whisk thoroughly to break down the ice crystals. Return to the freezer for 1–2 hours or until completely firm.
5. If the ice cream has been in the freezer for 24 hours or longer, transfer to the refrigerator 15 minutes before serving to soften slightly. To serve, form balls of the ice cream using a scoop.

From the left: Coppa Cleopatra; Coffee granita with vanilla ice cream

Coppa Cleopatra

100 g (4 oz) sugar
1 tablespoon water
small pinch of cream of tartar
50 ml (2 fl oz) double cream
50 ml (2 fl oz) cognac
4 pieces crystallized stem ginger, finely diced
4 scoops Vanilla Ice Cream (page 88) or Hazelnut Parfait (page 95)

Preparation time: *15 minutes, plus cooling*

1. Put the sugar and water into a pan with the cream of tartar. Heat until the sugar has completely dissolved. Bring to the boil, stirring, until the sugar turns to a mid-amber caramel.
2. Remove the pan from the heat and whisk in the cream. Beat in the cognac and leave to cool.
3. Put a scoop of ice cream in each of 4 glass coupes. Pour over the sauce and sprinkle the chopped ginger on top.

Coffee Granita With Vanilla Ice Cream

50 g (2 oz) sugar
450 ml (3/4 pint) strong black coffee
4 scoops Vanilla Ice Cream (page 88)
4 teaspoons liqueur (Tia Maria, Sambuco, Amoretti di Saronno) (optional)

Preparation time: *10 minutes, plus freezing*

1. Stir the sugar into the coffee until it has dissolved.
2. Pour the sweetened coffee into a shallow-sided tray. As soon as the coffee is cool, transfer the tray to the freezer or freezing compartment of the refrigerator.
3. After about 30 minutes, when it starts to freeze, scrape the ice crystals from the side of the tray to the centre. Return the tray to the freezer and repeat the scraping at regular intervals until all the mixture has a grainy texture.
4. Divide the granita between 4 glass coupes or sundae dishes. Spoon or arrange scoops of vanilla ice cream on top. Spoon a little liqueur over the ice cream if desired and serve immediately.

Coffee and Date Soufflé Glacé

150 g (5 oz) fresh dates, stoned
2 teaspoons instant coffee
30 ml (1 fl oz) boiling water
2 egg whites
1 tablespoon caster sugar
100 g (4 oz) sugar
200 ml (7 fl oz) double cream

Preparation time: *30 minutes, plus freezing*

1. Cut out 4 sheets of non-stick silicone paper 25 × 7.5 cm (10 × 3 inches). Fit the papers around four 120 ml (4 fl oz) ramekins to form a collar at least 4 cm (1½ inches) higher than the rim of the ramekin. Secure the papers with string or an elastic band.
2. Blend the dates to a purée, then combine with the coffee dissolved in the water.
3. Whisk the egg whites and caster sugar until stiff.
4. Place the sugar in a pan with sufficient water to moisten then boil hard for 3 minutes.
5. Whisking the egg whites continuously, pour the boiling sugar on to the whites in a steady stream. Whisk for a further 5 minutes.
6. Whisk the cream until it holds its shape on the whisk.
7. Fold the coffee and date mixture into the cooked meringue, then fold the cream into the meringue.
8. Spoon the mixture into the ramekins and place in the freezer. Freeze for about 1 hour or until set.
9. To serve, remove the paper collar and decorate with a rosette of whipped cream sprinkled with coffee granules, if liked. Serve within 15 minutes.

Coffee and date soufflé glacé

From the left: Coupe glacé à la mangue; Strawberries cocteau

Coupe Glacé à la Mangue

8 dessertspoons Vanilla Ice Cream (page 88)
1 mango, peeled, stoned and quartered
50 g (2 oz) caster sugar
juice of 1 orange
1 quantity Crème Chantilly (page 189)

Preparation time: *15 minutes*

1. Put 2 spoonfuls of ice cream into each of 4 coupes. Set them aside in a refrigerator.
2. Cut half the mango into fine slices for decoration.
3. Pass the remaining mango through a sieve or purée in a blender. Whisk in the sugar and orange juice.
4. Arrange the mango slices around the ice cream. Pour the mango purée on top.
5. To decorate, pipe rosettes of crème chantilly on top.

Strawberries Cocteau

4 Chocolate Macaroons (page 184)
2 tablespoons Kirsch
225 g (8 oz) alpine or common strawberries
4 scoops Vanilla Ice Cream (page 88)
1 quantity Crème Chantilly (page 189)
candied violets

Preparation time: *15 minutes*

1. Dip the macaroons in Kirsch. Put them in 4 dessert bowls or glass coupes.
2. Cover them with a layer of strawberries.
3. Put a scoop of ice cream on top.
4. Arrange more strawberries on top, reserving a few for decoration.
5. Pile the crème chantilly on top of the ice cream and strawberries.
6. Decorate with candied violets and the remaining strawberries. Serve immediately.

Kirsch Meringue Gâteau

100 g (4 oz) caster sugar
300 ml (1/2 pint) double cream
25 ml (1 fl oz) Kirsch
55 g (2 oz) Chocolate Fairy Fingers (page 185)
100 ml (4 fl oz) Fruit Coulis
(page 188), to decorate

Preparation time: *20 minutes, plus freezing*

1. Line a 15 cm (6 inch) soufflé dish with aluminium foil.
2. Whisk the sugar, cream and Kirsch until it holds its shape on the whisk.
3. Break up the chocolate meringue into small pieces and fold into the cream.
4. Spoon the mixture into the prepared soufflé dish and place in the freezer. Freeze for 3–4 hours or until firm.
5. If the gâteau has been in the freezer for 24 hours or longer, transfer to the refrigerator 15 minutes before serving to soften slightly. To serve, turn out the gâteau on to a serving dish. Remove the foil, and pour the fruit coulis over the top. Serve immediately.

Kirsch meringue gâteau

From the top: Hazelnut parfait with a caramel sauce; Ginger parfait

Ginger Parfait

3 egg yolks
75 g (3 oz) caster sugar
300 ml (1/2 pint) double cream
75 g (3 oz) stem ginger, finely diced

Preparation time: *20 minutes, plus freezing*

1. Whisk the egg yolks until they whiten. Whisk in the caster sugar.

2. In a separate bowl, whisk the cream until it holds its shape on the whisk.

3. Fold the yolks and sugar into the double cream and fold in the ginger.

4. Transfer the mixture to a freezer container and place in the freezer. Freeze for about 2–3 hours or until almost set.

5. Remove from the freezer and beat well, then freeze for a further 1–2 hours or until completely firm.

6. To serve, scoop a ball of the parfait into a coupe. Pour over a teaspoon of the stem ginger syrup and serve each with a Brandysnap (page 183).

7. If the parfait has been in the freezer for 24 hours or longer, transfer to the refrigerator 15 minutes before serving to soften slightly.

Hazelnut Parfait With a Caramel Sauce

75 g (3 oz) hazelnuts
75 g (3 oz) sugar
Parfait:
3 egg yolks
75 g (3 oz) caster sugar
300 ml (½ pint) double cream
Sauce:
75 g (3 oz) sugar
125 ml (4 fl oz) double cream

Preparation time: *1 hour, plus cooling and freezing*
Cooking time: *15 minutes*
Oven: *200°C, 400°F, Gas Mark 6*

1. Place the nuts in a roasting tin and roast in the oven for 15 minutes. Remove from the oven and rub off the hazelnut skins. Discard the skins.
2. Make the praline following the recipe on page 188, using the hazelnuts and sugar, then grind to a powder.
3. Whisk the egg yolks until they whiten. Whisk in the caster sugar and continue whisking until the mixture thickens.
4. In a separate bowl, whisk the cream until it holds its shape on the whisk.
5. Fold the yolks and sugar into the double cream then fold in half the hazelnut praline.
6. Transfer the mixture to a freezer container and place in the freezer. Freeze for 2–3 hours until almost set. Beat well and return to the freezer for 1–2 hours or until completely firm.
7. To make the sauce, place the sugar in a pan with sufficient water to moisten. Boil until a mid-amber caramel. Remove from the heat then reserve.
8. Bring the cream to the boil as quickly as possible. Whisk into the hot caramel. Allow to cool until just warm.
9. If the parfait has been in the freezer for 24 hours or longer, transfer to the refrigerator 15 minutes before serving, to soften slightly.
10. Pour the sauce over the scoops of parfait and sprinkle with the remaining praline.

Basic Vanilla Parfait

3 egg yolks
50 g (2 oz) vanilla sugar
300 ml (½ pint) double cream

Preparation time: *15 minutes, plus freezing*

1. Whisk the egg yolks until they whiten. Add the vanilla sugar and continue whisking until the mixture thickens.
2. In a separate bowl, whisk the cream until it holds its shape on the whisk.
3. Fold the yolks and sugar into the double cream, then pour into a freezer container and place in the freezer. Freeze for 2–3 hours or until almost set, but not solid.
4. Remove from the freezer and beat well to break down any ice crystals. Return to the freezer for 1–2 hours or until firm.
5. If the parfait has been in the freezer for 24 hours or longer, transfer to the refrigerator 15 minutes before serving to soften slightly.

Sorbet Syrup

300 g (11 oz) sugar
300 ml (½ pint) water

Preparation time: *10 minutes*

1. Place the sugar and water in a pan.
2. Heat to boiling point, stirring continuously to dissolve the sugar.
3. Cool, and store in an airtight container until ready for use.

Light Sugar Syrup

225 g (8 oz) sugar
600 ml (1 pint) water
few strips of lemon rind

1. Dissolve the sugar in the water, then add the lemon rind.
2. Bring to the boil, then reduce to a simmer and use for poaching fruit.

Loganberry Parfait

225g (8oz) loganberries, thawed if frozen
140g (5½oz) caster sugar
3 egg yolks
300ml (½ pint) double cream

Preparation time: *25 minutes, plus cooling and freezing*

1. Liquidize the loganberries until smooth, then strain to remove the seeds. Add 65g (2½oz) of the caster sugar to the purée.
2. Whisk the egg yolks until they whiten. Whisk in the remaining caster sugar and continue whisking until the mixture becomes thick and light.
3. In a separate bowl, whisk the cream until it holds its shape on the whisk.
4. Fold the yolks and sugar into the cream.
5. Beat in three-quarters of the purée a little at a time. The mixture should hold its shape on the whisk.
6. Transfer the mixture to a freezer container and place in the freezer. Freeze for 2–3 hours or until almost set. Beat well and return to the freezer for 1–2 hours or until completely firm.
7. If the parfait has been in the freezer for 24 hours or longer, transfer to the refrigerator 15 minutes before serving to soften slightly. To serve, scoop the parfait into individual bowls, then pour a little of the remaining purée over the top. Serve immediately.

From the left: Chestnut parfait; Loganberry parfait

Chestnut Parfait

165g (5½oz) chestnuts
200ml (7fl oz) milk
65g (2½oz) sugar
Parfait:
3 egg yolks
75g (3oz) caster sugar
300ml (½ pint) double cream

Preparation time: *45 minutes, plus cooling and setting*
Cooking: *1 hour 10 minutes*
Oven: *190°C, 375°F, Gas Mark 5*

1. Using a sharp knife slit the chestnuts and place in a roasting tin and roast in a preheated oven for 25 minutes. Remove from the oven, cool slightly, then peel the outer and inner chestnut skins. Discard the peel and skins.
2. In a pan bring the milk and sugar to the boil. Add the chestnuts and poach gently for 45 minutes. Blend the chestnuts and liquid to a purée and allow to cool.
3. To make the parfait, whisk the egg yolks until they whiten. Add the caster sugar and continue whisking until the mixture thickens.
4. In a separate bowl, whisk the cream until it holds its shape.
5. Whisk the chestnut purée, the yolks and sugar into the cream. The mixture should be stiff enough to hold its shape.
6. Transfer the mixture to a freezer container and place in the freezer. Freeze for 2–3 hours or until almost set. Beat well and return to the freezer for 1–2 hours or until firm.
7. If the parfait has been in the freezer for 24 hours or longer, transfer to the refrigerator 15 minutes before serving, to soften slightly.
8. To serve, scoop the parfait into a tall glass or parfait glass.

Basic Lemon Sorbet

grated rind of 2 lemons
juice of 3 lemons
200 ml (7 fl oz) prepared Sorbet Syrup (page 95)
100 ml (4 fl oz) water
1 egg white
1 teaspoon caster sugar

Preparation time: *20 minutes, plus freezing*

1. Place the rind, juice, syrup and water in a freezer container and blend thoroughly. Place in the freezer and freeze for about 2–3 hours or until almost solid.
2. Whisk the egg white and caster sugar until stiff. Remove the sorbet from the freezer and beat in the whisked egg white. Return to the freezer for 1–2 hours or until firm.
3. If the sorbet has been in the freezer for 24 hours or longer, transfer to the refrigerator 15 minutes before serving to soften slightly.

Ananas Givré

1 ripe pineapple, about 1 kg (2¼ lb)
200 ml (7 fl oz) prepared Sorbet Syrup (page 95)
To decorate:
1 tangerine, sliced
½ banana, sliced

Preparation time: *25 minutes, plus freezing*

1. Lay the pineapple on its side. Slice off the top third of the pineapple, cutting just above the level of the leaves.
2. Cut out the pineapple flesh from the top in a single piece and reserve for decoration.
3. Cut out the remaining pineapple flesh from the main segment, without damaging the skin. Freeze the pineapple shell.
4. Blend the pineapple flesh from the bottom segment to obtain about 400 g (14 oz) purée. Add the syrup.
5. Pour the puréed mixture into a freezer container and place in the freezer. Freeze for 3–4 hours or until almost solid. Beat the mixture thoroughly and return to the freezer for 1–2 hours or until set.
6. Spoon the sorbet into the frozen pineapple skin.
7. To decorate, slice the reserved pineapple into thin segments. Arrange all the sliced fruit on top of the sorbet and serve.

Ananas givré

Passionfruit Sorbet

10 passionfruit
juice of ½ lime
100 ml (4 fl oz) water
300 ml (½ pint) prepared Sorbet Syrup (page 95)
1 egg white
1 teaspoon caster sugar

Preparation time: *15 minutes, plus freezing*

1. Scoop the flesh out of the passionfruit. Liquidize with the lime juice and water for about 10 seconds. Strain the juice into a freezer container and combine with the syrup.
2. Place the freezer container in the freezer and freeze for 2–3 hours or until almost solid.
3. Whisk the egg white and caster sugar until stiff.
4. Remove the sorbet from the freezer and beat in the egg white, return the sorbet to the freezer for 1–2 hours or until set.
5. If the sorbet has been in the freezer for 24 hours or longer, transfer to the refrigerator 15 minutes before serving to soften slightly.

Cherry Brandy Sorbet

250 ml (8 fl oz) prepared Sorbet Syrup (page 95)
juice of 1 lemon
200 ml (7 fl oz) water
1 egg white
100 ml (3½ fl oz) cherry brandy
4 teaspoons cherry brandy, to serve

Preparation time: *15 minutes, plus freezing*

1. Mix the syrup, lemon juice and water in a freezer container. Place in the freezer and freeze for 3–4 hours or until almost solid.
2. Whisk the egg white until stiff, then whisk into the freezing sorbet. Add the cherry brandy, then return the sorbet to the freezer for 1–2 hours or until completely set.
3. To serve, scoop the sorbet into portions, and pour a teaspoon of cherry brandy over each.
4. If the sorbet has been in the freezer for 24 hours or longer, transfer to the refrigerator 15 minutes before serving to soften slightly.

Punch à la Romaine

400 ml (14 fl oz) prepared Sorbet Syrup (page 95)
50 ml (2 fl oz) orange juice
50 ml (2 fl oz) lemon juice
100 ml (4 fl oz) dry white wine
1 egg white
1 teaspoon caster sugar
6–8 teaspoons white rum

Makes 6–8 portions
Preparation time: *15 minutes, plus freezing*

1. In a freezer container combine the syrup, fruit juices and wine and place in the freezer. Freeze for 3–4 hours or until almost solid.
2. Whisk the egg white and sugar until stiff and beat into the sorbet. Return to the freezer for 1–2 hours or until completely firm.
3. If the punch has been in the freezer for 24 hours or longer, transfer to the refrigerator 15 minutes before serving to soften slightly. To serve, scoop the mixture into individual bowls and pour a teaspoon of rum over each portion.

Cranberry Sorbet

200 g (7 oz) cranberries
300 ml (½ pint) prepared Sorbet Syrup (page 95)
100 ml (3½ fl oz) orange juice

Preparation time: *15 minutes, plus cooling and freezing*
Cooking time: *15 minutes*

1. Poach the cranberries in the sorbet syrup for 15 minutes. Cool slightly, then blend the cranberries, syrup and orange juice to a purée.
2. Strain the purée into a freezer container, then place in the freezer. Freeze for 2–3 hours or until almost solid.
3. Remove from the freezer and beat thoroughly to break down the ice crystals.
4. Return to the freezer for 1–2 hours or until completely set.
5. If the sorbet has been in the freezer for 24 hours or longer, transfer to the refrigerator 15 minutes before serving to soften slightly.

From the left: Orange givré; Melon and grape sorbet

Orange Givré

4 oranges
200 ml (1/3 pint) prepared Sorbet Syrup (page 95)
1 egg white
1 teaspoon caster sugar

Preparation time: *25 minutes, plus freezing*

1. Cut the tops off the oranges, about two-thirds of the way up. Trim the bottoms so that the oranges stand upright.
2. Squeeze the juice from the oranges without damaging the outer peel. Scrape away the flesh and any membranes sticking to the peel with a grapefruit knife then blend and sieve the juice. Stand the hollowed shells and caps in the freezer.
3. Pour the juice and syrup in to a freezer container and place in the freezer. Freeze the sorbet for 2–3 hours or until almost firm.
4. Whisk the egg white and caster sugar until stiff.
5. Remove the sorbet from the freezer and beat in the whisked egg white. Return to the freezer for 1–2 hours or until set.
6. Spoon the sorbet into the frozen orange shells and place the orange lids on top.
7. If the givré has been in the freezer for 24 hours or longer, transfer to the refrigerator 15 minutes before serving, to soften slightly.

Melon and Grape Sorbet

120 g (4½ oz) black or white grapes, seeded
120 g (4½ oz) ripe melon flesh, cut into cubes
2 fresh mint leaves, finely chopped
40 g (1½ oz) sugar
3 tablespoons water
2 ogen melons, halved and seeds removed, to serve
To decorate:
2–4 sprigs of mint
black grapes, halved and deseeded

Preparation time: *25 minutes, plus freezing*

1. Pass the grapes, melon and mint leaves through a sieve or purée in a blender. Strain to remove the grape skins.
2. Put the sugar and water in a small saucepan over a gentle heat and bring to the boil, stirring constantly, so that the sugar is completely dissolved.
3. Add the syrup to the fruit purée. Pour the mixture into an ice cube tray and put in a freezer or the ice making compartment of a refrigerator until almost set. Beat well to break down the ice crystals and return to the freezer to set.
4. Fill the ogen melons with the sorbet and decorate with halved grapes and sprig of mint. Serve immediately.

Iced Mango Soufflé

3 eggs
100 g (4 oz) caster sugar
1 large mango, peeled and stoned
300 ml (½ pint) double cream, whipped

Preparation time: *30 minutes, plus freezing*

1. Put the eggs and caster sugar in a bowl over a pan of simmering water. Whisk them for 15 to 20 minutes until they are light and fluffy. Leave to cool for 10 minutes.
2. Weigh out 250 g (9 oz) of mango. Blend it in the liquidizer. Reserve the remaining fruit for decoration.
3. Whisk the mango purée into the cream a little at a time.
4. Fold the sugar and egg mixture into the cream and mango.
5. Fit a paper collar round the rim of a 750 ml (1¼ pint) soufflé dish and secure with string or an elastic band. Fill the dish with the mixture. Freeze for 5 hours.
6. To serve, remove the paper collar and decorate with mango slices. If liked, pipe rosettes of whipped cream around the top edge just before serving.

Honey and Rhubarb Sorbet

250 g (8 oz) rhubarb, chopped
140 g (scant 5 oz) clear honey
1 egg white
1 teaspoon caster sugar

Preparation time: *20 minutes, plus cooling and freezing*

1. Place the rhubarb, honey and a little water in a pan. Cover and poach until tender.
2. Blend the rhubarb with the poaching liquid to a smooth purée and allow to cool.
3. Transfer the mixture to a freezer container and place in the freezer. Freeze for 2–3 hours until almost solid.
4. Whisk the egg white and caster sugar until stiff. Remove the sorbet from the freezer and beat the egg white into the rhubarb. Return to the freezer for 1–2 hours or until completely firm.
5. If the sorbet has been in the freezer for 24 hours or longer, transfer to the refrigerator 15 minutes before serving to soften slightly.

From the left: Iced mango soufflé; Honey and rhubarb sorbet

Pancakes, Waffles & Sweet Omelettes

Apple Pancakes

12 Pancakes (page 104)
Apple Filling:
75 g (3 oz) unsalted butter
1 kg (2 lb) dessert apples such as Russets or Cox's Orange Pippins, peeled, cored and thinly sliced
50 g (2 oz) demerara sugar
150 ml (¼ pint) double cream

Serves 6
Preparation time: *20 minutes*
Cooking time: *15–20 minutes*
Oven: *200°C, 400°F, Gas Mark 6*

1. Have the Pancakes ready.
2. To make the filling, melt 50 g (2 oz) of the butter in a frying pan, and gently cook the apple slices until they are golden brown. Sweeten with 25 g (1 oz) of the sugar.
3. Spoon a little of the apple mixture in each pancake dividing it equally between them. Roll up the pancakes and place in a baking dish greased with the remaining butter.
4. Pour the cream evenly over the pancakes and sprinkle them with the remaining sugar.
5. Bake in a preheated oven for 15–20 minutes until golden brown.
6. Serve immediately.

Variation:
Poach 1 kg (2 lb) fresh apricots or peaches until tender. Drain, skin, stone and chop into chunky pieces. Melt the butter and 25 g (1 oz) sugar together and mix with the fruit. Use in place of the apple mixture as above.

Crêpes Soufflé

12 Pancakes (page 104)
Soufflé Filling:
3 eggs, separated
50 g (2 oz) caster sugar
20 g (¾ oz) plain flour
few drops of vanilla essence
250 ml (8 fl oz) milk
2 tablespoons Grand Marnier

Serves 6
Preparation time: *15 minutes*
Cooking time: *10 minutes*
Oven: *200°C, 400°F, Gas Mark 6*

1. Have the Pancakes ready.
2. To make the filling, beat the egg yolks and sugar together until they are light and creamy. Stir in the flour.
3. Put a few drops of vanilla essence in the milk. Bring the milk to the boil in a small pan and stir it slowly into the egg mixture.
4. Return the mixture to a clean pan over a low heat stirring constantly until it has thickened.
5. Remove the pan from the heat and add the Grand Marnier.
6. Whisk the egg whites until they are stiff. Fold them into the custard.
7. Place about a tablespoon of mixture on one half of each crêpe and fold over the other half. Arrange them in a buttered, shallow baking dish.
8. Bake in a preheated oven for 10 minutes until golden and risen. Serve immediately.

From the left: Apple pancakes; Crêpes soufflé

Crêpes Suzette

12 Pancakes (see below)
Orange Butter:
4 sugar lumps
2 oranges
75 g (3 oz) butter
50 g (2 oz) caster sugar
1 tablespoon Curaçao
2 tablespoons brandy, to serve

Serves 6
Preparation time: *15 minutes*

Pancake Batter

100 g (4 oz) plain flour
pinch of salt
2 eggs
300 ml (½ pint) milk
25 g (1 oz) butter, melted
1 tablespoon brandy or orange liqueur (optional)

Makes approximately 12 pancakes, each 15–18 cm (6–7 inches) in diameter

1. Sift the flour and salt into a mixing bowl. Make a well in the centre and drop in the eggs.
2. Using a wooden spoon, gradually stir in the eggs, adding a little milk from time to time. Drawing in the flour, stir until a smooth batter is formed.
3. Stir in the melted butter and brandy or liqueur, if used. The batter should have the consistency of single cream.
4. Lightly oil a heavy pancake pan and set it over a medium heat. When it is very hot, pour in just enough batter to cover the base of the pan thinly and cook the pancake until golden underneath.
5. Free the edges of the pancake with a palette knife or spatula and turn it over. Cook on the second side until golden. Remove the pancake from the pan and keep warm.
6. Repeat the process until all the batter has been used. Oil the pan lightly only if it looks dry. Stir the batter before making each pancake.
7. Stack the pancakes on top of one another until required.

1. Have the Pancakes ready.
2. To make the orange butter, rub the sugar lumps over the skin of the oranges until they have absorbed the colour and the flavour of the zest.
3. Crush the sugar lumps in a mixing bowl. Add the butter and sugar and beat together until light and creamy.
4. Add the juice of 1 orange and the Curaçao and mix well.
5. To serve the crêpes, melt the orange butter in a frying pan or, if you are preparing them at the table, a chafing dish.
6. Place the pancakes in the pan one at a time and spoon a little orange butter over each.
7. Fold each crêpe in half and half again. Arrange them around the pan with the points towards the centre.
8. Simmer the crêpes in the remaining orange butter for a minute. Warm the brandy in a ladle, ignite it and pour it, still flaming, over the crêpes. Serve at once.

Crêpes Suzette

Crêpes à la Crême Frangipane

12 Pancakes (see opposite)
Almond Butter Cream Filling:
150g (5oz) butter
100g (4oz) caster sugar
2 eggs, beaten
1 egg yolk
150g (5oz) ground almonds
few drops of almond essence
1 tablespoon Kirsch (optional)
25g (1oz) caster sugar, to sprinkle

Serves 6
Preparation time: *10 minutes*
Cooking time: *10–15 minutes*
Oven: *200°C, 400°F, Gas Mark 6*

1. Prepare the pancakes and set aside.
2. To make the filling, cream 100g (4oz) of the butter and sugar together until light and creamy.
3. Add the eggs, egg yolk, ground almonds, almond essence and Kirsch, if used, and mix to a smooth consistency.
4. Spoon the filling on to the pancakes, roll them up and place in a buttered dish.
5. Dot the pancakes with the remaining butter and sprinkle with sugar.
6. Bake in a preheated oven for 10–15 minutes until the almond cream has set. Serve with whipped cream.

From the top:
Chocolate pancakes with chocolate sauce; Crêpes à la crême frangipane

Chocolate Pancakes With Chocolate Sauce

100g (4oz) plain flour
1 tablespoon cocoa powder
pinch of salt
1 tablespoon caster sugar
2 eggs
300ml (½ pint) milk
1 tablespoon brandy (optional)
Filling:
100g (4oz) dark plain chocolate
25ml (1floz) strong black coffee
2 tablespoons brandy
300ml (½ pint) double cream
1 quantity Chocolate Sauce from French Christmas Pudding (page 127)

Serves 6
Preparation time: *20 minutes*

1. Sift the flour, cocoa powder, salt and caster sugar into a bowl. Make a well in the centre and drop in the eggs.
2. Using a wooden spoon, gradually stir in the eggs, adding a little milk at a time. Drawing in the flour slowly, stir until a smooth batter is formed. Add 1 tablespoon of brandy if liked.
3. Make 12 pancakes in the usual way (see Pancakes, opposite) and keep them hot.
4. To make the filling, put the chocolate, coffee and brandy in a small basin over a pan of simmering water. Stir until the chocolate has melted and a smooth paste is formed. Leave to cool slightly.
5. Whip the cream until it begins to thicken. Add the cooled chocolate and continue to whip until it holds it shape.
6. Spoon the chocolate filling into the warm pancakes. Arrange them on a serving dish and pour a little sauce on top.
7. Serve immediately, and hand the rest of the sauce separately.

Almond Crêpes With Praline Butter

100 g (4 oz) plain flour
pinch of salt
2 eggs
300 ml (½ pint) milk
25 g (1 oz) butter, melted
1 tablespoon caster sugar
100 g (4 oz) ground almonds, toasted
Praline Butter:
175 g (6 oz) unsalted butter
3 tablespoons caster sugar
1 quantity ground Praline (page 188)
caster sugar, for baking

Serves 6
Preparation time: *20 minutes*
Cooking time: *15 minutes*
Oven: *200°C, 400°F, Gas Mark 6*

1. Sift the flour and salt into a bowl. Make a well in the centre and drop in the eggs.
2. Using a wooden spoon, gradually stir in the eggs, adding a little milk at a time. Drawing in the flour slowly, stir until a smooth batter is formed. Add the melted butter, sugar and almonds.
3. Make 12 pancakes in the usual way (see Pancakes, page 104) and keep them hot.
4. To make the Praline Butter, cream the butter and the sugar together. Add the praline.
5. Spread a little praline butter on each crêpe and roll it up.
6. Place them in a buttered baking dish, with a dot of praline on top.
7. Sprinkle with caster sugar and bake in a preheated oven for 15 minutes.
8. Serve immediately with whipped cream if desired.

From the top: Almond crêpes with praline butter; Buckwheat pancakes

Buckwheat Pancakes

120 g (4½ oz) buckwheat flour
small pinch of salt
300 ml (½ pint) milk
3 eggs
2 tablespoons groundnut oil
oil, for frying

Makes 12–15 pancakes
Preparation time: *5 minutes, plus resting*
Cooking time: *about 1 minute per pancake*

Serve buckwheat pancakes with lemon and sugar, fruit purées, chocolate sauce, jams or liqueurs. Fold the cooked pancake in half and in half again so that it looks like a slice of cake.

1. Sift the flour and salt into a mixing bowl. Make a well in the middle.
2. Beat the milk with the eggs.
3. Pour half of the mixture into the flour. Stir in well, gradually adding the rest of the milk and eggs. Beat in the oil. Cover the bowl and leave the batter to rest for 2 hours.
4. Heat a 20 cm (8 inch) frying pan and brush with a little oil.
5. Pour about 3 tablespoons of batter into the pan, turning the pan to ensure that the pancakes are of even thickness. Cook the pancake for about half a minute. Turn it over and cook on the other side.
6. As soon as it is ready, slide the pancake from the pan to a hot plate. Keep warm. Repeat the process until all the batter has been used.

Apricot and praline pancake tower

Apricot and Praline Pancake Tower

12 small Pancakes (page 104)
Filling:
100 g (4 oz) dried apricots, soaked overnight
100 g (4 oz) caster sugar
4 egg yolks
300 ml (½ pint) double cream
grated rind of 1 lemon
175 g (6 oz) ground Praline (page 188)
butter, for greasing
25 g (1 oz) fresh, fine white breadcrumbs
50 g (2 oz) flaked almonds, toasted, to decorate

Serves 8
Preparation time: *20 minutes*
Cooking time: *1–1¼ hours*
Oven: *180°C, 350°F, Gas Mark 4*

When making the pancakes, use the same diameter as the soufflé dish if possible; otherwise trim the finished pancakes to fit the dish. This dessert is equally delicious eaten hot, in which case it should not be turned out.

1. Prepare the pancakes and set aside.
2. Simmer the apricots in their soaking liquid until they are tender. Pass them through a sieve or liquidize in a blender to make a purée. Add 1 tablespoon caster sugar.
3. Cream the egg yolks and remaining sugar together in a mixing bowl until light and thick. Add the cream and lemon rind and whisk together.
4. Transfer about 8 tablespoons of the mixture to a clean bowl and stir the ground Praline into it.
5. Transfer about 4 tablespoons of the mixture to a clean bowl and add to it the apricot purée. Reserve the remaining egg and cream mixture.
6. Butter a 900 ml (1½ pint) soufflé dish and sprinkle the inside with fresh white breadcrumbs.
7. Place a pancake in the bottom of the dish. Spoon a layer of praline cream over it and place another pancake on top. Spoon a layer of apricot cream over it. Layer the pancakes in this way, alternating with filling, finishing with a pancake on top.
8. Using a knife, push the pancakes away from the sides of the dish and pour the remaining egg and cream mixture over and down the sides of the pancakes.
9. Cover with buttered non-stick silicone paper and bake in a preheated oven for 1–1½ hours until the filling has set.
10. Leave to cool. Turn out carefully on to a serving dish. Sprinkle with almonds.

Beignets Bourguignons

175 g (6 oz) self-raising flour
50 g (2 oz) caster sugar
2 eggs, lightly beaten
2 tablespoons dark rum
75 g (3 oz) unsalted butter
oil, for deep frying
caster sugar, to decorate

Makes 24
Preparation time: *15 minutes, plus resting*
Cooking time: *about 5 minutes*

This delicious recipe originates from in the Burgundy region of France.

1. Mix the flour and sugar in a mixing bowl. Work in the eggs and add the rum.
2. Cream the butter and combine it with the batter to make a soft pastry. Cover the bowl and leave the pastry to rest for about 2 hours.
3. Roll out the pastry on a floured work surface and cut it into 24 diamond-shaped pieces.
4. Heat the oil in a large heavy saucepan to 190°C (375°F) or until a cube of bread turns brown in 30 seconds. Fry the pieces a few at a time for 5 minutes until golden brown. Lift them out with a slotted spoon and drain on paper towels. Dust them with caster sugar and serve immediately, with a sweetened apple sauce if desired. Serve hot.

Apricot Fritters in Brandy

225 g (8 oz) sugar
450 ml (3/4 pint) water
12 ripe apricots, peeled and stoned
4 tablespoons brandy
fritter batter (see Fruit Fritters, below)
oil, for deep frying
icing sugar, to decorate

Serves 4
Preparation time: *30 minutes, plus 2 hours marinating*

1. Put the sugar and water in a saucepan over a medium heat and bring to the boil, stirring constantly. Simmer for 1 minute.
2. Add the apricots to the syrup and poach for 10 to 15 minutes until they are completely tender.
3. Strain the apricots and marinate them in 3 tablespoons of the brandy for 2 hours.
4. Heat the oil in a large heavy saucepan to 190°C, 375°F or until a cube of bread turns brown in 30 seconds.
5. Add the remaining brandy to the fritter batter. Dip the apricots in the batter and fry them a few at a time, until they are crisp and golden.
6. Lift the fritters out of the pan and drain them on paper towels.
7. Sprinkle with icing sugar and serve immediately.

Fruit Fritters

4 dessert apples, peeled, cored and sliced or 1 small pineapple, peeled, cored and sliced or 6 bananas, peeled and sliced lengthways (or a mixture of all 3)
50 g (2 oz) caster sugar
Fritter Batter:
100 g (4 oz) plain flour
pinch of salt
25 g (1 oz) butter, melted
1 egg, separated
150 ml (1/4 pint) milk
oil, for deep frying
icing sugar, to serve

Serves 4
Preparation time: *15 minutes*

1. Sprinkle the fruit with the sugar.
2. Sift the flour and salt into a bowl. Make a well in the centre and drop in the butter and egg yolk. Using a wooden spoon, gradually incorporate the butter and eggs, adding the milk little by little until a smooth batter has formed.
3. Whisk the egg white until it is stiff and fold it into the batter.
4. Heat the oil in a large heavy saucepan to 190°C (375°F) or until a cube of bread turns brown in 30 seconds.
5. Dip the pieces of fruit in the batter and fry them a few at a time, until they are crisp and golden.
6. Lift the fritters out of the pan and drain them on paper towels. If liked, place the fritters on a baking sheet lined with paper towels. Place in a heated oven to keep hot.
7. Sprinkle with icing sugar and serve immediately.

From the top left, clockwise: Beignets bourguignons; Apricot fritters in brandy; Clafoutis; Fruit fritters

Clafoutis

175 g (6 oz) plain flour
2 eggs
75 g (3 oz) caster sugar
300 ml (½ pint) milk
2 tablespoons brandy
450 g (1 lb) black or red cherries, stoned

Serves 6
Preparation time: *15 minutes*
Cooking time: *40 minutes*
Oven: *190°C, 375°F, Gas Mark 5*

1. Sift the flour into a bowl. Make a well in the centre and add the eggs, sugar and a little milk. Beat, gradually adding the rest of the milk and brandy, until smooth.
2. Grease a 1 litre (1¾ pint) baking dish and pour in half the batter.
3. Arrange the cherries in a single layer and pour over the rest of the batter.
4. Bake in a preheated oven for 40 minutes or until set. To test the pudding, insert a skewer. If the skewer comes out clean, the pudding is ready.
5. Serve warm with pouring cream.

From the left: Orange and rum soufflé omelette; Soufflé omelette
Right, from the top: Waffles with maple syrup; Nut waffles

Orange and Rum Soufflé Omelette

4 eggs, separated
1 tablespoon caster sugar
1 tablespoon rum
15 g (½ oz) butter
Filling:
1 orange, peeled, pith removed, and divided into segments
2 tablespoons orange marmalade
3 tablespoons rum, to flambé

Serves 2
Preparation time: *20 minutes*
Cooking time: *5 minutes*
Oven: *200°C, 400°F, Gas Mark 6*

1. Prepare the omelette in the same way as for a Soufflé Omelette (see next column), substituting rum for the cream.
2. To make the filling, mix the orange segments with the marmalade.
3. Spread the orange and marmalade on the cooked omelette. Fold it in half and turn out on to a warmed serving dish.
4. Warm the rum in a ladle and ignite it. Pour the rum, still flaming over the omelette and serve immediately.

Soufflé Omelette

4 eggs, separated
1 tablespoon caster sugar
25 ml (1 fl oz) double cream
15 g (½ oz) butter
4 tablespoons red jam or thick fruit purée
a few strawberries, sliced (optional)
icing sugar, to decorate

Serves 2
Preparation time: *15 minutes*
Cooking time: *5 minutes*
Oven: *200°C, 400°F, Gas Mark 6*

1. Whisk the egg yolks, sugar and cream together.
2. Whisk the egg whites until they are stiff and fold them into the egg mixture.
3. Melt the butter in a small omelette pan. When it begins to sizzle, pour in the mixture and cook until it is golden underneath.
4. Transfer the pan quickly to a preheated oven. Bake for 5 minutes until set.
5. Remove the pan from the oven. Spread the omelette with warmed jam and the sliced strawberries, if using, or fruit purée and fold it in half.
6. Turn out on to a warmed serving dish, dust with icing sugar and serve.

Waffles With Maple Syrup

75g (3oz) plain flour
2 teaspoons baking powder
50g (2oz) caster sugar
1 teaspoon ground cinnamon
2 eggs, separated
300ml (1/2 pint) milk
25g (1oz) butter, melted
To serve:
300ml (1/2 pint) double cream, whipped
maple syrup

Serves 4–6
Preparation time: *10 minutes*
Cooking time: *1–1 1/2 minutes for each waffle*

Leftover waffles can be toasted briefly to crisp them up and heat them through.

1. Sift the flour, baking powder, sugar and cinnamon into a bowl. Make a well in the centre and drop in the egg yolks.
2. Gradually stir in the yolks, adding a little milk from time to time, until a smooth batter is formed. Add the melted butter.
3. Whisk the egg whites until they are stiff and fold them into the batter.
4. Heat a well-greased waffle iron until a drop of batter placed on it sizzles immediately.
5. Pour some batter on to the iron and cook until golden brown on both sides.
6. Sandwich the waffles immediately with whipped cream and serve with maple syrup poured over the top.

Nut Waffles

75g (3oz) plain flour
2 teaspoons baking powder
50g (2oz) caster sugar
2 eggs, separated
300ml (1/2 pint) milk
50g (2oz) nuts, (walnuts, pecan nuts or hazelnuts), chopped
25g (1oz) butter, melted

Serves 4–6
Preparation time: *10 minutes*
Cooking time: *1–1 1/2 minutes for each waffle*

1. Prepare the batter in the same way as for Waffles with Maple Syrup (see above).
2. Fold the chopped nuts into the batter and cook as for plain waffles.
3. Serve immediately, sandwiched with whipped cream or Praline Cream (see Praline Pears, page 64), with a Fruit Coulis (page 188).

Perfect Pies, Flans & Pastries

Treacle Tart

½ quantity Shortcrust Pastry (page 114)
225 g (8 oz) golden syrup
juice of ½ small lemon
55 g (2 oz) fresh breadcrumbs

Preparation time: *25 minutes, plus resting*
Cooking time: *35 minutes*
Oven: *190°C, 375°F, Gas Mark 5*

1. Roll out the pastry on a lightly floured surface and use to line a 20 cm (8 inch) flan ring.
2. Trim the excess pastry and roll again. Cut into four 25 cm (10 inch) strips. Rest the flan-case and strips for 30 minutes.
3. Gently warm the syrup and lemon juice in a pan and add the crumbs. Mix well and pour into the flan-case.
4. Decorate with the strips of pastry and bake in a preheated oven for 35 minutes.
5. Allow to cool slightly and serve warm with custard or cream.

Lattice work:
A lattice pattern is a traditional decoration for open flans and tarts. Roll out pastry trimmings to about 25 cm (10 inches) long for a 20 cm (8 inch) flan. Cut the pastry into 1 cm (½ inch) strips. Moisten the edges of the flan with water. Lay half the strips over the flan an equal distance apart in one direction. Place the remaining strips an equal distance apart in a criss-cross fashion to form diamond or square spaces between the strips. Trim the strips to shape into the pastry at the outer edge. Glaze the strips with milk or little beaten egg and milk for a golden brown result.

Pecan Tart

½ quantity Pâte Brisée (page 120)
75 g (3 oz) pecan nuts, ground
50 g (2 oz) sponge cake crumbs
65 g (2½ oz) caster sugar
150 ml (¼ pint) milk
2 eggs
To decorate:
1 pink grapefruit
12 pecan nuts

Preparation time: *20 minutes, plus cooling*
Cooking time: *40 minutes*
Oven: *190°C, 375°F, Gas Mark 5*

For the best flavour grind the nuts just before using. Ground nuts deteriorate rapidly once processed.
Pink grapefruit come from the United States and are available all the year round. They add a delicate decoration and fragrance to the tart. Add to the tart just before serving so the juices do not soak into the filling. If pink grapefruit are not available, use ordinary grapefruit as an alternative.

1. Line a 20 cm (8 inch) flan ring with the pâte brisée.
2. Combine the ground pecan nuts with the cake crumbs in a mixing bowl. Beat the sugar, milk and eggs together in another bowl and stir this mixture into the pecans and crumbs.
3. Pour the mixture into the flan ring.
4. Place in a preheated oven and bake for 40 minutes. Leave to cool.
5. Peel the grapefruit and divide into segments. Using a sharp, pointed knife, carefully remove the skin from the segments, leaving them whole.
6. Arrange the grapefruit segments in the centre of the tart, and decorate the edge with whole pecan nuts.

From the top: Treacle tart; Pecan tart

From the left: Prune and Madeira tart; Walnut treacle tart; Apple plate pie

Shortcrust pastry

350 g (12 oz) plain flour
pinch salt
75 g (3 oz) hard maragarine, chopped into small pieces
75 g (3 oz) lard, chopped into small pieces
4 tablespoons milk

Makes about 450 g (1 lb) pastry
Will line 2 × 20 cm (8 inch) flan rings
Preparation time: *10 minutes*
Storage time: *5 days foil-wrapped in the refrigerator*

1. Sieve the flour and salt into a mixing bowl. Rub the butter and lard into the flour until the mixture resembles fine breadcrumbs. Avoid squeezing the fat into the flour, but rub it delicately between the thumbs and fingers.
2. Gradually stir in the milk until the mixture begins to bind. With the fingers mix the pastry to a smooth dough. Rest for 30 minutes.

Prune and Madeira Tart

350 g (12 oz) canned or stewed prunes, stoned
150 ml (1/4 pint) Madeira
120 g (4½ oz) caster sugar
½ quantity Shortcrust Pastry (see left)

Preparation time: *20 minutes, plus soaking*
Cooking time: *30 minutes*
Oven: *190°C, 375°F, Gas Mark 5*

1. Wipe the prunes with paper towels and leave to steep in the Madeira for 2 hours. Drain and reserve the liquid.
2. Blend the prunes with half the sugar to produce a purée.
3. Roll out the pastry on a lightly floured surface and use to line a 20 cm (8 inch) flan ring. Prick the base with a fork. Trim the excess pastry.
4. Roll out the excess pastry and cut into thin strips.
5. Spread the purée evenly in the pastry and decorate the top with strips of pastry.
6. Bake in a preheated oven for 30 minutes.
7. Add the remaining sugar to the Madeira. Boil in a small saucepan until reduced to a sticky glaze. Spoon over the tart. Cool and serve with Crème chantilly (page 189).

Walnut Treacle Tart

½ quantity Shortcrust Pastry (see opposite)
175 g (6 oz) maple syrup
50 g (2 oz) treacle
150 g (5 oz) walnuts, ground
25 g (1 oz) brown breadcrumbs

Preparation time: *25 minutes, plus resting*
Cooking time: *35 minutes*
Oven: *190°C, 375°F, Gas Mark 5*

Pure maple syrup is expensive but is well worth buying for its superior flavour. It is available from health food stores, delicatessens and some supermarkets.

1. Roll out the pastry on a lightly floured surface and use to line a 20 cm (8 inch) flan ring.
2. Trim off the excess pastry and roll it out again. Cut into four 25 cm (10 inch) strips. Leave the flan case and strips to rest for 30 minutes.
3. Warm the syrup and treacle in a saucepan over a low heat. Add the walnuts and breadcrumbs. Mix well and pour into the flan case.
4. Decorate with the strips of pastry and bake in a preheated oven for 35 minutes or until the pastry is golden.

Apple Plate Pie

½ quantity Shortcrust Pastry (see opposite)
25 g (1 oz) unsalted butter
1 teaspoon ground semolina
250 g (9 oz) cooking apples, peeled, cored and roughly chopped
2 Cox's Orange Pippin apples, peeled, cored and roughly chopped
65 g (2½ oz) sugar
To glaze:
milk
granulated sugar

Preparation time: *25 minutes*
Cooking time: *35 minutes*
Oven: *200°C, 400°F, Gas Mark 6*

1. Roll out ⅔rds of the pastry on a floured work surface and use to line a 20 cm (8 inch) pie plate or tin. Prick the base with a fork. Melt half the butter in a small container and brush over the base of the pastry making sure the pastry is completely covered. Sprinkle with the semolina.
2. Stew the cooking apples in the remaining butter until soft. Mash with a fork.
3. Mix the eating apples, sugar and cooked apples. Pour into the prepared pastry.
4. Roll out the rest of the pastry to a 20 cm (8 inch) circle. Brush the edges of the pastry case with water and position the pastry lid over the apple. Press the 2 pastry edges together, trim and crimp to finish. Make a hole in the centre of the lid.
5. Brush the pastry with milk and sprinkle liberally with granulated sugar.
6. Bake in a preheated oven for 35 minutes.

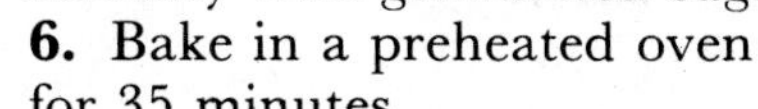

Tarte Tatin

10 g (¼ oz) unsalted butter
150 g (5 oz) sugar
250 g (9 oz) Cox's Orange Pippin apples peeled, cored and sliced
½ teaspoon ground ginger
150 g (5 oz) prepared Puff Pastry (see below)

Preparation time: *20 minutes*
Cooking time: *25 minutes*
Oven: *220°C, 425°F, Gas Mark 7*

1. Brush a 20 cm (8 inch) cake tin (with a fixed base) with butter.
2. Place the sugar in the cake tin with enough water to moisten it.
3. Place the cake tin containing the sugar over a moderate heat until it becomes a golden brown caramel. Using oven gloves remove from the heat and dip the base in a bowl of cold water to stop the caramel from burning.
4. Arrange the apple slices neatly on the caramel base and sprinkle with the ginger.
5. Roll the pastry into a circle to fit the tin and lay it over the apples.
6. Bake in a preheated oven for 25 minutes.
7. Turn the tart out upside down on to a plate. If some of the caramel sticks to the tin, heat it for a few moments and pour it over the apples.

Puff Pastry

450 g (1 lb) salted butter
450 g (1 lb) strong white flour
300 ml (10 fl oz) water, chilled
1 teaspoon lemon juice

Makes about 1.25 kg (2½ lb) pastry
Preparation time: *30 minutes, plus resting*
Storage time: *about 1 week foil-wrapped in the refrigerator*

It is sensible to make a large quantity and divide it into four. Wrap up three of the pieces in foil and freeze until required.

1. Rub 1/3rd of the butter into the flour.
2. Combine the water and lemon juice and mix with the flour. Work into a smooth, elastic paste.
3. On a floured surface roll out into a large neat rectangle about 1 cm (½ inch) thick.
4. Mark the pastry across in 3 equal sections. Spread the remaining butter over ⅔rds of the pastry leaving a 2.5 cm (1 inch) margin at the edges.
5. Fold the unbuttered ⅓rd back over half the butter. Fold over again enclosing the rest of the butter. Seal the edges to trap the air by pressing them together with the rolling pin.
6. Put the pastry on the floured work surface with one of the short folded sides facing and roll to form a large oblong as before. Fold into 3 again. Rest for 15 minutes.
7. Repeat the last stage 4 more times, resting the pastry 15 minutes each time.

Tart tatin

From the left: Dartois aux peches; Maids of honour

Dartois aux Pêches

2 large or 3 small fresh peaches
300 g (11 oz) prepared Puff Pastry (see opposite)
1 egg, separated
40 g (1½ oz) vanilla sugar

Preparation time: *15 minutes, plus resting*
Cooking time: *35 minutes*
Oven: *240°C, 475°F, Gas Mark 9; 190°C, 375°F, Gas Mark 5*

1. Drop the peaches in to boiling water and leave for 45 seconds. Using a slotted draining spoon, lift out, skin and dice.
2. On a lightly floured surface roll out half the pastry to form an oblong 20 × 15 cm (8 × 6 inches). Wind round the rolling pin and transfer to a greased baking sheet. Lay flat and prick with a fork.
3. Brush the rolled pastry with the egg white, then pile the peaches in the middle of the pastry leaving a 2.5 cm (1 inch) margin at the edges. Sprinkle with the sugar.
4. Roll out the second half of the pastry a little larger than the first and use to cover the peaches and first piece of pastry. Seal the edges well, knock up and flute. Rest for 20 minutes.
5. Brush with the egg yolk and bake in a preheated oven for 15 minutes. Reduce the heat and bake for a further 20 minutes.

Maids of Honour

165 g (5½ oz) prepared Puff Pastry (see opposite)
100 g (4 oz) ground almonds
50 g (2 oz) caster sugar
¼ teaspoon cinnamon
¼ teaspoon nutmeg
grated rind of ¼ lemon
1 egg
15 g (½ oz) self-raising flour
2 tablespoons double cream
25 g (1 oz) currants soaked in 2 tablespoons Cognac (optional)

Makes 4
Preparation time: *30 minutes, plus resting*
Cooking time: *30–35 minutes*
Oven: *200°C, 400°F, Gas Mark 6*

1. Divide the pastry into four. Roll out the pastry very thinly and use to line 12 deep patty tins. Rest for 30 minutes.
2. Mix the almonds, sugar, spices, rind and egg. Fold in the flour, cream and currants, if using.
3. Pour the mixture into the pastry cases and bake in a preheated oven for 25–30 minutes.

From the left: Spiced bramble pie; Poires en douillons

Spiced Bramble Pie

300 g (11 oz) blackberries, hulled
200 g (7 oz) cooking apples, peeled, cored and thinly sliced
juice of ½ lemon
½ teaspoon ginger
¼ teaspoon mace
½ teaspoon mixed spice
75 g (3 oz) soft brown sugar
300 g (11 oz) prepared Puff Pastry (page 116)
1 egg yolk

Preparation time: *20 minutes*
Cooking time: *45 minutes*
Oven: *240°C, 475°F, Gas Mark 9; 190°C, 375°F, Gas Mark 5*

1. Mix all the ingredients together except for the puff pastry and egg yolk. Transfer to a 900 ml (1½ pint) pie dish.
2. Roll the pastry into an oval shape roughly 5 cm (2 inches) wider than the pie dish.
3. Cut a 2.5 cm (1 inch) band from the circumference of the rolled pastry and use to cover the entire rim of the pie dish. Trim.
4. Brush the rim with water then cover with the lid of pastry. Trim the edges with kitchen scissors or a very sharp knife.
5. Press the edges together and flute the pastry. Make a hole in the centre of the pie to let the steam escape during cooking.
6. Decorate the top with trimmings cut into leaf shapes. Brush with the egg yolk.
7. Bake for 20 minutes in a preheated oven. Reduce the heat and bake for 25 minutes.

Poires en Douillons

275 g (10 oz) prepared Puff Pastry (page 116)
1 tablespoon semolina
1 tablespoon caster sugar
1 teaspoon ground cinnamon
4 dessert pears, peeled and cored
1 egg yolk, beaten with 1 teaspoon water

Preparation time: *20 minutes*
Cooking time: *40 minutes*
Oven: *220°C, 425°F, Gas Mark 7; 190°C, 375°F, Gas Mark 5*

1. Roll the puff pastry out into a square on a floured work surface to a thickness of 5 mm (¼ inch). Divide it into 4 equal squares.
2. Mix the semolina, sugar and cinnamon.
3. Level the rounded bases of the pears so they will stand upright and roll the pears in the semolina mixture.
4. Wrap each pear in a square of pastry. Seal the pastry by brushing the edges with water and pressing them together. Trim the pastry to obtain a neat finish.
5. Roll out the pastry trimmings and cut out 8 long strips with a pastry cutter. Moisten the strips with a little water and wind them in a spiral around the wrapped pears to decorate.
6. Stand the pears on a baking sheet and brush them with egg yolk.
7. Bake in a preheated oven for 30 minutes. Reduce the heat and bake for 10 minutes.
8. Serve hot with whipped cream or Chocolate sauce (page 188).

Choux Pastry

70g ($2\frac{1}{2}$oz) flour
pinch of salt
1 teaspoon caster sugar
125ml ($4\frac{1}{2}$fl oz) water and milk mixed
60g (2oz) unsalted butter
2 eggs

Makes 375g (13oz)
Preparation time: *10 minutes*
Storage time: *5 days in the refrigerator*

Large quantities of this pastry can be made. When completely cold transfer to plastic freezer bags and freeze.

1. Sift the flour, salt and sugar on to a plate.
2. Put the water, milk and butter in a pan and heat gently until the fat has melted.
3. Bring to the boil and when bubbling vigorously, remove from the heat, add the flour mixture all at once and beat quickly with a wooden spoon until a smooth paste forms drawing away from the sides of the pan.
4. Beat in one egg until thoroughly mixed, then beat in the second.

Paris Brest

1 quantity choux pastry (see left)
icing sugar, to dredge
25g (1oz) flaked almonds
75g (3oz) Praline (page 188)
50g (scant 2oz) unsalted butter, creamed
about 250g (9oz) Crème Pâtissière (page 189)

Preparation time: *40 minutes, plus cooling*
Cooking time: *30 minutes*
Oven: *220°C, 425°F, Gas Mark 7*
190°C, 375°F, Gas Mark 5

1. Mark a 20cm (8 inch) circle on a sheet of greaseproof paper. Grease the paper and place on a baking sheet.
2. Fill a piping bag with the choux pastry and pipe 2 rings touching each other, following the line of the traced circle. Pipe a third ring on top of the other two. Sprinkle with icing sugar and flaked almonds.
3. Bake in a preheated oven for 20 minutes then reduce the heat for the remainder of the cooking time. Check after 20 minutes and if the almonds are starting to burn cover the pastry with a sheet of foil. Cool the pastry prior to filling, about 20 minutes.
4. Beat the praline and butter into the crème pâtissière. Spoon into a piping bag.
5. Split the choux ring into two by cutting horizontally through the middle of the cooked pastry and remove the top.
6. Pipe the cream into the bottom half. Replace the top and serve.

Paris brest

Plum and Almond Tart

½ quantity Pâte Brisée (see below)
120 g (4½ oz) unsalted butter
120 g (4½ oz) soft golden brown sugar
2 eggs
120 g (4½ oz) ground almonds
2–3 drops almond essence
1 tablespoon cornflour
5 Victoria plums (or greengages), halved and stoned
1 tablespoon golden soft brown sugar, for sprinkling
10 whole almonds, blanched

Preparation time: *25 minutes, plus resting*
Cooking time: *55 minutes*
Oven: *200°C, 400°F, Gas Mark 6; 190°C, 375°F, Gas Mark 5*

1. Roll the pastry on a lightly floured surface and use to line a 20 cm (8 inch) flan ring. Rest for 30 minutes. Bake blind for 20 minutes in a preheated oven. Remove the greaseproof paper and beans.
2. Cream the butter and sugar until fluffy.
3. Beat in the eggs one at a time, then fold in the ground almonds, almond essence and cornflour. Pour into the pastry case.
4. Sprinkle the cut surface of the plums with sugar and arrange on top of the flan case skin side downwards. Place an almond in the centre of each half plum.
5. Reduce the oven temperature and bake for 35 minutes.
6. Remove the ring and serve hot with Crème anglaise (page 189) or cold with Crème chantilly (page 189).

Pâte Brisée

275 g (10 oz) plain flour
225 g (8 oz) unsalted butter, cut into 1 cm (½ inch) cubes
2 teaspoons caster sugar
pinch of salt
1 egg, size 6, lightly beaten
approximately 1 tablespoon cold water

Makes about 500 g (1¼ lb) pastry
Will line 2 × 20 cm (8 inch) flan rings
Preparation time: *10 minutes, plus resting*
Storage: *5 days foil-wrapped in the refrigerator*

1. Place the flour in a mixing bowl and make a well in the centre. Place the butter, sugar and salt in the well and mix lightly with the flour.
2. Add the egg and mix to a paste, handling as little as possible. Add a little water if necessary.
3. Transfer to a floured work surface and flatten the mixture using the heel of the hand. Fold in half, then in half again.
4. Work into a ball shape and rest for 1 hour.

Pear Flan

½ quantity Pâte Brisée (see left)
3 pears, Bartlett or Williams, weighing 400 g (14 oz), peeled, halved and cored
½ bay leaf
1 clove
slice of lemon peel
400 ml (14 fl oz) water
200 g (7 oz) sugar
1 quantity Crème Pâtissière (page 189)

Preparation time: *30 minutes, plus resting*
Cooking time: *35 minutes*
Oven: *200°C, 400°F, Gas Mark 6*

Ensure that the pears are thoroughly poached and tender, otherwise they will brown once sliced. Drain thoroughly.

1. Roll out the pastry on a lightly floured surface and use to line a 20 cm (8 inch) flan ring. Rest for 30 minutes. Bake blind for 20 minutes in a preheated oven. Remove the beans and greaseproof paper and bake for a further 5 minutes. Cool.
2. Put the bay leaf, clove, lemon peel, water and sugar into a pan. Stirring continuously, bring to simmering point.
3. When the sugar has dissolved, add the pears and poach until tender, about 10 minutes.
4. Drain the pears on paper towels, then slice thinly. Reserve the liquid.
5. Spread the crème pâtissière on the tart, then arrange the pear slices on top.
6. Boil the syrup rapidly until thick then brush the pears with the syrup. Remove the ring and serve immediately.

From the top, clockwise: Pear flan; Plum and almond tart; Clafoutis aux kiwis

Clafoutis aux Kiwis

½ quantity Pâte Brisée (see opposite)
2 kiwi fruit, peeled and cut into thin slices
2 eggs
80 g (3 oz) vanilla sugar
75 ml (scant 3 fl oz) double cream
75 ml (scant 3 fl oz) milk
icing sugar, for dusting

Preparation time : *15 minutes, plus resting*
Cooking time: *40 minutes*
Oven: *200°C, 400°F, Gas Mark 6; 190°C, 375°F, Gas Mark 5*

1. Line a 20 cm (8 inch) flan ring with pastry and rest for 30 minutes. Bake blind in a preheated oven for 10 minutes.
2. Wipe the kiwi fruit with paper towels, then layer the fruit in the pastry case.
3. Beat the eggs, sugar, cream and milk in a mixing bowl and pour over the fruit.
4. Reduce the oven temperature and bake the flan for 30 minutes.
5. Dust the flan with icing sugar. Glaze to a golden brown under a preheated grill. Remove the flan ring and serve hot or chilled with a custard (page 189) or a pouring cream.

Lemon meringue pie

Lemon Meringue Pie

3 lemons scrubbed
200 ml (7 fl oz) boiling water
65 g (2½ oz) plain flour
75 g (3 oz) clear honey
75 g (3 oz) caster sugar
3 egg yolks
½ quantity Pâte Brisée (page 120)
½ quantity Swiss meringue (page 46)

Preparation time: *40 minutes, plus resting*
Cooking time: *40 minutes*
Oven: *200°C, 400°F, Gas Mark 6;*
160°C, 325°F, Gas Mark 3

1. Remove the zest of the lemons using a vegetable peeler. Infuse the peel in the boiling water for 4 minutes then strain.
2. Squeeze the lemons and combine the juice and the water in which the zests infused.
3. Blend the flour with the liquid, then pour into a *stainless steel* or *enamel* pan and bring to the boil stirring continuously. Simmer until thickened.
4. Add the honey and sugar and bring to the boil.
5. Away from the heat, beat in the yolks and cool.
6. Line a 20 cm (8 inch) flan ring with the pastry. Rest for 30 minutes. Bake blind for 20 minutes in a preheated oven. Remove the beans and greaseproof paper.
7. Pour the lemon cream into the pastry and spoon or pipe the meringue on top of the lemon cream.
8. Reduce the oven temperature and bake for a further 20 minutes. Cool slightly and remove the ring.

Variations:
1. Orange meringue pie: use 3 medium oranges or 3 tangerines in place of the lemons.
2. Lime meringue pie: use 2 limes and 1 lemon in place of the lemons.
3. Citrus meringue pie: use 1 lemon, 1 lime and 1 orange or tangerine in place of the lemons.
4. Pineapple meringue pie: use 1 lemon only. Add 100 g (4 oz) finely chopped fresh pineapple to the lemon cream. Scatter the meringue with a little chopped crystallized pineapple just before baking.

Pâte Sablée

300 g (11 oz) flour
150 g (5½ oz) unsalted, butter, chopped into small pieces
125 g (4½ oz) caster sugar
2 eggs

Makes 675 g (1½ lb) pastry
Will line 2 × 20 cm (8 inch) flan rings
Preparation time: *10 minutes, plus resting*
Storage time: *5 days foil-wrapped in the refrigerator*

1. Rub the flour and butter together in a mixing bowl until the mixture resembles fine breadcrumbs.
2. Lightly beat the sugar and egg and add to the butter and flour mixture. Work the paste into a smooth ball.
3. Rest for 30 minutes before use.

Bakewell Tart

½ quantity Pâte Sablée (see opposite)
40 g (1½ oz) seedless raspberry jam
115 g (4 oz) caster sugar
2 eggs
115 g (4 oz) ground almonds
115 g (4 oz) unsalted butter, melted

Preparation time: *20 minutes, plus resting*
Cooking time: *35 minutes*
Oven: *190°C, 375°F, Gas Mark 5*

1. Line a 20 cm (8 inch) flan ring with the pastry and prick the base.
2. Spread the jam evenly over the pastry base.
3. Whisk the sugar and eggs in a mixing bowl until the mixture doubles in volume and leaves a trail when the whisk is lifted.
4. Using a metal spoon, fold in the almonds, then the melted butter. It is necessary to work very delicately or the butter will fall during cooking and the tart will be stodgy.
5. Pour the mixture into the pastry case and bake in a preheated oven for 35 minutes, until the filling is well risen and golden brown.

Apricot Tart

½ quantity Pâte Sablée (see opposite)
8 large fresh apricots, halved, reserve 4 stones
150 g (5 oz) vanilla sugar
250 ml (8 fl oz) water
1 quantity Crème Pâtissière (page 189)

Preparation time: *35 minutes, plus resting*
Cooking time: *25 minutes*
Oven: *200°C, 400°F, Gas Mark 6; 190°C, 375°F, Gas Mark 5*

1. Line a 20 cm (8 inch) flan ring with the pastry. Rest for 30 minutes. Bake blind in a preheated oven for 15 minutes. Remove the greaseproof paper and baking beans. Reduce the heat and bake for a further 10 minutes. Remove the ring and cool.
2. Crack 4 of the apricot stones and remove the kernels.
3. Put the kernels, vanilla sugar and water in a pan and simmer for 5 minutes. Add the apricots and poach for about 10 minutes until tender. Drain the apricots on paper towels.
4. Spread the crème pâtissière in to the flan and arrange the apricot halves on top.

From the left: Bakewell tart; Apricot tart

Traditional Steamed & Baked Puddings

Almond and Apricot Puddings

butter, for greasing
4 tablespoons apricot jam
50 g (2 oz) butter
1 tablespoon caster sugar
100 g (4 oz) ground almonds
a few drops of almond essence
2 eggs, separated

Preparation time: *15 minutes*
Cooking time: *40 minutes*

1. Lightly grease 4 ramekin dishes with butter. Place a tablespoon of jam in each.
2. Cream the butter and sugar together until light and fluffy.
3. Add the ground almonds, almond essence and egg yolks and mix together.
4. Whisk the egg whites until they are stiff, then cut and fold them into the almond mixture.
5. Divide the mixture between the 4 ramekin dishes and cover each one with a piece of pleated, buttered aluminium foil. Tie with string.
6. Place the dishes in a heavy saucepan. Pour in enough boiling water to come half way up the side of the dishes. Cover the pan and simmer for 30–40 minutes, topping up with hot water if necessary.
7. To serve, remove the string and foil and turn the puddings out on to warmed individual plates. Serve with whipped cream.

Variation:
Hazelnut and Raspberry Puddings: make the recipe as above replacing the apricot jam with raspberry jam and the ground almonds with freshly ground hazelnuts. Omit the almond essence.

From the top, clockwise: Apricot rice mould; Apricot sauce; Almond and apricot puddings

Apricot Rice Mould

600 ml (1 pint) milk
2 strips of orange rind
75 g (3 oz) short-grain rice
50 g (2 oz) caster sugar
2 eggs, separated
150 ml (5 fl oz) double cream
100 g (4 oz) dried apricots, soaked overnight
300 ml (½ pint) water
sugar, to taste
about 85 ml (3 fl oz) orange juice

Serves 6
Preparation time: *40 minutes, plus soaking*
Cooking time: *45 minutes*
Oven: *180°C, 350°F, Gas Mark 4*

1. Pour the milk into a saucepan and bring to the boil over a gentle heat. Add the strips of orange rind and the rice. Simmer, stirring occasionally, for 30 minutes or until the rice is tender. Add the sugar.
2. Remove the saucepan from the heat and let the mixture cool a little. Stir in the egg yolks and the cream.
3. Whisk the egg whites until they form soft peaks, and fold them into the rice.
4. Pour the mixture into a 1.2 litre (2 pint) greased ring mould.
5. Cover with a piece of greased aluminium foil and place in a bain-marie. Bake in a preheated oven for 45 minutes.
6. Meanwhile, make the apricot sauce. Put the apricots in a pan with the water in which they have been soaking and simmer until tender. Pass the apricots through a nylon sieve or liquidize in a blender. Add sugar to taste and thin the sauce with orange juice if necessary.
7. Test the rice mould to see if it is cooked by piercing it. The skewer will come out clean if the rice is cooked.
8. Let the rice mould stand for 10 minutes before turning it out on to a warmed dish.
9. Serve hot with the apricot sauce handed round separately in a jug or sauce boat. Fill the centre and decorate the sides with canned apricot halves, if liked.

Christmas Pudding

75 g (3 oz) self-raising flour
pinch of salt
1 teaspoon mixed spice
1 teaspoon grated nutmeg
1 teaspoon ground cinnamon
150 g (5 oz) stoned raisins
100 g (4 oz) sultanas
75 g (3 oz) currants
75 g (3 oz) candied peel
50 g (2 oz) dates, chopped
50 g (2 oz) candied pineapple
50 g (2 oz) candied papaya
25 g (1 oz) glacé cherries
1 dessert apple, peeled and grated
1 carrot, peeled and grated
50 g (2 oz) almonds, blanched and chopped
200 g (7 oz) shredded suet
175 g (6 oz) fresh white breadcrumbs
100 g (4 oz) soft dark brown sugar
3 eggs, beaten
3 tablespoons brandy
85 ml (3 fl oz) brown ale
juice and grated rind of 1 orange
butter, for greasing
1 tablespoon brandy, to serve

Serves 8–10
Preparation time: *1 hour*
Cooking time: *6 hours, plus 3 hours on the day*

This unusually light Christmas Pudding is just what one wants after a traditionally filling main course. Candied pineapple and papaya are available from health food shops. The pudding can be made in advance and left to mature in the same way as heavier puddings.

1. Sift the flour, salt and spices into a large bowl. Add the dried and candied fruits, the apple, carrot, almonds, suet, breadcrumbs and sugar and mix well. Stir in the eggs, brandy, beer and the orange juice and rind.
2. Grease a 1.5 litre (2½ pint) pudding basin with butter. Line the base with a circle of greaseproof paper, buttered on both sides. Spoon the mixture into the basin, packing it in tightly, and level the top.
3. Cover with greased greaseproof paper and a piece of aluminium foil, pleated to allow for expansion, and tie on with string.
4. Place the basin in a large, heavy saucepan. Pour in boiling water to come two-thirds up the side of the basin.
5. Cover the saucepan and steam steadily for 6 hours, topping up with hot water when necessary.
6. At the end of the cooking time, remove the basin from the saucepan and leave to cool. Take off the string, paper and foil and replace them with a fresh cover. Store in a cool, dry place.
7. On the day of serving, steam the pudding again for 3 hours.
8. Remove the string, paper and foil and turn the pudding out on to a warmed dish.
9. Decorate the pudding with a sprig of holly.
10. Just before serving, remove the holly, pour a tablespoon of warmed brandy over the pudding and light with a match.
11. Serve with brandy butter.

To make Brandy butter, cream 75 g (3 oz) unsalted butter with 75 g (3 oz) caster sugar and the grated rind of half an orange until light and fluffy. Gradually beat in the brandy until thoroughly mixed. Chill for 2–3 hours or until the butter is firm.

From the left:
Christmas pudding; French Christmas pudding

French Christmas Pudding

1 × 425 g (15 oz) can chestnut purée
100 g (4 oz) unsalted butter, softened
4 eggs, separated
175 g (6 oz) caster sugar
2 tablespoons brandy (optional)
Chocolate sauce:
150 ml (1/4 pint) double cream
225 g (8 oz) plain dark chocolate, broken into pieces
2 tablespoons brandy
4 marrons glacés, sliced, to decorate (optional)

Serves 8
Preparation time: *30 minutes*
Cooking time: *2 hours*
Oven: *180°C, 350°F, Gas Mark 4*

1. Cream the chestnut purée and the butter together.
2. Beat in the egg yolks and the sugar.
3. Whisk the egg whites until stiff and fold them into the chestnut purée mixture.
4. Grease a 1.2 litre (2 pint) non-stick or enamel loaf tin and line the bottom with a piece of greased greaseproof paper. Pour the mixture into the tin.
5. Place the tin in a bainmarie and bake in a preheated oven for 2 hours until set. If the top of the pudding looks as if it is browning too quickly, cover with a piece of buttered foil.
6. Meanwhile, prepare the sauce. Heat the cream in a small heavy saucepan over a gentle heat. Do not let it boil. Add the broken chocolate and brandy. Stir over a very gentle heat until the chocolate has melted and the sauce is smooth.
7. Remove the pudding from the oven and let it cool in the tin for about 5–10 minutes. Run a knife around the edge to loosen it and turn out on to a warmed dish.
8. Coat the pudding with a little chocolate sauce and decorate with the sliced marrons glacés. Hand the remaining sauce separately.

Brioche Apricot Bake

butter, for spreading
4 slices of slightly stale brioche
6 apricots, halved and stoned
100 g (4 oz) sugar
whipped cream, to serve (optional)

Preparation time: *10 minutes*
Cooking time: *20–30 minutes*
Oven: *180°C, 350°F, Gas Mark 4*

A brioche is a fancy, sweet bread or rich yeast dough originating from France. Sometimes it contains dried and candied fruits. Brioches come in various shapes and sizes. The traditional shape is similar to a cottage loaf, large or small, but square and cylinder shapes are available.

1. Lightly butter each slice of brioche and place on a baking sheet buttered side up.
2. Place 3 apricot halves on each slice and sprinkle the sugar in the spaces between the apricot halves.
3. Bake near the top of a preheated oven for 20–30 minutes.
4. Serve with whipped cream if desired.

From the left: Apricot brown betty; Brioche apricot bake; Bread and butter pudding

Apricot Brown Betty

450 g (1 lb) fresh apricots or 225 g (8 oz) dried apricots, soaked overnight
100 g (4 oz) fresh white breadcrumbs
75 g (3 oz) butter, melted
75 g (3 oz) caster sugar
grated rind of 1 orange

To serve:

2 tablespoons demerara sugar
1 quantity Fruit Coulis (page 188) made with stewed or poached apricots.

Serves 4–6
Preparation time: *20 minutes*
Cooking time: *40 minutes*
Oven: *190°C, 375°F, Gas Mark 5*

1. If using fresh apricots, halve them and remove the stones.
2. Toss the breadcrumbs in the melted butter.
3. Spread a thin layer of crumbs in the bottom of a greased 1.2 litre (2 pint) ovenproof dish.
4. Cover the crumbs with a shallow layer of fruit, sprinkled with sugar and orange rind.
5. Continue to layer the fruit and crumbs alternately, finishing with a layer of crumbs, and a sprinkling of sugar.
6. Bake in a preheated oven for 40 minutes until crisp and golden.
7. Sprinkle with the demerara sugar and serve with the fruit coulis.

Bread and Butter Pudding

8 slices of slightly stale white bread, crusts removed
50 g (2 oz) butter
75 g (3 oz) sultanas
grated rind of 1 orange
50 g (2 oz) caster sugar
2 eggs
600 ml (1 pint) milk
grated nutmeg, for sprinkling

Serves 4–6
Preparation time: *15 minutes, plus soaking*
Cooking time: *1 hour*
Oven: *180°C, 350°F, Gas Mark 4*

1. Spread the bread fairly thickly with butter on both sides and cut each slice into 4 triangles.
2. Arrange half the bread in a 1.2 litre (2 pint) buttered ovenproof dish. Sprinkle with the sultanas, grated orange rind and half the sugar.
3. Cover with the remaining bread.
4. Beat the eggs and milk together and strain over the pudding.
5. Sprinkle with the remaining sugar and grated nutmeg and leave to soak for 15 minutes.
6. Bake in a preheated oven for about 1 hour until golden.
7. Serve with Vanilla ice cream (page 88) or whipped cream.

Golden Treacle Sponge

100 g (4 oz) butter
100 g (4 oz) caster sugar
grated rind of 1 orange
2 eggs, beaten
150 g (5 oz) self-raising flour
4 tablespoons golden syrup

Serves 4–6
Preparation time: *20 minutes*
Cooking time: *1½ hours*

1. Grease a 900 ml (1½ pint) pudding basin.
2. Cream the butter, sugar and orange rind together until they are light and fluffy.
3. Add the eggs gradually and beat well between each addition.
4. Sift the flour and fold it into the mixture.
5. Spoon the syrup into the bottom of the pudding basin and pour the sponge mixture on top.
6. Cover the basin with a pleated piece of greased, greaseproof paper and aluminium foil large enough to allow for expansion and tie with string.
7. Place the basin in a heavy saucepan, two-thirds full of hot water, cover and steam steadily over a low heat for approximately 1½ hours. Top up with hot water if necessary during the cooking time.
8. To serve, remove the string, paper and foil and turn the sponge out on to a warmed dish. Serve with custard.

From the left: Golden treacle sponge; Steamed chocolate sponge; Queen of puddings

Steamed Chocolate Sponge

100 g (4 oz) butter
100 g (4 oz) caster sugar
2 eggs, beaten
150 g (5 oz) self-raising flour
20 g (¾ oz) cocoa powder mixed with 2 tablespoons milk
Chocolate Sauce (page 188), to serve

Serves 4–6
Preparation time: *30 minutes*
Cooking time: *1½ hours*

1. Grease a 900 ml (1½ pint) pudding basin.
2. Cream the butter and sugar together in a mixing bowl until they are light and fluffy.
3. Add the eggs gradually and beat well between each addition.
4. Sift the flour and fold it in using a figure of eight motion until thoroughly blended. Add the cocoa mixed with milk.
5. Spoon the sponge mixture into the pudding basin.
6. Cover the basin with a pleated piece of greased greaseproof paper and aluminium foil large enough to allow for expansion, and tie with string.
7. Place the basin in a heavy saucepan, two-thirds full of hot water, cover and steam steadily over a low heat for approximately 1½ hours. Top up with hot water if necessary during the cooking time.
8. While the pudding is steaming, prepare the chocolate sauce.
9. To serve, remove the string, paper and foil and turn the pudding out on to a warmed dish. Pour a little hot chocolate sauce over the pudding and serve the rest separately.

Queen of Puddings

300 ml (½ pint) milk
200 g (7 oz) caster sugar
3 eggs, separated
a few drops of vanilla essence
75 g (3 oz) fresh white breadcrumbs
3 tablespoons raspberry jam
juice of ½ lemon
175 g (6 oz) caster sugar

Serves 6
Preparation time: *30 minutes, plus soaking*
Cooking time: *50–60 minutes*
Oven: *180°C, 350°F, Gas Mark 4*

1. Put the milk, 25 g (1 oz) of the sugar, egg yolks and vanilla essence in a mixing bowl and whisk together.
2. Pour the mixture over the breadcrumbs and leave for 15 minutes.
3. Transfer to a 900 ml (1½ pint) greased ovenproof dish and bake in a preheated oven for 30 minutes.
4. Remove from the oven and leave to cool slightly.
5. Mix the jam and lemon juice together and spread evenly over the surface of the pudding.
6. Beat the egg whites until they are stiff. Add the remaining sugar a tablespoon at a time, whisking well between each addition until the mixture is thick and glossy.
7. Pipe or spoon the meringue on top of the pudding and return to the oven for about 20 minutes until the meringue is crisp and lightly coloured.
Serve hot.

Flamri

Flamri

450 ml (¾ pint) milk
2 tablespoons semolina
2 strips of orange rind
1 tablespoon caster sugar
25 g (1 oz) butter
2 eggs, separated
1 quantity Fruit Coulis (page 188) made with raspberries
100 g (4 oz) fresh raspberries, to decorate

Serves 4–6
Preparation time: *20 minutes, plus cooling*
Cooking time: *30 minutes*
Oven: *180°C, 350°F, Gas Mark 4*

1. Bring the milk to the boil in a saucepan. Add the semolina and orange rind and simmer, stirring continuously, for 10 minutes.
2. Stir in the sugar and butter. Leave the mixture to cool slightly.
3. Work in the egg yolks.
4. Whisk the egg whites until stiff and cut and fold them into the mixture.
5. Pour into a well-greased 600 ml (1 pint) mould and set in a bain-marie.
6. Cover the mould with a piece of greased aluminium foil and bake in a preheated oven for 30 minutes until the Flamri is firm to the touch.
7. Leave the pudding to cool before turning it out on to a serving dish.
8. Decorate with the raspberries and pour a little fruit coulis on top. Serve the rest of the sauce separately.

Rhubarb and Ginger Crumble

1 kg (2 lb) rhubarb
100 g (4 oz) caster sugar
2 pieces of stem ginger, chopped
2 tablespoons stem ginger syrup
Crumble:
225 g (8 oz) plain flour
100 g (4 oz) butter
50 g (2 oz) caster sugar
25 g (1 oz) demerara sugar

Serves 6
Preparation time: *20 minutes*
Cooking time: *40 minutes*
Oven: *190°C, 375°F, Gas Mark 5*

1. Top and tail the rhubarb and remove the stringy skin.
2. Cut the rhubarb into 2.5 cm (1 inch) lengths, put it into a large ovenproof dish and sprinkle with sugar. Add the stem ginger and its syrup.
3. To make the crumble, sift the flour into a mixing bowl and rub in the butter until the mixture looks like fine breadcrumbs. Mix in the caster sugar.
4. Cover the rhubarb with the crumble and press it down lightly. Sprinkle the surface with demerara sugar.
5. Bake in a preheated oven for 40 minutes until golden brown.
6. Serve hot with whipped cream or custard. This crumble is delicious served cold with Vanilla ice cream (page 88).

Apple and Blackberry Charlotte

1 quantity Apple and Blackberry Purée (page 71)
1 slightly stale medium sliced white sandwich loaf, crusts removed
100 g (4 oz) butter, melted

Serves 8
Preparation time: *40 minutes*
Cooking time: *40 minutes*
Oven: *200°C, 400°F, Gas Mark 6*

1. Prepare the fruit purée.
2. Cut enough slices of the bread into narrow rectangles to line the sides of a 900 ml (1½ pint) charlotte mould. Dip one side of each rectangle in melted butter and use to line the mould, with the buttered side facing the mould.
3. Cut the remaining bread in triangles and dip in melted butter. Reserve enough bread to make a lid, then lay the remaining slices of bread buttered side down overlapping in the base of the mould.
4. Pack the purée into the bread-lined mould. Make a lid with the remaining bread, buttered side uppermost.
5. Bake in a preheated oven for 40 minutes until golden brown.
6. Leave to cool slightly and turn out on to a serving dish.
7. Serve with hot Crème anglaise (page 189) or a pouring cream.

From the top: Apple and blackberry charlotte; Rhubarb and ginger crumble

Glorious Gâteaux

Pistachio Cake with Kiwi Fruit

3 eggs
100g (4oz) caster sugar
75g (3oz) plain flour
50g (2oz) pistachio nuts, blanched, peeled and finely chopped
300ml (½ pint) double cream, whipped
3 kiwi fruit, peeled and sliced
To decorate:
icing sugar
whole pistachio nuts
slices of kiwi fruit, halved

Serves 6–8
Preparation time: *20 minutes*
Cooking time; *20 minutes*
Oven: *180°C, 350°F, Gas Mark 4*

1. Grease and flour three 18cm (7 inch) sandwich tins and line the bases with greased non-stick silicone paper.
2. Place the eggs and sugar in a mixing bowl set over a pan of simmering water.
3. Whisk until the mixture is very thick and light and leaves a trail on the whisk. Remove the bowl from the pan and whisk until cool.
4. Gently fold in the flour and chopped nuts and divide the mixture between the 3 tins.
5. Bake in a preheated oven for 20 minutes until golden and springy to the touch.
6. Turn the cakes out on to a wire tray and leave to cool.
7. Sandwich the cake layers with two-thirds of the cream and kiwi fruit.
8. Dust the top of the cake with icing sugar and decorate with rosettes of cream, pistachio nuts and halved slices of kiwi fruit.

From the top: Pistachio cake with kiwi fruit; Chocolate boxes

Chocolate Boxes

225g (8oz) plain dark chocolate
3 eggs
75g (3oz) caster sugar
grated rind of 1 orange
75g (3oz) plain flour
pinch of salt
2 tablespoons Curaçao
4 tablespoons apricot jam, warmed and sieved
150ml (¼ pint) double cream, whipped
6 strawberries, halved
12 chocolate leaves

Serves 6
Preparation time: *30 minutes*
Cooking time: *10 minutes*
Oven: *220°C, 425°F, Gas Mark 7*

As an alternative, decorate each box with half a glacé cherry and angelica leaves.

1. Melt the chocolate in a bowl set over a pan of hot water. Pour it on to a piece of waxed paper to make a 30 × 23cm (12 × 9 inch) rectangle and leave to cool.
2. Whisk the eggs, sugar and orange rind in a bowl set over a pan of simmering water, until they are thick and light.
3. Sift in the flour and salt, and fold in gently.
4. Turn the mixture into a greased and lined 28 × 18 × 4cm (11 × 7 × 1½ inch) Swiss roll tin and bake in a preheated oven for 10 minutes until light golden in colour and springy to the touch. Turn out to cool on a wire tray.
5. Sprinkle the cake with the orange curaçao and cut it into 12 equal cubes 5 × 6cm (2 × 2½ inches).
6. Brush the sides of each square with a little melted jam.
7. Cut the chocolate into 48 squares to fit the sides of the cakes, and press them on to the sides.
8. Spoon or pipe whipped cream into the boxes and top each with a strawberry and chocolate leaf.

Savarin Aux Fruits En Kirsch

225 g (8 oz) strong plain flour
pinch of salt
10 g (1/4 oz) instant dried yeast
1 teaspoon sugar
150 ml (1/4 pint) milk
4 eggs, beaten
100 g (4 oz) butter, creamed

Syrup:

175 g (6 oz) sugar
250 ml (8 fl oz) water
strip of lemon rind
6 tablespoons Kirsch

Filling:

225 g (8 oz) fresh fruit (pineapple, strawberries, cherries), marinated in
3 tablespoons Kirsch
sugar, to taste
300 ml (1/2 pint) double cream

Serves 8
Preparation time: *25 minutes, plus proving*
Cooking time: *30–40 minutes*
Oven: *200°C, 400°F, Gas Mark 6*

Instant yeast is available from supermarkets. It does not require pre-mixing with water, unlike other dried yeasts. If you wish to use fresh yeast, double the quantity.

1. Sift the flour and salt into a large warmed bowl. Add the yeast and sugar.
2. Mix the milk and eggs together and add them to the flour. Using the hands, work the mixture to a smooth dough.
3. Knead the dough vigorously until the texture is smooth and elastic.
4. Cover the dough with oiled clingfilm and leave in a warm place for 45 minutes to rise.
5. Beat the creamed butter into the risen dough until it is thoroughly incorporated.
6. Turn the dough into a greased ring mould 20 cm (8 inches) in diameter. Cover with oiled clingfilm and leave in a warm place until the dough has risen to the top of the mould.
7. Bake in a preheated oven for 30–40 minutes until golden and firm to the touch.
8. Leave the savarin to cool in the mould. When the sides have shrunk away from the tin, turn it out on to a wire tray.
9. To prepare the syrup, gently heat the sugar with the water in a small saucepan, stirring frequently until the sugar has dissolved. Add the lemon rind and boil for 5 minutes.
10. Stir in the Kirsch and remove the pan from the heat.
11. Prick the savarin all over with a fork. Pour the syrup evenly over the top. As it soaks through, spoon it over until the savarin has soaked up all the syrup.
12. Fill the centre of the savarin with fruit and sugar to taste. If preferred, pipe the whipped cream with a large star nozzle.

Rum Babas

100 g (4 oz) strong plain flour
pinch of salt
10 g (1/4 oz) dried instant yeast (see Savarin aux Fruits en Kirsch, (opposite))
1 teaspoon sugar
3 tablespoons milk
2 eggs, beaten
50 g (2 oz) butter, softened
175 g (6 oz) sugar
250 ml (8 fl oz) water
strip of lemon rind
3 tablespoons dark rum

To decorate:

150 ml (1/4 pint) double cream, whipped
4 glacé cherries, cut in half
8 angelica leaves

Serves 8
Preparation time: *20 minutes, plus proving*
Cooking time: *15 minutes*
Oven: *200°C, 400°F, Gas Mark 6*

1. Grease 8 small ring moulds.
2. Place the flour, salt, yeast and sugar in a warm mixing bowl.
3. Add the milk, eggs and butter and beat vigorously for 5 minutes until the dough is smooth and elastic.
4. Half fill each ring mould with dough and cover with oiled clingfilm. Leave in a warm place until the dough has risen two thirds of the way up the moulds.
5. Bake in a preheated oven for 15 minutes until they are golden brown.
6. To prepare the syrup, gently heat the sugar with the water in a small saucepan, stirring frequently until the sugar has dissolved. Add the lemon rind and boil for 5 minutes. Stir in the rum and remove the pan from the heat.
7. Turn the babas out of the moulds. When they are cool, spoon over the rum syrup until they are well saturated.
8. Using a piping bag fitted with a rose nozzle, fill the centres with whipped cream. Top each one with half a glacé cherry and angelica leaves.

From the left: Savarin aux fruits en Kirsch; Rum babas

Raspberry Hazelnut Cake

4 eggs
100 g (4 oz) caster sugar
100 g (4 oz) plain flour
50 g (2 oz) hazelnuts, toasted and chopped

Filling:

300 ml (½ pint) double cream, whipped
225 g (8 oz) raspberries

Serves 6
Preparation time: *20 minutes*
Cooking time: *40 minutes*
Oven: *180°C, 350°F, Gas Mark 4*

1. Grease and flour a 20 cm (8 inch) loose-bottomed cake tin.
2. Place the eggs and sugar in a bowl set over a pan of simmering water.
3. Whisk until the mixture is very thick and light and leaves a trail. Remove the bowl from the pan and continue to whisk until the mixture is cool.
4. Sift in the flour and carefully fold it in with the nuts.
5. Pour the mixture into the prepared cake tin and bake in a preheated oven for 40 minutes until firm to the touch.
6. Leave to cool in the tin for 5 minutes then turn out and cool completely.
7. Cut the cake in half horizontally. Sandwich the layers with two thirds of the cream and the raspberries, reserving some of the best berries for decoration.
8. Spread the remaining cream on top of the cake and make a circular pattern with the prongs of a fork. Decorate with raspberries, and if liked, a few blanched and toasted hazelnuts left whole.

From the top, clockwise:
Gâteau regent; Raspberry hazelnut cake; Coffee and walnut cake

Gâteau Regent

4 eggs
100 g (4 oz) caster sugar
75 g (3 oz) flour
25 g (1 oz) cocoa powder
25 g (1 oz) melted butter

Filling:

250 g (9 oz) chestnuts, peeled
1 egg
1 egg yolk
75 g (3 oz) caster sugar
15 g (½ oz) flour
250 ml (8 fl oz) milk

To decorate:

200 g (7 oz) apricot jam
1 tablespoon water
1 tablespoon dark rum
8 apricot halves, sliced
8 whole chestnuts, reserved from the filling

Preparation time: *50 minutes, plus cooling*
Cooking time: *25 minutes*
Oven: *190°C, 375°F, Gas Mark 5*

1. Whisk the eggs and sugar in a bowl set over a pan of simmering water until they have trebled in volume.
2. Sift the flour with the cocoa powder. Fold half of it into the eggs. Gently stir in the melted butter. Fold in the remaining flour and cocoa powder.
3. Pour the mixture into a greased 20 cm (8 inch) cake tin. Bake in a preheated oven for 25 minutes. Turn out on to a wire tray to cool.
4. To make the filling, put the chestnuts in a saucepan of simmering water, reserving 8 of them for decoration. Poach for 20 minutes or until tender. Pass the chestnuts through a sieve, or purée in a blender.
5. Beat the egg, egg yolk, sugar and flour in a mixing bowl.
6. Heat the milk to simmering point. Pour it into the egg mixture, stirring constantly. Mix well.
7. Transfer the mixture to a clean pan. Stirring throughout, cook over a low heat until thickened.
8. Add the sauce to the chestnut purée and mix well.
9. Cut the sponge in three horizontally. Sandwich the layers together with the chestnut filling.
10. To make the decoration, heat the apricot jam with the water in a small saucepan to simmering point. Pass the warmed jam through a sieve and add the rum. Coat the cake with apricot glaze, arrange the whole chestnuts and apricot slices on top.

Coffee and Walnut Cake

100 g (4 oz) butter
100 g (4 oz) caster sugar
2 eggs, beaten
100 g (4 oz) self-raising flour
50 g (2 oz) walnuts, chopped
1 tablespoon coffee essence

Filling:

3 egg yolks
75 g (3 oz) sugar
50 ml (2 fl oz) water
100 g (4 oz) butter, softened
2 teaspoons coffee essence

To decorate:

icing sugar
walnut halves

Serves 6
Preparation time: *25 minutes*
Cooking time: *about 30 minutes*
Oven: *180°C, 350°F, Gas Mark 4*

1. Grease and flour two 18 cm (7 inch) sandwich tins.
2. Cream the butter and the sugar together in a mixing bowl until light and fluffy.
3. Gradually beat in the eggs.
4. Fold in the flour and chopped walnuts and add the coffee essence.
5. Divide the mixture equally between the two tins, and bake in a preheated oven for 30 minutes or until risen and springy to the touch.
6. Turn the cakes out on to wire trays to cool.
7. To make the filling, whisk the egg yolks until they are light and thick.
8. Put the sugar in a small saucepan with the water and bring to the boil, stirring constantly to dissolve the sugar. Boil to the thread stage (107°C, 225°F on a sugar thermometer). The syrup should form a fine short thread off the side of a spoon.
9. Beating continuously, pour the hot syrup into the whisked egg yolks in a thin, steady stream. Whisk until the mixture cools, and is thick and pale.
10. Beat in the butter until the mixture is smooth and shiny. Stir in the coffee essence.
11. Sandwich the cakes together with half the filling.
12. Put the remaining filling into a piping bag fitted with a ribbon nozzle and pipe lines to section the top of the cake. Lightly dust with icing sugar then decorate with walnut halves.

Gâteau au Chocolat

100 g (4 oz) butter
175 g (6 oz) caster sugar
175 g (6 oz) plain dark chocolate
6 eggs, separated
75 g (3 oz) plain flour
1 teaspoon baking powder
Filling:
225 g (8 oz) plain dark chocolate
250 ml (8 fl oz) double cream
2 tablespoons brandy
To decorate:
chocolate scrolls
icing sugar

Serves 8
Preparation time: *30 minutes*
Cooking time: *1 hour*
Oven: *180°C, 350°F, Gas Mark 4*

1. Grease and flour a 20 cm (8 inch) loose-bottomed cake tin.
2. Cream the butter and the sugar together until they are light and creamy.
3. Melt the chocolate in a bowl set over a pan of hot water.
4. Add the melted chocolate to the creamed butter.
5. Sieve the flour and baking powder together. Add the egg yolks to the creamed mixture one by one, incorporating a little flour mixture each time and beat together well. Stir in the rest of the flour.
6. Whisk the egg whites until they stand in soft peaks.
7. Fold the egg whites gently into the chocolate mixture. (It is easier to do this using your hand.)
8. Pour the mixture into the prepared tin and bake in a preheated oven for 1 hour until the surface is firm.
9. Leave the cake to cool in the tin for a while before turning it out on to a wire tray.
10. Meanwhile prepare the filling. Melt the chocolate in a bowl set over a pan of hot water and stir in the cream and brandy. Leave to cool and thicken.
11. When cool, whisk the mixture until it becomes lighter in texture and increases in volume.
12. Slice the cake horizontally into 3 layers and sandwich each layer with a little chocolate cream.
13. Set the bowl of remaining chocolate cream over the pan of hot water to melt it down again, if necessary.
14. Pour the chocolate cream over the cake. Decorate with chocolate scrolls and dust lightly with the icing sugar.

Almond Layer Cake

3 egg whites
175 g (6 oz) caster sugar
a few drops of vanilla essence
½ teaspoon lemon juice
75 g (3 oz) ground almonds
Cake:
100 g (4 oz) butter
100 g (4 oz) caster sugar
3 eggs, beaten
75 g (3 oz) ground almonds
40 g (1½ oz) self-raising flour
a few drops of almond essence
Filling:
3 quantities Praline (page 188)
600 ml (1 pint) double cream, whipped
chocolate leaves, to decorate

Serves 8–10
Preparation time: *45 minutes*
Cooking time: *1¼–1½ hours*
Oven: *150°C, 300°F, Gas Mark 2*

1. Prepare the meringue, in the same way as the Almond Meringue Cake (page 44) and set aside.
2. Grease and flour a 20 cm (8 inch) loose-bottomed cake tin.
3. Cream the butter and the sugar together until light and fluffy. Gradually add the eggs and the ground almonds and beat well. Fold in the flour and the almond essence.
4. Spoon the mixture into the tin and bake in a preheated oven for 45 minutes or until a skewer comes out dry and clean. Turn the cake out on to a wire tray.
5. Fold 225 g (8 oz) of the praline, selecting the smallest pieces, into 450 ml (¾ pint) of the cream.
6. Slice the almond cake in half horizontally and spread one half with a little praline cream. Place a meringue layer on top. Repeat the layers of praline cream, meringue and cake, ending with a meringue layer.
7. Spread the remaining praline cream around the side of the cake and press on the reserved praline.
8. To decorate the cake, put the remaining cream into a piping bag and pipe rosettes of cream over the top and arrange chocolate leaves around the edge.

From the top: Gâteau au chocolat: Almond layer cake

Pineapple Meringue Cake

50 g (2 oz) plain flour
pinch of salt
2 eggs
50 g (2 oz) caster sugar

Meringue:

3 egg whites
175 g (6 oz) caster sugar
a few drops of vanilla essence
1 teaspoon lemon juice
75 g (3 oz) hazelnuts, ground and toasted

Filling:

250 ml (8 fl oz) double cream, whipped
1 pineapple, peeled, cored and sliced

To decorate:

250 ml (8 fl oz) double cream, whipped
75 g (3 oz) hazelnuts, chopped and toasted

Serves 8
Preparation time: *1 hour*
Cooking time: *55 minutes*
Oven: *Cake: 190°C, 375°F, Gas Mark 5*
Meringue: 180°C, 350°F, Gas Mark 4

1. Grease and flour four 18 cm (7 inch) sandwich tins.
2. Sift the flour and salt twice on to a piece of non-stick silicone paper and set aside.
3. Place the eggs and sugar in a bowl and set over a pan of simmering water. Whisk until the mixture is thick and pale and leaves a trail.
4. Sift the flour into the mixture and fold it in gently.
5. Divide the mixture between 2 of the sandwich tins and bake in a preheated oven for 15 minutes until golden brown and springy to the touch.
6. Prepare the meringue in the same way as Almond Meringue Cake but substitute hazelnuts for almonds. Turn the meringue mixture into the 2 remaining sandwich tins, reduce the oven temperature and bake for 40 minutes.
7. Set aside 1 slice of pineapple for decoration. To assemble the cake, spread one layer with cream, place a few slices of pineapple on top, and cover with a meringue layer. Spread with more filling. Repeat the cake and filling layers. Complete the cake with a meringue layer only.
8. To decorate the gâteau, spread a little cream on the sides and coat with the chopped, toasted hazelnuts.
9. Put the remaining cream into a piping bag fitted with a rose nozzle and pipe a rope around the edges. Divide the reserved pineapple slices into pieces and arrange them on top. Dust with a little icing sugar.

Caramel and Orange Gâteau

4 eggs
100 g (4 oz) caster sugar
grated rind of 1 orange
90 g (3½ oz) plain flour, sifted
50 g (2 oz) butter, melted and slightly cooled

Filling:

3 tablespoons Grand Marnier or Curaçao
300 ml (½ pint) double cream, whipped
6 oranges, peeled, pith removed and divided into segments

To decorate:

75 g (3 oz) sugar
85 ml (3 fl oz) water
crystallized orange slices (optional)

Serves 6
Preparation time: *40 minutes*
Cooking time: *30 minutes*
Oven: *190°C, 375°F, Gas Mark 5*

1. Grease a 20 cm (8 inch) cake tin, line the base with a piece of greased non-stick silicone paper and dust with flour.
2. Place the eggs, sugar and orange rind in a bowl and set over a pan of simmering water.
3. Whisk until the mixture is very thick and light and leaves a trail. Remove the bowl from the pan and whisk the mixture until cool.
4. Fold in half the flour. Pour in the melted butter in a thin stream and gently fold in the remaining flour.
5. Pour the mixture into the tin and bake in a preheated oven for 30 minutes until it is springy to the touch and begins to shrink from the sides of the tin. Turn the cake on to a wire tray to cool.
6. Cut the cake in half horizontally.
7. Sprinkle the chosen liqueur on the bottom layer. Spread it with two-thirds of the cream and arrange the orange segments on top.
8. To decorate the cake, put the sugar and water in a small saucepan and bring slowly to the boil, stirring constantly so that the sugar is completely dissolved. Boil the syrup until it turns to a golden caramel then pour it immediately on to the top layer of sponge. Spread it out and mark it into portions with an oiled knife.
9. When the caramel glaze is cool, pipe rosettes with the reserved cream on each portion and top each with a slice of crystallized orange, if liked.

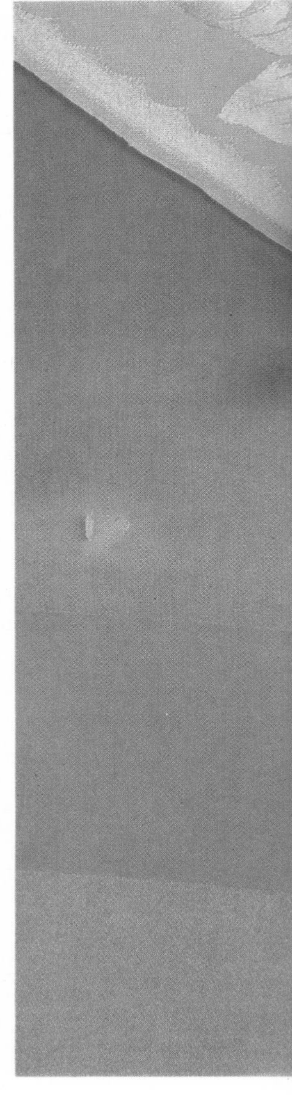

From the top left, clockwise: Caramel and orange gâteau; Pineapple meringue cake; Pineapple and Kirsch upside down cake

Pineapple and Kirsch Upside Down Cake

25 g (1 oz) butter
50 g (2 oz) soft light brown sugar
7 thin slices pineapple, fresh or canned, marinaded for 3 hours in
3 tablespoons Kirsch
7 glacé cherries
6 almonds, blanched

Cake Mixture:

100 g (4 oz) butter
100 g (4 oz) caster sugar
grated rind of 1 lemon
2 eggs, beaten
150 g (5 oz) self-raising flour
2 tablespoons Kirsch (optional)

Serves 6
Preparation time: *20 minutes*
Cooking time: *50–55 minutes*
Oven: *180°C, 350°F, Gas Mark 4*

1. Lightly grease a 20 cm (8 inch) cake tin.
2. Melt the butter with the soft brown sugar in a small saucepan over a gentle heat, stirring until the sugar has dissolved.
3. Spread the glaze over the bottom of the tin. Place the pineapple on top and put a cherry or an almond alternately in the centre of each pineapple ring.
4. Cream the butter, sugar and lemon rind together until light and fluffy.
5. Add the eggs, a little at a time, beating thoroughly between each addition.
6. Sift in the flour and fold it in gently. Stir in the Kirsch if desired.
7. Spoon the mixture on to the pineapple rings. Bake in a preheated oven for 50–55 minutes until the sponge springs back when lightly pressed.
8. Turn out on to a serving dish and serve hot or cold with whipped cream.

Raspberry shortcake gâteau

Raspberry Shortcake Gâteau

150 g (5 oz) butter
75 g (3 oz) caster sugar
grated rind of 1 lemon
1 egg yolk
225 g (8 oz) plain flour
300 ml (½ pint) double cream, whipped
225 g (8 oz) raspberries
icing sugar, for dusting

Serves 6
Preparation time: *30 minutes, plus cooling*
Cooking time: *20 minutes*
Oven: *180°C, 350°F, Gas Mark 4*

1. Cream the butter and sugar together until soft and fluffy. Stir in the grated lemon rind and the egg yolk.
2. Fold in the flour and knead to a soft dough.
3. Divide the dough into 3. Roll out each piece between two pieces of non-stick silicone paper to make a circle 20 cm (8 inches) in diameter. Remove the top piece of paper from each circle and flute the edges with the fingers.
4. Set each circle on a baking sheet and bake in a preheated oven for 15–20 minutes until lightly golden.
5. Leave to cool for 2–5 minutes. Divide one circle of shortcake into 8 equal sections.
6. Lift all the shortcake layers off the paper and leave them on a wire tray until completely cool.
7. Sandwich the two uncut layers with two thirds of the cream and the raspberries, reserving some for the top layer.
8. Put the remaining cream into a piping bag fitted with a rose nozzle. Pipe 8 equally spaced rosettes of cream on top of the gâteau. Prop a shortcake section against each one. Decorate with raspberries and dust with icing sugar. Serve within 1–2 hours once assembled.

Valentine Gâteau

5 eggs, separated
165 g (5½ oz) caster sugar
65 g (2½ oz) cornflour
65 g (2½ oz) flour
1 × 450 g (1 lb) can apricots, drained and chopped
2 tablespoons Kirsch
2 quantities Crème Chantilly (page 189)
2 tablespoons pistachio nuts, shelled and chopped
24 strawberries

Serves 8–10
Preparation time: *1½ hours*
Cooking time: *40 minutes*
Oven: *160°C, 325°F, Gas Mark 3*

1. Beat the egg yolks and sugar together until the mixture thickens and leaves a trail when it falls off the whisk.
2. Sift the cornflour and flour together until well blended.
3. Whisk the egg whites until they are very stiff and stand in peaks.
4. Fold the flour carefully into the egg yolks using a figure of eight motion.
5. Fold the egg whites into the mixture and pour it into a buttered 20 cm (8 inch) cake tin. Bake in a preheated oven for 40 minutes. Turn out on to a wire tray and leave to cool.
6. Pass the apricots through a sieve or purée in a blender.
7. Trim the cake to a heart shape. Cut into 4 horizontal slices and sprinkle a little Kirsch over each layer.
8. Spread apricot purée over each cake layer. Put the layers back together and place the cake on a serving dish.
9. Spread crème chantilly over the top and sides of the cake. Decorate the top with the chopped pistachio nuts. If liked, arrange some strawberries around the bottom edge of the cake.

Valentine gâteau

Strawberry Choux Gâteau

1 quantity Choux Pastry (page 119)
25 g (1 oz) almonds, blanched and shredded

Filling:

300 ml (½ pint) double cream, whipped
225 g (8 oz) strawberries
icing sugar, for dusting

Serves 4–6
Preparation time: *20 minutes*
Cooking time: *50 minutes*
Oven: *200°C, 400°F, Gas Mark 6*
190°C, 375°F, Gas Mark 5
120°C, 250°F, Gas Mark ½

1. Grease an 18 cm (7 inch) sandwich tin.
2. Spoon in the choux pastry, leaving a hole in the middle about 4 cm (1½ inches) wide. Scatter the ring with almonds.
3. Bake in a preheated oven for 20 minutes. Reduce the oven temperature and bake for a further 20–30 minutes.
4. Slice the choux ring in half and scoop out any uncooked pastry. Return the halves to a very cool oven to dry out for about 10–15 minutes. Cool on a wire tray.
5. Sandwich the gâteau with whipped cream and strawberries, reserving a few for decoration.
6. Dust the top lightly with icing sugar, and decorate with the strawberries.

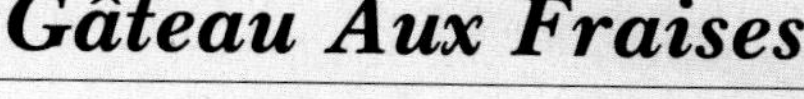

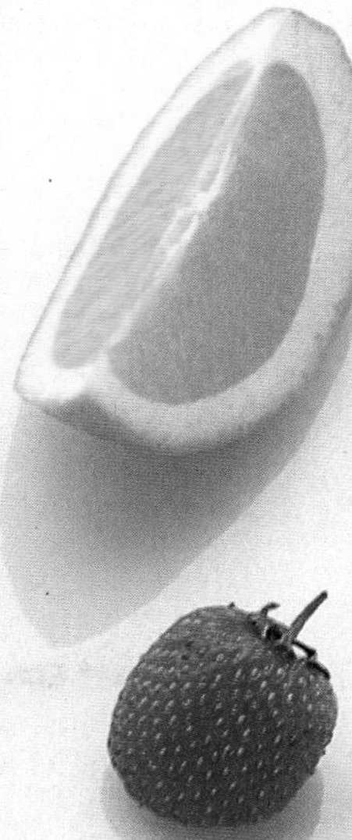

Gâteau Aux Fraises

100 g (4 oz) butter
100 g (4 oz) caster sugar
2 eggs, (sizes 1, 2) beaten
100 g (4 oz) self-raising flour
25 g (1 oz) ground almonds
a few drops of almond essence
300 ml (½ pint) double cream, lightly whipped
225 g (8 oz) strawberries, halved

Serves 6
Preparation time: *30 minutes*
Cooking time: *25–30 minutes*
Oven: *180°C, 350°F, Gas Mark 4*

1. Grease and flour two 18 cm (7 inch) sandwich tins.
2. Cream the butter and the sugar together until light and fluffy.
3. Gradually beat in the eggs, stirring well between each addition.
4. Sift in the flour, add the ground almonds and almond essence and fold into the creamed butter and sugar.
5. Divide the mixture between the tins and bake in a preheated oven for 25–30 minutes until golden brown and springy.
6. Leave the cakes to cool in the tins for 5 minutes, then turn them out on to a wire tray to cool.
7. Sandwich the layers together with half the cream and strawberries.
8. Decorate the top with rosettes of cream and the remaining strawberries.

From the top left: Gâteau aux fraises; Strawberry choux gâteau; Angel cake with orange

Angel Cake with Orange

50 g (2 oz) plain flour
175 g (6 oz) caster sugar
6 egg whites
1 teaspoon cream of tartar
grated rind of 1 orange
300 ml (½ pint) double cream, whipped
3 oranges, peeled and divided into segments

Serves 6
Preparation time: *20 minutes*
Cooking time: *35 minutes*
Oven: *190°C, 375°F, Gas Mark 5*

1. Sift the flour and half the sugar 3 times.
2. Whisk the egg whites with the cream of tartar until they stand in soft peaks.
3. Gradually whisk in the remaining sugar, whisking well between each addition, until the egg whites are thick and glossy.
4. Gently fold in the sifted flour and sugar and the orange rind.
5. Spoon the mixture into an ungreased 1.2 litre (2 pint) ring mould and bake in a preheated oven for 35 minutes.
6. Loosen the cake around the edges and turn it out on to a wire tray.
7. When the cake is completely cool, slice it horizontally through the middle and sandwich the 2 halves together with half the whipped cream and half of the orange segments.
8. Cover the cake with the remaining cream and decorate with the segments.

Desserts Around the World

AUSTRALIA

Pavlova

4 egg whites
250 g (9 oz) caster sugar
2 teaspoons cornflour
few drops of vanilla essence
2 teaspoons lemon juice

Filling:

300 ml (½ pint) double or whipping cream
450 g (1 lb) mixed fresh fruit (e.g. strawberries, raspberries, mango, kiwi fruit, passion fruit, grapes, peaches)

Serves 6–8
Preparation time: *30 minutes*
Cooking time: *1½ hours*
Oven: *150°C, 300°F, Gas Mark 2*

Pavlova originated in Australia and was created in honour of the great ballerina. The light meringue base is built up at the sides to suggest the dancer's tutu. It is filled with fresh cream and fruit.

1. Draw a 20 cm (8 inch) circle on rice paper or non-stick silicone paper and place on a baking sheet.
2. Whisk the egg whites until standing in stiff peaks, then gradually add half the sugar, 1 tablespoon at a time, whisking between each addition, until thick and glossy.
3. Sift the remaining sugar and the cornflour and fold into the meringue with the vanilla essence and lemon juice.
4. Spoon the meringue on to the prepared baking sheet following the line of the circle and hollow out the centre slightly.
5. Place the baking sheet in a preheated oven for 1½ hours until crisp and lightly coloured. Cool, then remove the paper.
6. To make the filling, whip the cream until it forms soft peaks. Spoon it into the hollow of the meringue, then top with the prepared fruit and chill lightly before serving.

From the top: Hexenschaum; Pavlova

AUSTRIA

Hexenschaum

450 g (1 lb) Cox's Orange Pippin apples
100 g (4 oz) canned apricots, drained
65 g (2½ oz) sugar
2 egg whites
25 g (1 oz) caster sugar

To decorate:

4 canned apricot halves
a few flaked almonds

Preparation time: *25 minutes, plus cooling*
Cooking: *about 15 minutes*

Hexenschaum is a popular Austrian dish which literally means 'witches' foam'. It is a dessert which is particularly liked by children because of its smooth, refreshing fruity flavour.

1. Peel, core and chop the apples and put them in a pan with 1 tablespoon of water. Simmer over a gentle heat until tender.
2. Blend the apricots and the cooked apple to a smooth purée. Combine the mixture with the sugar and cool.
3. Whisk the egg whites and caster sugar until very stiff and fold into the fruit purée. Spoon into 4 glasses or glass coupes and chill.
4. For serving, place an apricot half on top of the mousse, the rounded side uppermost and arrange almonds around the apricot like flower petals.

Variations:
1. Add 1 teaspoon of cinnamon to the stewed apples.
2. Blend 1 tablespoon dark rum with the apples and apricots.
3. Use 550 g (1¼ lb) plums, stewed and stoned, in place of the apple and apricots. Use brown sugar in place of the caster sugar.
4. Use 450 g (1 lb) gooseberries in place of the apples and stew with a small sprig of elderflowers.

AUSTRIA

Apfelstrudel

150 g (5 oz) strong white flour
1 tablespoon groundnut oil
75 ml (3 fl oz) water
a small pinch of salt
oil, for brushing

Filling:

65 g (2½ oz) unsalted butter
65 g (2½ oz) white breadcrumbs
750 g (1½ lb) cooking apples, grated
120 g (4½ oz) caster sugar
75 g (3 oz) raisins
2 tablespoons ground cinnamon
25 g (1 oz) butter, melted, to glaze
icing sugar, to dust

Preparation time: *45 minutes, plus resting*
Cooking time: *30 minutes*
Oven: *190°C, 375°F, Gas Mark 4*

1. Sift the flour into a mixing bowl. Add the oil, water and salt and knead to make a supple paste. Return the ball of dough to the mixing bowl. Brush it with a little oil and leave it to rest for 30 minutes.
2. Put a clean cotton tablecloth, at least 1 metre (39 inches) square, in the middle of a table. Dust the cloth with flour.
3. Put the dough in the middle of the cloth and roll it out until it is about 3 mm (⅛ inch) thick.
4. Stretch the dough a little at a time until it is paper-thin and transparent, by putting your hands palm side down, under the sheet of pastry lifting up and moving your fingers apart. Work slowly, carefully and evenly until the square of strudel pastry just reaches the sides of the cloth.
5. To make the filling, heat the butter in a frying pan. Fry the crumbs until golden.
6. Spoon the grated apple over two-thirds of the square of pastry, leaving a narrow margin at the edges and one-third of the pastry uncovered. Sprinkle the sugar, raisins, breadcrumbs and cinnamon over the apples.
7. Lift two corners of the tablecloth nearest to the section of pastry covered with apple. Go on lifting and as you lift, roll the pastry into a Swiss roll shape.
8. Line a baking sheet with non-stick silicone paper. Arrange the strudel on the sheet in the shape of a horseshoe.
9. Bake in a preheated oven for about 30 minutes. Halfway through cooking, brush with melted butter. Serve hot, warm or cold, dusted with icing sugar and with cream handed separately.

AUSTRIA

Topfenknoedel

65 g (2½ oz) unsalted butter
25 g (1 oz) caster sugar
2 eggs
100 g (4 oz) curd cheese
50 ml (2 fl oz) double cream or 50 g (2 oz) clotted cream
grated rind of ½ lemon
65 g (2½ oz) white breadcrumbs
65 g (2½ oz) flour

Sauce:

250 g (9 oz) plums
120 g (4½ oz) caster sugar

Topping:

50 g (2 oz) white breadcrumbs
25 g (1 oz) unsalted butter
1 tablespoon soft brown sugar

Preparation time: *45 minutes, plus chilling*
Cooking time: *about 5 minutes*

These two stages are easier and quicker if you have a food processor.

1. Cream the butter and sugar in a mixing bowl. Beat in the eggs one by one.
2. Beat in the cheese, cream, grated rind, crumbs and flour to form a smooth paste. Chill in the refrigerator.
3. To make the sauce, slit the plums, and put them in a saucepan with the sugar and a little water. Poach until tender. Remove the stones and sieve the plums. Chill.
4. To make the topping, fry the breadcrumbs in butter until golden. Allow to cool and stir in the brown sugar.
5. Spoon the plum sauce on to 4 dessert plates.
6. Fill a large saucepan with water and bring to the boil. Fit a piping bag with a 2 cm (¾ inch) plain tube and fill it with the cheese mixture. Pipe dumplings about 2.5 cm (1 inch) long into the simmering water. Snip each one off the nozzle of the piping bag with a pair of sharp kitchen scissors. Poach the dumplings for about 5 minutes. Lift them out with a slotted spoon and drain on paper towels.
7. Arrange the dumplings on the plum sauce, sprinkle the toasted crumbs on top and serve immediately.

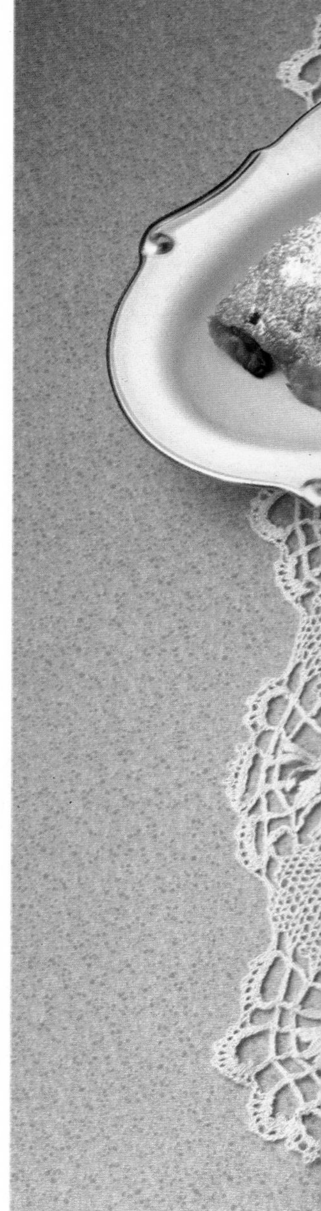

From the top left: Apfelstrudel; Topfenknoedel; Mandelcreme

AUSTRIA

Mandelcreme

65 g (2½ oz) sugar
pinch of cream of tartar
10 g (¼ oz) unsalted butter, melted
4 egg whites
150 g (5 oz) caster sugar
65 g (2½ oz) ground almonds
1 quantity Crème Chantilly (page 189), to decorate

Preparation time: *20 minutes, plus cooling*
Cooking time: *35 minutes*
Oven: *160°C, 325°F, Gas Mark 3*

1. Butter a 600 ml (1 pint) ring mould.
2. Moisten a pan with water then add the sugar, cream of tartar and sufficient water to moisten in a pan and boil to a mid-amber caramel. Remove from the heat and add 1 tablespoon of cold water. Return the caramel to the heat for a few seconds, then pour into the prepared mould or cake tin. Coat the bottom and sides.
3. Whisk the egg whites with 25 g (1 oz) of the caster sugar until very stiff. Fold in the ground almonds and the remaining sugar. Spoon into the mould. Bake in a preheated oven for 35 minutes.
4. To serve, turn out on to a serving dish and leave to cool. Decorate with the crème chantilly.

From the left: Brazilian meringue cake; Caribbean sponge

BRAZIL

Brazilian Meringue Cake

1 teaspoon coffee essence, or strong black coffee
1 quantity Swiss Meringue (page 46)

Filling:

1 quantity Vanilla Ice Cream (page 88)
2 tablespoons coffee essence, or strong black coffee, cooled

To decorate:

icing sugar
few candied coffee beans

Serves 8
Preparation time: *30 minutes*
Cooking time: *1–1¼ hours*
Oven: *120°C, 250°F, Gas Mark ½*

1. Line 3 baking sheets with non-stick silicone or lightly greased greaseproof paper and draw a 20 cm (8 inch) circle on each.
2. Carefully fold the coffee flavouring into the Swiss meringue.
3. Divide the meringue equally between the 3 sheets and spread evenly within the marked circles. Bake in a preheated oven for about 1–1¼ hours or until crisp.
4. Remove the vanilla ice cream from the freezer and leave for 10 minutes to soften.
5. Beat the ice cream, then gradually add the coffee flavouring, beating thoroughly between each addition. Return the ice cream to the freezer for about 15 minutes.
6. When the meringues are cold, sandwich them together with ⅔rds of the ice cream. The ice cream should not be too firm or it will break the meringue when spread. Sprinkle the top with icing sugar.
7. Beat the remaining ice cream until smooth and a piping consistency, then pipe rosettes around the edge of the cake. Decorate with candied coffee beans.
8. Return the cake to the freezer to firm. If made well in advance, transfer to the refrigerator 15 minutes before serving.

CARIBBEAN

Caribbean Sponge

100g (4oz) butter
100g (4oz) caster sugar
grated rind and juice of 1 lime
2 eggs, beaten
150g (5oz) self-raising flour
50g (2oz) desiccated coconut
1 tablespoon dark rum (optional)

Serves 4–6
Preparation time: *30 minutes*
Cooking time: *1½ hours*

1. Grease a 900ml (1½ pint) pudding basin.
2. Cream the butter, sugar and lime rind in a mixing bowl until they are light and fluffy.
3. Add the eggs gradually and beat well between each addition.
4. Sift in the flour and fold in the desiccated coconut. Add the lime juice and a little rum if desired.
5. Pour the mixture into a greased 900ml (1½ pint) pudding basin. Cover with a sheet of buttered aluminium foil, pleated to allow for expansion, and tie with string.
6. Place in a large saucepan and pour in enough boiling water to come half-way up the side of the basin. Cover the pan and steam over a gentle heat for 1½ hours, topping up with hot water if necessary.
7. Remove the foil and string and turn the sponge out on to a warmed serving dish. Serve with rum-flavoured whipped cream.

Chinese toffee apples

CHINA

Chinese Toffee Apples

100g (4oz) plain flour
1 tablespoon cornflour
pinch of salt
2 eggs, beaten
150ml (¼ pint) water
4 dessert apples, peeled and cored
a little cornflour, for coating
oil, for deep frying
Toffee:
225g (8oz) sugar
300ml (½ pint) water
2 tablespoons groundnut oil
50g (2oz) sesame seeds

Preparation time: *30 minutes*

1. Sift the flour, cornflour and salt into a bowl and make a well in the centre. Mix in the egg, and gradually whisk in the water until a smooth batter is formed.
2. Cut each apple into 6 wedges.
3. Toss the apples wedges in a little cornflour.
4. In a large heavy saucepan heat the fat to 200°C, 400°F, or so that a cube of bread will brown in 30 seconds.
5. Fry the apple wedges until they are golden brown. Lift them out of the oil with a slotted spoon and drain on paper towels. Keep warm.
6. To make the toffee, stir the sugar into the water in a heavy pan over a low heat. When the sugar has dissolved add the groundnut oil and increase the heat. Boil until golden caramel.
7. Remove the pan from the heat. Tip in the apple wedges and the sesame seeds and turn the pieces of apple carefully until coated with toffee.
8. Dip the toffee apples quickly in iced water and serve immediately. The toffee should be crisp.

Bondepige med slör

DENMARK

Bondepige Med Slör

500 g (1¼ lb) cooking apples, peeled, cored and chopped
120 g (4½ oz) soft light brown sugar
50 g (2 oz) unsalted butter
100 g (4 oz) brown breadcrumbs
150 ml (¼ pint) double cream
2 tablespoons raspberry jam (optional)

Preparation time: *20 minutes, plus cooling*
Cooking time: *15 minutes*

1. Put the apples in a pan with a tablespoon of water. Simmer until tender.
2. Press the cooked apples through a sieve. Add 90 g (3½ oz) of soft brown sugar.
3. Heat the butter in a small pan and fry the breadcrumbs until they are crisp. Remove the pan from the heat and combine the crumbs with the remaining brown sugar.
4. Put one third of the sweetened crumbs in the bottom of a trifle dish. Spoon half the apple on top. Cover with half the remaining crumbs. Spread the rest of the apple on top. Cover with the remaining crumbs.
5. Whip the cream until it holds its shape on the whisk and spread it on top. Warm the jam slightly, if using, and spoon it over the cream.

FRANCE

Gâteau St Honoré

175 g (6 oz) Shortcrust Pastry (page 114)
1 quantity Choux Pastry (page 119)
300 ml (½ pint) double cream, whipped
100 g (4 oz) sugar
85 ml (3 fl oz) water
300 ml (½ pint) Crème Pâtissière (page 189)
To decorate:
150 ml (¼ pint) double cream, whipped
chopped angelica, glacé cherries or crystallized violets

Serves 6
Preparation time: *40 minutes*
Cooking time: *30 minutes*
Oven: *220°C, 425°F, Gas Mark 7*
190°C, 375°F, Gas Mark 5

This speciality originated in Paris and is called after the patron saint of pastrycooks, St Honoré. It consists of a base of shortcrust pastry and a wall of caramel-coated choux buns filled with whipped cream. The centre is filled with Crème Pâtissière.

1. Grease 2 large baking sheets.
2. Roll out the shortcrust pastry to a thickness of about 5 mm (¼ inch) and cut out an 18 cm (7 inch) circle. Place the circle on a baking sheet, prick it with a fork, and dampen the edges with water.
3. Spoon the choux pastry into a piping bag fitted with a 1 cm (½ inch) plain nozzle. Pipe the dough around the rim of the pastry circle. Pipe the remaining dough on to the second baking sheet in small buns the same width as the choux ring.
4. Place both sheets in a preheated oven, the second on a lower shelf than the first. After 15 minutes, reduce the temperature, and bake for a further 15 minutes.
5. Remove the baking sheets from the oven and slit the choux ring and buns to allow the steam to escape. Leave to cool.
6. Spoon the whipped cream into a piping bag fitted with a rose nozzle and pipe some cream into each cooled bun.
7. To prepare the caramel, put the sugar and water in a small saucepan and heat slowly until the sugar is dissolved. Boil to a rich caramel.
8. Dip the base of each bun in caramel and place them around the choux ring. Trickle the remaining caramel on top of the buns.
9. Spoon the crème pâtissière into the base of the gâteau and pipe rosettes of cream on top. Decorate with angelica leaves, halved glacé cherries or crystallized violets.

FRANCE

Galette Valencienne

165 g (5½ oz) strong white flour
15 g (½ oz) caster sugar
1 teaspoon dried yeast
25 ml (1 fl oz) milk
2 eggs, lightly beaten
65 g (2½ oz) unsalted butter, cut into cubes
grated rind of ½ orange
juice of 1 lemon
2 eggs
120 g (4½ oz) caster sugar
65 g (2½ oz) unsalted butter, melted
icing sugar, to dust

Preparation time: *40 minutes, plus proving*
Cooking time: *30 minutes*
Oven: *200°C, 400°F, Gas Mark 6*

1. Sift the flour and sugar together into a mixing bowl.
2. Heat the milk to blood temperature and dissolve the yeast in it.
3. Mix the yeast and eggs together and add them to the flour. Knead to a dough.
4. Work in the butter for about 10 minutes until the dough is smooth and elastic. Cover with a clean linen cloth and leave to prove in a warm place for 1 hour.
5. Knock back the dough. Roll it on a floured work surface and line a 28 × 18 × 4 cm (11 × 7 × 1½ inch) shallow-sided baking tin. Leave to prove for 45 minutes.
6. Put the orange rind, lemon juice, eggs and sugar in a bowl set over a pan of simmering water and whisk until the mixture is pale and frothy. Fold in the butter.
7. Pour the mixture over the dough to cover it evenly.
8. Bake in a preheated oven for 30 minutes. After one-third of the cooking time, cover the pastry with a sheet of aluminium foil, folded at the edges so that it does not touch the topping. Serve either hot or cold, dusted with icing sugar.

From the left: Gâteau St Honoré; Galette valencienne

FRANCE

Tarte Tropezienne

250 g (9 oz) flour
75 g (3 oz) unsalted butter
15 g (½ oz) caster sugar
2 teaspoons dried yeast
120 ml (4 fl oz) milk, heated to body temperature
3 eggs, lightly beaten
250 g (9 oz) Crème Pâtissière (page 189)
150 g (5 oz) Butter Cream (page 188)
icing sugar, to dust

Preparation time: *30 minutes, plus proving*
Cooking time: *20 minutes*
Oven: *220°C, 425°F, Gas Mark 7*

1. Sift the flour into a mixing bowl and rub in the butter. Add the sugar.
2. Dissolve the yeast in the warm milk.
3. Add the yeast and eggs to the flour. Knead to a smooth, slightly sticky dough.
4. Butter and flour a 25 cm (10 inch) flan dish. Spread the dough over the base of the flan dish. Leave in a warm place to prove, covered with a clean linen cloth, until the dough doubles its size.
5. Bake in a preheated oven for 20 minutes. Cover the tart with a piece of aluminium foil halfway through the cooking time.
6. Turn the tart on to a tray. Leave to cool.
7. Beat the crème into the butter cream 1 tablespoon at a time. Split the tart horizontally through the middle. Spread the lower half with the filling and place the other half on top. Dust with icing sugar.

From the left: Tarte tropezienne; Nid d'Abeilles; Millefeuille gâteau

FRANCE

Nid d'Abeilles

300 g (11 oz) flour
100 g (4 oz) butter
120 ml (4 fl oz) milk
10 g (¼ oz) dried yeast
1 egg, lightly beaten
50 g (2 oz) unsalted butter
75 g (3 oz) caster sugar
25 g (1 oz) honey
25 g (1 oz) flaked almonds
1 tablespoon Kirsch
300 g (11 oz) Crème Pâtissière (page 189)

Preparation time: *30 minutes, plus proving*
Cooking time: *30 minutes*
Oven: *200°C, 400°F, Gas Mark 6*

1. Sift the flour into a mixing bowl and rub in the butter.
2. Heat the milk to body temperature. Dissolve the yeast in the milk.
3. Add the egg and milk to the flour and knead to form a smooth dough. Leave to prove in a warm place until it doubles its volume. Knock back the dough. Put it in a buttered 20 cm (8 inch) cake tin. Leave to prove again until well risen.
4. Melt the unsalted butter, sugar and honey in a saucepan over a gentle heat, stirring until the sugar dissolves. Spread the mixture over the risen dough and sprinkle the almonds on top.
5. Bake in a preheated oven for 30 minutes. After 20 minutes of the cooking time, cover the cake with buttered aluminium foil.
6. Remove the cake from the oven and turn out on to a wire tray. Leave to cool.
7. When the cake is cold, split it in half horizontally.
8. Beat the Kirsch into the cold Crème Pâtissière. Spread the crème over the lower half of the cake and put the other half back on top.

FRANCE

Millefeuille Gâteau

350 g (12 oz) prepared Puff Pastry (page 116)

Filling:

150 ml (1/4 pint) double cream, whipped
450 g (1 lb) strawberries, sliced
6 tablespoons redcurrant jelly
juice of 1/2 lemon

Serves 6
Preparation time: *15 minutes*
Cooking time: *15–20 minutes*
Oven: *220°C, 425°F, Gas Mark 7*

1. Roll the pastry out to a large rectangle 3 mm (1/8 inch) thick.
2. Cut the pastry into 3 equal rectangles and place them on baking sheets.
3. Prick the pastry with a fork, cover with clingfilm and chill for 20 minutes.
4. Bake in a preheated oven for 15–20 minutes until crisp and golden.
5. Leave the pastry layers to cool on wire trays. Trim them to an even size.
6. Sandwich the pastry layers together with whipped cream and strawberries, setting aside enough strawberries to cover the top of the gâteau.
7. Arrange the strawberries on top of the gâteau in neat rows.
8. Melt the redcurrant jelly in a small saucepan with the lemon juice and simmer until slightly thickened. Brush it over the strawberries. Use a very sharp knife to cut the gâteau so the pastry does not shatter. Lift the slices carefully, to serve.

Left: Doboschtorte; *right:* Schwartzwalder kirschtorte

GERMANY

Doboschtorte

3 eggs
100 g (4 oz) caster sugar
pinch of salt
100 g (4 oz) plain flour

Butter Cream:

50 g (2 oz) sugar
50 ml (2 fl oz) water
2 egg yolks
175 g (6 oz) unsalted butter
75 g (3 oz) dark plain chocolate, melted

Caramel:

350 g (12 oz) sugar
300 ml (½ pint) water

Serves 6
Preparation time: *40 minutes*
Cooking time: *5–6 minutes for each batch*
Oven: *190°C, 375°F, Gas Mark 5*

1. Grease and flour 3 baking sheets and mark an 18 cm (7 inch) circle on each.
2. Place the eggs and sugar in a bowl set over a pan of simmering water. Whisk until the mixture is very thick and pale and leaves a trail.
3. Sift the salt and flour into the mixture and fold in gently.
4. Divide half the mixture equally between the baking trays and spread it out within the marked circles. Bake in a preheated oven for 5–6 minutes. Carefully transfer the cake layers to a wire tray.
5. Clean, regrease and flour the baking sheets and repeat the process with the remaining mixture.
6. Trim the 6 cakes to the same size. Set 1 layer on a lightly oiled baking sheet ready for glazing. Have ready a second baking sheet, lightly oiled.
7. Prepare the butter cream in the same way as the recipe for Coffee and Walnut Cake (page 139) substituting melted chocolate for coffee essence.
8. To prepare the caramel, put the sugar and water in a small saucepan and bring slowly to the boil, stirring constantly so that the sugar is completely dissolved. Boil to a golden caramel.
9. Pour enough caramel over the single layer on the baking sheet to completely cover the top.
10. Pour the remaining caramel on to the second baking sheet and spread it out thinly. When it has set, crush the caramel with a rolling pin.
11. Before the caramel on the cake sets hard, mark it into 8 sections with an oiled knife and trim the edges if necessary.
12. Sandwich the 6 layers with two-thirds of the chocolate butter cream, putting the caramel-covered layer on top.
13. Spread the sides with a little of the remaining butter cream and press on the crushed caramel.
14. Pipe a border of butter cream around the top edge.

GERMANY

Schwartzwalder Kirschtorte

6 eggs
175 g (6 oz) caster sugar
175 g (6 oz) plain flour
50 g (2 oz) cocoa powder
8 tablespoons Kirsch or cherry brandy
2 × 450 g (15 oz) cans black cherries, drained, stoned and halved, juice reserved

Filling:

600 ml (1 pint) double cream, whipped
2 teaspoons arrowroot
150 ml (1/4 pint) juice from the cherries
75 g (3 oz) plain dark chocolate, grated, or *chocolate scrolls, to decorate*

Serves 8–10
Preparation time: *50 minutes, plus overnight soaking*
Cooking time: *30–40 minutes*
Oven: *190°C, 375°F, Gas Mark 5*

1. Grease and flour two 20 cm (8 inch) round cake tins.
2. Place the eggs and the sugar in a bowl and set over a pan of simmering water.
3. Whisk the eggs and sugar until they are pale and thick enough to leave a trail. Remove the bowl from the pan of water and continue to whisk until the mixture is cool.
4. Sift in the flour and cocoa powder and fold them gently into the egg mixture.
5. Divide the mixture between the 2 tins and bake them in a preheated oven for 30–40 minutes or until firm and spongy.
6. Leave the cakes to cool in the tins. Turn them out on to wire trays. When they are completely cold, split the cakes in half horizontally.
7. Sprinkle 2 tablespoons of Kirsch and 4 tablespoons of cherry juice on each layer. Soak overnight.
8. Sandwich a third of the cream and half the black cherries between each layer of chocolate cake.
9. Spread half the remaining cream around the sides of the cake. Arrange the remaining cherries in concentric circles on top of the cake, leaving a border for rosettes of whipped cream.
10. Slake the arrowroot with a little water and stir it into the reserved cherry juice. Bring the juice gently to the boil, stirring continuously until it clears and thickens.
11. Pour the cherry sauce over the cherries on top of the cake.
12. Pipe a border of cream rosettes round the edge of the cake and cover the sides of the cake with grated chocolate or chocolate scrolls.

GERMANY

Griestorte with Spiced Apples

6 eggs, separated
200 g (7 oz) caster sugar
juice and grated rind of 1 lemon
150 g (5 oz) fine semolina
50 g (2 oz) ground almonds

Filling:

4 dessert apples, peeled and cored
Light Sugar Syrup flavoured with a few cloves and a cinnamon stick (page 95)
pinch of mixed spice
300 ml (1/2 pint) double cream, whipped

To decorate:

50 g (2 oz) whole almonds, blanched
icing sugar

Serves 6
Preparation time: *40 minutes*
Cooking time: *45 minutes*
Oven: *180°C, 350°F, Gas Mark 4*

1. Grease a 20 cm (8 inch) loose-botomed cake tin, line the base with a piece of greased non-stick silicone paper and dust with flour.
2. Beat the egg yolks, sugar, lemon juice and rind with an electric beater until light.
3. Fold in the semolina and ground almonds. Rest for 10 minutes.
4. Whisk the egg whites until they form soft peaks and fold them into the mixture.
5. Turn the mixture into the tin and bake in a preheated oven for 45 minutes until the cake is light golden brown. Turn the cake out on to a wire tray and leave to cool.
6. Cut each apple into 8 slices. Poach them in the syrup until tender. When cool, strain and sprinkle with mixed spice.
7. Slice the cake in half horizontally and sandwich it with whipped cream, spiced apples and almonds.
8. To decorate the cake, place a patterned doily on top and lightly sprinkle it with icing sugar. Carefully remove the doily to leave a lacy pattern behind.

From the left: Griestorte with spiced apples; Kastanienreis

Baclava

GREECE

Baclava

75 g (3 oz) almonds
75 g (3 oz) walnuts
40 g (1½ oz) pistachios
1 tablespoon pine kernels
1 teaspoon cinnamon
65 g (2½ oz) unsalted butter
65 g (2½ oz) sugar
50 ml (2 fl oz) water
300 g (11 oz) prepared Puff Pastry (page 116)
For the syrup:
100 g (4 oz) sugar
100 g (4 oz) honey
100 ml (4 fl oz) water
juice of ½ lemon

Makes 8–12 pieces
Preparation time: *45 minutes, plus soaking*
Cooking time: *55 minutes*
Oven: *220°C, 425°F, Gas Mark 7: 190°C, 375°F, Gas Mark 5*

Filo paste, which is traditionally used for making baclava can be used in place of puff pastry. It can be bought from good delicatessens or Greek food specialist shops. Cut the filo sheets to fit the baking tin. Place 2 or 3 sheets on the base of the buttered tin, brushing each sheet with melted mixture. Layer the tin as below ending with 3 layers of buttered pastry. Bake at 180°C, 350°F, Gas Mark 4 for 30 minutes.

1. Finely chop the almonds, walnuts, pistachios and pine kernels by hand and mix with the cinnamon.
2. Place the butter, sugar and water in a pan and boil for 3 minutes.
3. Line a rectangular baking tin, 20 × 30 cm (8 × 12 inches) with foil.
4. Divide the pastry into 4 equal pieces and roll each one into a rectangle 20 × 30 cm (8 × 12 inches). Line the base of the tin with one sheet of pastry, then brush with the butter and sugar mixture. Cover with a third of the nuts. Repeat the layers twice ending with the fourth sheet of pastry.
5. Bake in a preheated oven for 15 minutes. Reduce the heat and bake for a further 40 minutes.
6. Meanwhile make the syrup. Place the sugar, honey, water and lemon juice in a pan. Boil until the sugar dissolves.
7. Remove the baclava from the oven and cut it into 8–12 equal squares. Pour over the syrup and leave to soak in the tin for at least 6 hours. To serve, lift the slices carefully using a cake slice.

GERMANY

Kastanienreis

25 g (1 oz) plain chocolate
25 g (1 oz) unsalted butter
25 g (1 oz) caster sugar
1 tablespoon rum
125 g (4½ oz) unsweetened chestnut purée
⅓ quantity (about 250 g (9 oz)) prepared Pâte Sablée (page 122)
1 quantity Crème Chantilly (page 189)

Makes 4
Preparation time: *30 minutes, plus resting*
Cooking time: *10 minutes*
Oven: *200°C, 400°F, Gas Mark 6; 190°C, 375°F, Gas Mark 5*

1. Melt the chocolate and butter in a bowl over a pan of simmering water. Add the sugar, rum and purée and beat until smooth. Wipe the base of the bowl, cool slightly, then place in the refrigerator while you prepare the pastry.
2. Divide the pastry into four. On a lightly floured surface roll out the pastry and use to line 4 buttered tartlet or patty pans and rest for 30 minutes. Bake blind in a preheated oven for 10 minutes. Remove the beans and greaseproof paper. Reduce the heat and bake for a further 10 minutes. Cool.
3. Pile the chantilly into the tartlet cases.
4. Remove the chestnut mixture from the freezer. Spoon the mixture into a piping bag fitted with a small writing nozzle. Force the mixture directly onto the cream so that it falls like vermicelli. These tarts are best eaten on the day of making.

Hungarian crêpe cake

HUNGARY

Hungarian Crêpe Cake

12 Pancakes (page 88)
Filling:
1 kg (2 lb) cooking apples, peeled, cored and sliced
50 g (2 oz) unsalted butter
75 g (3 oz) brown sugar
1 teaspoon ground cinnamon
grated rind of 1 lemon
Glaze:
6 tablespoons apricot jam
2 tablespoons rum
grated rind and juice of 1 lemon
50 g (2 oz) flaked almonds

Serves 6
Preparation time: *20 minutes*
Cooking time: *10 minutes*
Oven: *180°C, 350°F, Gas Mark 4*

1. Prepare the pancakes and set aside.
2. To make the filling, fry the apples gently in the butter until they soften and colour.
3. Add the sugar, cinnamon and rind.
4. Place one pancake on a greased baking dish. Spoon a little of the apple on to it and top with a second pancake. Put a spoon of apple filling on top and continue to make layers of apple and pancakes, ending with a pancake.
5. To make the glaze, combine the apricot jam, rum, lemon rind and juice. Spoon a little glaze on top of the pile of pancakes.
6. Scatter the top with almonds. Place in a preheated oven and bake for 10 minutes.
7. Serve immediately with whipped cream and the rest of the apricot glaze.

INDIA

Gulab Jaman

175 g (6 oz) sugar
350 ml (12 fl oz) water
2 drops rosewater
40 g (1½ oz) low-fat milk powder
20 g (¾ oz) self-raising flour
1 teaspoon semolina
15 g (½ oz) unsalted butter, melted
4 small green cardamoms, shelled and ground
125 mg (1 small sachet or large pinch) saffron powder
25 ml (1 fl oz) milk
oil, for deep frying

Preparation time: *20 minutes, plus cooling and steeping*
Cooking time: *about 12 minutes*

1. Put the sugar and water in a saucepan and bring to the boil slowly, stirring all the time so that the sugar is completely dissolved. Boil for 2 minutes.
2. Add the rosewater. Pour the syrup into a serving bowl and leave to cool.
3. Put the powder, flour, semolina, butter, cardamoms and saffron in a mixing bowl. Work in the milk. Knead to a smooth dough and divide into 16 small balls each about the size of a large hazelnut.
4. Heat the oil in a saucepan to 190°C, 375°F on a frying thermometer. Fry the balls gently for 10 minutes until cooked through. Lift them out of the pan with a slotted spoon and drain on absorbent paper towels.
5. Put the balls into the syrup and leave to steep overnight. To serve, spoon the balls and syrup into individual dishes.

ISRAEL

Almond Pudding

3 eggs, separated
100 g (4 oz) caster sugar
75 g (3 oz) ground almonds
2 tablespoons caster sugar
25 g (1 oz) slivered almonds

Preparation time: *20 minutes*
Cooking time: *45 minutes*
Oven: *180°C, 350°F, Gas Mark 4*

1. Whisk the egg yolks and sugar together until creamy. Add the ground almonds.
2. Whisk the egg whites until they form soft peaks and fold them into the mixture.
3. Pour the mixture into a buttered 900 ml (1½ pint) ovenproof dish and bake in a preheated oven for 20 minutes.
4. Sprinkle caster sugar and slivered almonds over the pudding. Return it to the oven and bake for a further 25 minutes. Serve hot with a Fruit coulis (page 188) or pouring cream flavoured with a little Cointreau.

From the left: Gulab jaman; Almond pudding

ITALY

Zabaglione

3 yolks
50 g (2 oz) caster sugar
6 tablespoons Marsala

Preparation: *15 minutes*

1. Whisk the yolks and sugar in a bowl until they become creamy and white. Add the Marsala.
2. Stand the bowl over a pan of simmering water (the bowl should not touch the water) and whisk the mixture until it thickens and becomes spongy.
3. Pour into 4 wine glasses and serve accompanied by a selection of Langues de chats (page 185) and Almond and ginger tuiles (page 186).

Zabaglione

ITALY

Melanzane al Cioccolato

250 g (9 oz) aubergines, finely sliced
75 g (3 oz) flour
oil, for deep frying
2 eggs, lightly beaten
65 g (2½ oz) caster sugar
2 quantities Chocolate Sauce (page 188)
To decorate:
8 sugared or silvered almonds
1 teaspoon silver balls

Preparation time: *15 minutes*
Cooking time: *about 5 minutes*

1. If the aubergine is large, cut the slices into quarters.
2. Sift the flour into a bowl. Heat the oil in a saucepan to 190°C, 375°F or until a cube of bread browns in 30 seconds.
3. Dip the aubergine pieces first in flour and then egg. Deep fry them for about 5 minutes. Turn them as soon as they colour.
4. When the aubergine slices are golden on both sides, lift them out of the pan with a slotted spoon and drain on paper towels. Dredge with sugar.
5. Arrange a layer in the bottom of a charlotte dish. Pour over a little hot chocolate sauce. Fill the dish with layers of aubergines coated with sauce.
6. Decorate the top with sugared almonds and silver balls. Serve hot.

ITALY

Zuppa Inglese

150 g (5 oz) sponge cake, cut into cubes
150 ml (5 fl oz) Marsala
65 g (2½ oz) raspberry jam, melted
½ quantity Chocolate Sauce (page 188)
½ quantity Italian Meringue mixture (page 49)

Preparation time: *15 minutes*
Cooking time: *2 minutes*
Oven: *240°C, 475°F, Gas Mark 9*

1. Arrange the sponge cake in the bottom of an ovenproof porcelain dish and pour over the Marsala. Spoon the jam over the sponge cake. Press the sponge slightly with the back of a spoon. Trail the warm chocolate sauce over the sponge cake.
2. Fit a piping bag with a star tube and fill it with the Italian meringue. Pipe stars or scrolls over the top of the sponge cake.
3. Bake in a preheated oven for 2 minutes, or just long enough to colour the meringue.

From the top, clockwise: Zuccotto; Zuppa inglese; Melanzane al cioccolato

ITALY

Zuccotto

1 × 20 cm (8 inch) round Madeira cake
3 tablespoons cognac
2 tablespoons orange Curaçao
2 tablespoons cherry brandy or Maraschino
50 ml (2 fl oz) Sorbet Syrup (page 95)
100 g (4 oz) whole almonds
150 g (5 oz) plain chocolate, grated
450 ml (¾ pint) double cream
75 g (3 oz) caster sugar
icing sugar, to decorate

Serves 8
Preparation time: *40 minutes, plus chilling*

1. Line a 1.5–2 litre (2½–3½ pint) soufflé dish with aluminium foil.
2. Slice the cake into three discs.
3. Cut 2 of the discs into 16 segments and just score the third.
4. Sprinkle the cake evenly with the liqueurs and syrup.
5. Line the base of the dish with the whole disc, scored side down, and arrange the segments around the side.
6. Mix the almonds, with 90 g (3½ oz) of the grated chocolate.
7. Whip the cream and caster sugar until it is stiff.
8. Put half the whipped cream into a clean bowl and fold in the chocolate and nut mixture. Spread this mixture around the inside of the madeira cake.
9. Melt the remaining chocolate and combine it with the rest of the whipped cream. Spoon it into the middle of the dish and smooth the top.
10. Cover with the remaining cake disc. Chill thoroughly in the refrigerator.
11. Turn the cake out carefully on to a serving dish. Peel away the foil and dust with icing sugar.

NORWAY

Riskrem

500 ml (18 fl oz) milk
1 vanilla pod
75 g (3 oz) caster sugar
90 g (3½ oz) pudding rice
50 ml (2 fl oz) water
15 g (½ oz) gelatine
40 g (1½ oz) unsalted butter
150 ml (¼ pint) double cream
50 g (2 oz) almonds, flaked

Preparation time: *15 minutes, plus cooling and setting*
Cooking time: *40 minutes*

1. Bring the milk to the boil in a stainless steel or enamel pan. Add the vanilla pod and sugar.
2. Rain in the rice. Half-cover the pan with a lid. Simmer very gently for 40 minutes.
3. Pour the water in a small heatproof bowl and sprinkle the gelatine over the top. Stand the bowl over a pan of simmering water. Heat gently, without boiling. Stir occasionally until the gelatine has completely dissolved. Remove from the heat.
4. Remove the vanilla pod from the cooked rice. Stir in the gelatine and the butter. Leave to cool.
5. Whip the cream until it holds its shape on the whisk.
6. Just before the rice reaches setting point, fold in the cream and the almonds.
7. Spoon into a 1.25 litre (2 pint) mould. Leave in a cool place. When the rice is set, turn it on to a serving dish. Serve with a Fruit Coulis (page 188).

PORTUGAL

Pudim Molokov

100 g (4 oz) sugar
2 egg whites (sizes 1, 2)
50 g (2 oz) flaked almonds, toasted
225 g (8 oz) soft fruit (optional)
150 ml (¼ pint) cream, to serve

Serves 4–6
Preparation time: *20 minutes, plus chilling*
Cooking time: *15 minutes*
Oven: *180°C, 350°F, Gas Mark 4*

1. Place the sugar in a heavy-based saucepan with 4 tablespoons of cold water. Heat gently, without boiling, stirring until all the sugar is dissolved. When dissolved, increase the heat and boil briskly, without stirring until the syrup turns a golden caramel colour.
2. Remove from the heat and stir in 2 tablespoons of hot water, stand back – it can spit – then add another 2 tablespoons. If the mixture is lumpy, return the pan to a low heat and stir until smooth.
3. Pour a little of the caramel into a warm, lightly greased 600 ml (1 pint) ring mould.
4. Reheat the remaining caramel to boiling point. Whisk the egg whites until stiff, then add the caramel, pouring in a steady stream and whisking continuously until the mixture is stiff and glossy. Fold in the nuts and spoon into the mould.
5. Stand the mould in a hot bain marie and bake in a preheated oven for 15 minutes.
6. Remove from the oven, cool slightly, then turn out on to a serving plate and chill.
7. Just before serving, fill the centre with soft fruit, if using, and serve with cream.

RUSSIA

Kisel

225 g (8 oz) redcurrants and blackcurrants, fresh or frozen
150 g (5 oz) sugar
900 ml (1½ pints) water
2 tablespoons potato flour

Preparation time: *30 minutes, plus cooling*

Kisel may be used as a sauce for a number of desserts. The redcurrants and blackcurrants can be mixed in any proportions.
1. Pass the currants through a nylon sieve to make a purée and set aside.
2. Stir the sugar into 300 ml (½ pint) of the water in a heavy saucepan. Bring to the boil, stirring until the sugar is dissolved.
3. Dissolve the potato flour in the remaining water and stir it into the syrup. Boil for 5 minutes.
4. Remove the syrup from the heat. Add the fruit purée and mix well.
5. Cool, pour into individual glasses and serve with cream.

SCOTLAND

Scotch Pancakes

100 g (4 oz) plain flour
2 teaspoons baking powder
50 g (2 oz) caster sugar
pinch of salt
1 egg, beaten
1 tablespoon lemon juice
75 ml (2½ fl oz) milk
25 g (1 oz) butter, melted

Sauce:

100 g (4 oz) clear honey
grated rind and juice of 1 lemon

Serves 6
Preparation time: *15 minutes*
Cooking time: *1–2 minutes on each side of the pancakes*

1. Sift the flour, baking powder, sugar and salt into a bowl.
2. Make a well in the centre and drop in the egg and lemon juice. Mix together to make a smooth batter, adding the milk little by little. Stir in the melted butter.
3. Heat a frying pan or griddle and grease lightly with butter.
4. Drop 3 or 4 tablespoons of batter on to the pan, keeping them well apart. Cook a few pancakes at a time. When they are golden brown on one side, turn them over and cook the other side. Keep them warm on a serving dish while cooking the others.
5. To prepare the sauce, heat the honey gently in a small pan with the lemon rind and juice. Serve the pancakes with the hot sauce poured over, and whipped cream handed separately.

From the top left, clockwise: Riskrem; Kisel; Pudim molokov; Scotch pancakes

SPAIN

Churros

300 ml (½ pint) water
175 g (6 oz) plain flour
pinch of salt
2 eggs, beaten
groundnut or sunflower oil, for deep frying
caster sugar mixed with ground cinnamon, to coat the churros

Serves 4–6
Preparation time: *10 minutes*
Cooking time: *3–4 minutes*

1. Bring the water to the boil in a heavy pan. When it is boiling furiously, tip in all the flour and the salt, and beat vigorously until the ball of dough leaves the side of the pan.
2. Beat in the egg gradually until the mixture is smooth and glossy.
3. Put the mixture into a large piping bag fitted with a large rose nozzle.
4. Heat the oil in a large saucepan to 180°C (350°F) or test by dropping in a 1 cm (½ inch) cube of bread. It should turn golden in 30 seconds.
5. Pipe sections of dough approximately 10 cm (4 inches) long and fry them until golden brown.
6. Remove the churros from the pan with a slotted spoon and toss in cinnamon sugar. Serve immediately.

SWITZERLAND

Swiss Waffles

100 g (4 oz) plain flour
1½ teaspoons baking powder
50 g (2 oz) caster sugar
pinch of salt
1 egg, separated
50 ml (2 fl oz) soured cream
25 ml (1 fl oz) milk
1 tablespoon Kirsch
juice and grated rind of 1 lemon

Serves 4–6
Preparation time: *10 minutes*
Cooking time: *1–1½ minutes for each waffle*

This batter makes very light waffles. Keep them hot by laying them on a baking sheet lined with paper towels and place them in the oven heated to 150°C, 300°F, Gas Mark 2 for up to 15 minutes.

1. Sift the flour, baking powder, sugar and salt into a bowl.
2. Whisk egg yolk, sour cream, milk, kirsch together. Beat mixture into the flour to form a smooth batter. Add lemon rind and juice.
3. Whisk the egg whites until they form stiff peaks and fold them into the batter.
4. Cook as for Waffles with Maple Syrup (page 111).
5. Serve with soured cream, jam or a Fruit coulis (page 188).

From the left: Churros; Swiss waffles

Rich Kentucky chocolate pie

U.S.A.

Rich Kentucky Chocolate Pie

½ quantity Pâte Brisée (page 120)
45 g (1½ oz) plain chocolate
45 g (1½ oz) ground rice
240 ml (8 fl oz) double cream
2 eggs
175 g (6 oz) caster sugar
50 g (2 oz) unsalted butter
25 ml (1 fl oz) rum
1 quantity Crème Chantilly (page 189), to decorate

Preparation time: *20 minutes, plus resting and cooling*
Cooking time: *25 minutes*
Oven: *200°C, 400°F, Gas Mark 6*

1. Line a 20 cm (8 inch) flan ring with the pastry. Rest for 30 minutes. Bake blind for 20 minutes in a preheated oven. Remove the baking beans and greaseproof paper. Bake for a further 5 minutes. Cool.
2. Melt the chocolate in a bowl over a pan of simmering water.
3. In a separate bowl, blend the ground rice with a third of the cream, then beat in the remaining cream, the eggs and sugar and stir into the melted chocolate.
4. Pour the mixture into a clean pan. Stirring continuously, heat until thickened.
5. Beat in the butter and rum, then cool for 10 minutes.
6. Pour the mixture into the pastry case. Leave to set in the refrigerator for at least 2–3 hours.
7. Before serving, pipe stars of crème chantilly around the inner rim of the pie.

Children's Favourites

Meringue Ducks

4 egg whites
225 g (8 oz) icing sugar
a few drops of vanilla essence
Filling:
300 ml (½ pint) double cream, whipped
12 chocolate drops
24 almond halves
6 thin chocolate biscuits

Serves 6
Preparation time: *30 minutes*
Cooking time: *1½–2 hours*
Oven: *140°C, 275°F, Gas Mark 1*

1. Line 2 baking sheets with non-stick silicone paper.
2. Prepare the meringue as for Strawberry Meringue Basket (page 41).
3. Spoon the mixture into a piping bag fitted with a 1 cm (½ inch) plain nozzle. On one sheet pipe out six 4 cm (1½ inch) diameter circles for the heads and six 6 cm (2½ inch) diameter circles for the bodies, joining the heads at slight angles. Pipe out six more pairs in the same way with the body joining the head on the opposite side.
4. Bake the meringues in a preheated oven for 1½–2 hours until they are crisp. Peel off the paper and leave them to cool on wire trays.
5. Sandwich the halves together with whipped cream.
6. Attach the chocolate drop eyes with a little cream and stick two almond halves in each duck to resemble an open beak.
7. Pipe some cream on each chocolate biscuit and sit a duck on top. Place two almond halves under each duck to represent the feet.

From the top: Meringue ducks; Chocolate blancmange rabbit

Chocolate Blancmange Rabbit

300 ml (½ pint) single cream
300 ml (½ pint) milk
100 g (4 oz) plain dark chocolate, broken into pieces
1 tablespoon vanilla sugar
3 tablespoons cornflour mixed with a little milk
To decorate:
about 100 g (4 oz) desiccated coconut
a few drops of green food colouring
a few chocolate drops for the eyes and nose
a little whipped cream (optional)

Serves 6
Preparation time: *15 minutes, plus setting*

1. Heat the cream, milk and chocolate in a saucepan over a low heat, stirring occasionally, until the chocolate melts completely.
2. Add the vanilla sugar and the cornflour mixture, stirring constantly until the mixture comes to the boil and thickens. Continue to simmer the thickened mixture for a few minutes.
3. Pour into a dampened 600 ml (1 pint) rabbit mould, and place in a refrigerator until set.
4. Place the desiccated coconut in a bowl and add a few drops of the food colouring. With a fork, mix the coconut thoroughly until the colouring is evenly blended. Tip the coloured coconut onto the serving dish making a slight well in the centre about the size of the rabbit.
5. Turn the rabbit out on to the plate and decorate with chocolate drops. If desired, pipe a little whipped cream for the tail.

Strawberry Meringues

4 egg whites
250 g (9 oz) caster sugar
few drops of vanilla essence
few drops of pink food colouring
Filling:
300 ml (½ pint) double cream
175 g (6 oz) fresh strawberries, hulled, sliced and sprinkled with caster sugar (optional)

Serves 6
Preparation time: *30 minutes*
Cooking time: *2–2½ hours*
Oven: *120°C, 250°F, Gas Mark ½*

If preferred, pipe out the meringues as 6 nests and put the filling inside.

1. Line 2 large baking sheets with non-stick silicone paper.
2. Whisk the egg whites until they form stiff peaks. Gradually whisk in half the sugar, beating well until it is thick and glossy. Fold in the remaining sugar, vanilla essence and colouring.
3. Spoon the mixture into a piping bag fitted with a large rose nozzle and pipe 12 swirls on to the prepared baking sheets. Bake in a preheated oven for 1½ hours until crisp. Leave to cool on a wire tray and peel off the paper.
4. Sandwich the meringues together with whipped cream and strawberries.

From the top left, clockwise: Multi-coloured marble cake; Fruity hedgehog; Strawberry meringues

Multi-Coloured Marble Cake

175 g (6 oz) butter
175 g (6 oz) caster sugar
3 eggs, beaten
175 g (6 oz) self-raising flour, sifted
grated rind and juice of 1 lemon
grated rind and juice of 1 orange
grated rind and juice of 1 lime
a few drops of yellow food colouring
a few drops of orange food colouring
a few drops of green food colouring

Serves 6
Preparation time: *30 minutes*
Cooking time: *50 minutes–1 hour*
Oven: *180°C, 350°F, Gas Mark 4*

1. Grease and flour a 20 cm (8 inch) loose-bottomed cake tin.
2. Cream the butter and the sugar together in a mixing bowl until light and fluffy.
3. Gradually add the eggs, beating well between each addition.
4. Fold in the flour.
5. Divide the mixture equally between 3 bowls. To the first add the rind and juice of a lemon with a few drops of yellow food colouring. To the second add the orange rind and juice and orange food colouring; to the third add the lime rind and juice and green food colouring.
6. Place spoonfuls of each coloured mixture in the prepared tin, keeping each colour apart. Bake in a preheated oven for 50 minutes–1 hour until risen and springy to the touch.
7. Turn the cake out and leave it to cool on a wire tray.

Variations:
Divide the cake mixture into 3 portions as above. Flavour and colour with a few drops of the suggested combinations:
1. Vanilla essence/plain
Peppermint essence/green colouring
1 tablespoon cocoa powder blended with 2 tablespoons hot water
2. Vanilla essence/plain
grated rind and juice of 1 orange/orange colouring
1 dessertspoon instant coffee powder blended with 1 tablespoon hot water
3. Vanilla essence/plain
Strawberry or raspberry flavouring/pink colouring
1 tablespoon cocoa powder blended with 2 tablespoons hot water

Fruity Hedgehog

3 egg whites
175 g (6 oz) caster sugar
Fruit jelly:
100 g (4 oz) caster sugar
600 ml (1 pint) raspberry purée made with fresh or frozen raspberries
15 g (½ oz) powdered gelatine
4 tablespoons water
150 ml (¼ pint) double cream, whipped
To decorate:
chocolate drops
chocolate peanuts
25 g (1 oz) toasted, flaked almonds

Serves 6
Preparation time: *40 minutes, plus setting*
Cooking time: *1½ hours*
Oven: *140°C, 275°F, Gas Mark 1*

1. Whisk the egg whites until stiff. Gradually whisk in half the sugar until the mixture is thick and glossy. Carefully fold in the remaining sugar.
2. Spoon the meringue into a piping bag fitted with a plain nozzle. Pipe out one 6 cm (2½ inch) diameter meringue for the head. Pipe the remaining meringue into 2.5 cm (1 inch) circles for the body. Bake in a preheated oven for 1½ hours or until they are crisp.
3. To prepare the jelly, add the sugar to the raspberry purée.
4. Sprinkle the gelatine over the water in a small heatproof bowl. Stand the bowl in a pan of hot water and heat gently without boiling, and stir until the gelatine has dissolved. Remove from the heat.
5. Mix the gelatine with the fruit purée and pour into a 300 ml (1 pint) mixing bowl or domed mould. Leave to set in a refrigerator.
6. Turn the jelly out on to a plate, and place the meringue head against the side. Cover the jelly and the meringue with whipped cream.
7. Stick flaked almonds into the head to resemble quills. Use chocolate drops for the eyes and a chocolate peanut for the nose.
8. Cover the body with the little meringues.

Jam Roly-Poly

225 g (8 oz) self-raising flour
50 g (2 oz) caster sugar
100 g (4 oz) shredded suet
1 egg, beaten
150 ml (1/4 pint) milk
100 g (4 oz) strawberry or raspberry jam
Glaze:
1 tablespoon milk
caster sugar

Serves 4–6
Preparation time: *20 minutes*
Cooking time: *45 minutes*
Oven: *190°C, 375°F, Gas Mark 5*

1. Mix the flour, sugar and suet together in a mixing bowl. Add the egg and enough milk to form a soft dough.
2. Roll the pastry out on to a floured surface to make a 20 × 25 cm (8 × 10 inch) rectangle.
3. Warm the jam a little and spread it over the pastry, leaving a narrow border.
4. Fold the edges over to prevent the jam oozing out.
5. Brush the edges with a little milk, and roll the dough up from the short edge.
6. Place the roll, seam side down, on to a baking sheet lined with a piece of buttered aluminium foil. Fold the foil to make a box half-way up around the roll.
7. Cut a few slanting slits on top of the roll.
8. Brush the roll with a little milk and sprinkle with sugar.
9. Bake in a preheated oven for 45 minutes or until golden brown and serve with hot custard.

From the top: Jam roly-poly; Spotted Dick

Spotted Dick

100 g (4 oz) self-raising flour
100 g (4 oz) shredded suet
50 g (2 oz) sugar
pinch of salt
100 g (4 oz) fresh white breadcrumbs
150 g (5 oz) currants
85–120 ml (3–4 fl oz) water

Serves 4–6
Preparation time: *15 minutes*
Cooking time: *2 hours*

1. Grease a 900 ml (1½ pint) pudding basin with butter or margarine.
2. Mix all the ingredients together to form a soft dough.
3. Turn out on to a floured board and knead gently into a ball.
4. Place the ball of dough into the pudding basin pushing it gently to fit.
5. Cover with a piece of buttered aluminium foil, pleated to allow for expansion, and secure with string.
6. Place the basin in a large saucepan and add enough boiling water to come half way up the side. Cover the pan and steam over a low heat for 2 hours, topping up with hot water if necessary.
7. To serve, remove the foil and string and turn the pudding out on to a warmed serving dish. Serve with custard.

Rice and Raisin Pudding

600 ml (1 pint) milk
50 g (2 oz) short-grain rice, rinsed under cold water
15 g (½ oz) butter
25 g (1 oz) vanilla sugar
150 ml (¼ pint) double cream, whipped
75 g (3 oz) raisins
raspberry jam, to decorate

Preparation time: *10 minutes*
Cooking time: *2 hours*
Oven: *150°C, 300°F, Gas Mark 2*

1. Bring the milk to the boil in a saucepan and stir in the rice.
2. Pour into a lightly buttered 900 ml (1½ pint) ovenproof dish. Dot with butter and sprinkle with vanilla sugar.
3. Bake in a preheated oven for 2 hours until set. Half-way through the cooking time, stir the pudding to separate the grains. Leave to cool a little.
4. Stir in the cream and raisins and serve topped with a swirl of raspberry jam.

Chocolate Semolina

600 ml (1 pint) milk
50 g (2 oz) semolina
100 g (4 oz) plain dark chocolate
1 tablespoon sugar
1 egg
caster sugar, for sprinkling

Serves 4–6
Preparation time: *10 minutes*
Cooking time: *20 minutes*
Oven: *190°C, 375°F, Gas Mark 5*

1. Bring the milk to the boil in a saucepan and stir in the semolina. Cook over a gentle heat, for 3–4 minutes, stirring constantly.
2. Remove the pan from the heat and add the chocolate and sugar. Stir until they are melted.
3. Let the mixture cool a little before beating in the egg.
4. Pour into a 900 ml (1½ pint) ovenproof dish and sprinkle with caster sugar. Bake in a preheated oven for 20 minutes until the surface is set. Serve hot or cold.

From the left: Rice and raisin pudding; Chocolate semolina

Chocolate Trifle

1 chocolate Swiss roll, cut into slices
3 oranges, peeled and segmented
Custard:
600 ml (1 pint) milk
50 g (2 oz) caster sugar
4 egg yolks
2 teaspoons cornflour
100 g (4 oz) plain chocolate, melted
150 ml (1/4 pint) double cream, whipped
chocolate buttons, to decorate

Serves 6
Preparation time: *20 minutes*

1. Place the Swiss roll slices at the bottom of a glass bowl and arrange the orange segments on top.
2. Prepare the custard in the same way as for the Harlequin Trifle (page 178). Stir in the melted chocolate and leave to cool.
3. Pour the chocolate custard over the orange segments. Leave to cool and set.
4. Pipe rosettes of cream around the trifle and decorate with chocolate buttons.

Chocolate Mousse Cake

175 g (6 oz) chocolate digestive biscuits, finely crushed
50 g (2 oz) butter, melted
2 egg yolks
2 tablespoons caster sugar
rind and juice of 1 orange
225 g (8 oz) full fat soft cheese
100 g (4 oz) plain dark chocolate, melted
10 g (¼ oz) powdered gelatine
150 ml (¼ pint) double cream, lightly whipped
3 egg whites, lightly whisked
To decorate:
150 ml (¼ pint) double cream, whipped
chocolate buttons
grated chocolate

Serves 6–8
Preparation time: *30 minutes*

1. Lightly grease a 20 cm (8 inch) loose-bottomed cake tin.
2. Mix the crushed biscuits with the melted butter. Spread them over the base of the tin and press down firmly. Chill until set.
3. Whisk the egg yolks, sugar and orange rind until they are thick and light. Beat in the cheese and melted chocolate.
4. Add the cream to the chocolate mixture.
5. Pour the orange juice into a small heat-proof bowl and sprinkle the gelatine over it. Stand the bowl in a pan of hot water and heat gently, stirring until the gelatine has dissolved. Add to the mixture.
6. Fold the egg whites into the chocolate mixture. Pour it over the chilled biscuit base and leave to set.
7. Unmould the cheesecake from the tin and decorate with rosettes of cream, chocolate buttons and grated chocolate.

Banana Split with Hot Chocolate Sauce

85 ml (3 fl oz) double cream
100 g (4 oz) dark plain chocolate, broken into pieces
Banana Split:
6 large ripe bananas
1 quantity Vanilla Ice Cream (page 88)
To decorate:
150 ml (¼ pint) double cream, whipped
50 g (2 oz) chocolate drops
glacé cherries

Serves 6
Preparation time: *15 minutes*

1. To make the sauce, put the cream in a small saucepan and heat it gently just to boiling point. Remove the pan from the heat and add the chocolate. Stir until it is melted. Set aside and keep warm.
2. Slice each banana in half lengthways. Place in a banana split boat and sandwich the halves together with scoops of ice cream.
3. Decorate with piped cream, chocolate drops and glacé cherries.
4. Pour a little chocolate sauce over the top and serve immediately.

Variation:
Caramel sauce: place 150 g (6 oz) sugar in a pan with sufficient water to moisten. Boil until a mid-amber caramel. Remove from the heat. Bring 250 ml (8 fl oz) double cream to the boil as quickly as possible. Whisk into the hot caramel. Cool until just warm. Use in place of the chocolate sauce.

From the top:
Chocolate mousse cake; Chocolate trifle; Banana split with hot chocolate sauce

Strawberry Cream Jelly

3 squares of strawberry jelly from a packet
150 ml (1/4 pint) boiling water
225 g (8 oz) fresh or frozen strawberries
50 g (2 oz) caster sugar
150 ml (1/4 pint) double cream, whipped
15 g (1/2 oz) powdered gelatine
4 tablespoons water
2 egg whites, lightly whisked

Serves 6
Preparation time: *20 minutes*

1. Melt the jelly cubes in the boiling water and pour into a dampened 900 ml (1½ pint) jelly mould. Leave to set in the refrigerator.
2. Pass the strawberries through a nylon sieve or purée them in a food processor. Add the sugar.
3. Fold the whipped cream into the purée.
4. Sprinkle the gelatine over the water in a small heatproof bowl. Stand the bowl in a pan of hot water and heat gently until dissolved. Add to the strawberry cream.
5. Fold in the egg white.
6. Pour the strawberry mixture over the set jelly and return to the refrigerator until completely set. Unmould and serve.

Nursery Trifle

120 g (4½ oz) sponge cake, cut in cubes
1 × 225 g (8 oz) can raspberries
1½ bananas, sliced
200 ml (1/3 pint) hot Crème Anglaise (page 189)
150 ml (1/4 pint) double cream
1 egg white
65 g (2½ oz) caster sugar
To decorate:
1 teaspoon silver balls
1 teaspoon hundreds and thousands

Preparation time: *30 minutes, plus cooling*

1. Put half the sponge cake in a trifle dish. Spoon the raspberries and their syrup on top. Cover with the rest of the sponge.
2. Arrange two-thirds of the banana slices on top of the sponge.
3. Liquidize the remaining banana slices in a blender with the crème anglaise. Pour over the trifle base and leave to cool. Chill in the refrigerator.
4. Whip the double cream, egg white and sugar until stiff. Heap on top of the custard.
5. Decorate the top of the trifle with silver balls and hundreds and thousands. To vary the decoration, use chocolate chips, drops buttons or vermicelli instead.

Harlequin Trifle

8 trifle sponges or *8 fingers of stale sponge cake*
4 tablespoons raspberry jam
350 g (12 oz) frozen raspberries, thawed
50 g (2 oz) caster sugar
1 × 150 g (5 oz) packet raspberry jelly
600 ml (1 pint) boiling water
Custard:
2 teaspoons cornflour
600 ml (1 pint) milk
50 g (2 oz) caster sugar
few drops of vanilla essence
4 egg yolks
To decorate:
300 ml (1/2 pint) double cream, whipped
glacé cherries
angelica

Serves 6–8
Preparation time: *30 minutes, plus setting*

1. Slice the trifle sponges or pieces of sponge cake in half horizontally and spread them with jam. Sandwich the halves together and place them in the bottom of a glass bowl.
2. Scatter the raspberries on top and sprinkle with sugar.
3. Melt the jelly in the boiling water and pour over the raspberries. Leave in a cool place to set.
4. To prepare the custard, blend the cornflour with the milk. Put the milk, sugar and the vanilla essence in a saucepan and bring to the boil, stirring frequently. Cool slightly.
5. Pour the milk over the eggs, stirring all the time. Return the mixture to a clean pan over a moderate heat. Stir continuously until the mixture coats the back of a wooden spoon. Leave to cool.
6. Pour the cool custard over the firm jelly. Leave to cool until the custard is set.
7. To decorate, spread a thin layer of cream over the custard. Pipe rosettes of cream on top and surround them with glacé cherries and pieces of angelica.

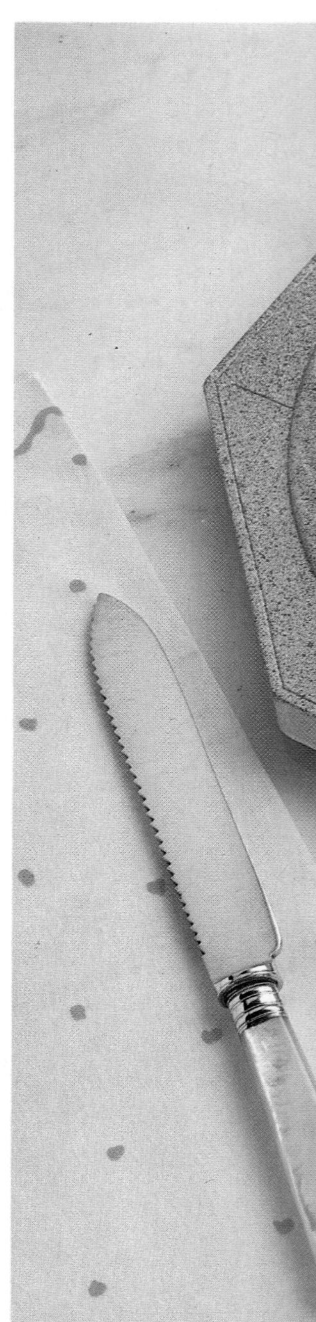

Smiley Face Tart

225 g (8 oz) prepared Shortcrust Pastry (page 114)
225 g (8 oz) strawberry or raspberry jam
1 egg yolk, lightly beaten with a little milk

Serves 6
Preparation time: *15 minutes*
Cooking time: *30 minutes*
Oven: *200°C, 400°F, Gas Mark 6*

1. Line the base of an 18 cm (7 inch) pie plate with half the pastry.
2. Spoon the jam evenly over the pastry.
3. Brush the rim of the pastry with a little beaten egg.
4. Roll out the remaining pastry to a circle the same size as the pie plate. Using a 2.5 cm (1 inch) plain round cutter, cut out two eyes. Cut out the mouth with a moon-shaped pastry cutter or a knife.
5. Carefully place the pastry 'face' on top of the jam, pressing it down around the edge with the fingers.
6. Flute the pastry around the rim and bake in a preheated oven for 30 minutes until golden brown.
7. Serve hot or cold with ice cream.

From the top left, clockwise: Smiley face tart; Nursery trifle; Strawberry cream jelly; Harlequin trifle

Toffee Apples

4 dessert apples (Cox's Pippins or russets)
4 sticks (the thickness of pencils or chopsticks)
450 g (1 lb) sugar
150 ml (¼ pint) water

Preparation time: *10 minutes*

Apples with a waxy shine, such as Granny Smith's, are not suitable for this recipe, because the toffee will not adhere to the apple. Toffee apples are best eaten on the day of making as the caramel may soften once covering the apple. Toffee apples look spectacular wrapped in a variety of coloured cellophane and as a centrepiece for children or Hallow'een parties.

1. Wash the apples and dry them completely. Push the sticks firmly into the cores of the apples.
2. Put the sugar and water in a pan and set over a gentle heat, stirring frequently.
3. When the sugar has completely dissolved, turn up the heat and let the syrup boil rapidly until it turns a golden caramel. Remove from the heat.
4. Quickly swirl each apple in the caramel and place them on to a lightly oiled sheet of mirror or glass. Leave until set. If the caramel hardens before all the apples are coated, return it to the heat to melt. When the caramel on the apples has become firm, wrap in coloured cellophane.

Above: Toffee apples

Pears with Chocolate Sauce

4 evenly sized Comice pears, peeled
225 g (8 oz) sugar
600 ml (1 pint) water
few strips of lemon rind
600 ml (1 pint) Vanilla Ice Cream (page 88)
Chocolate Sauce (see Banana Split, page 177)

Preparation time: *15 minutes*

1. To make the syrup, dissolve the sugar in the water, then add the lemon rind. Bring to the boil, then reduce to a simmer.
2. Poach the pears in syrup until they are tender. Leave to cool in the syrup.
3. Place 2 scoops of ice cream in the bottom of 4 sundae glasses and top each with a drained, cold poached pear.
4. Pour over the warm Chocolate Sauce and serve immediately.

Chocolate Chip Bombe

450 ml (3/4 pint) double cream
175 g (6 oz) plain dark chocolate, melted and slightly cooled
120 ml (4 fl oz) water
4 oz (100 g) raisins
50 g (2 oz) glacé cherries, quartered
75 g (3 oz) chocolate drops or *chocolate chips*
75 g (3 oz) plain dark chocolate, melted, to finish

Serves 6–8
Preparation time: *15 minutes, plus freezing overnight*

This dessert is a wonderful children's alternative to Christmas pudding. If desired, decorate with a sprig of holly. To vary the ice cream filling, add pieces of chopped angelica and other crystallized fruits to add colour and flavour.

1. To make the ice cream, whip the cream very lightly. Add the cooled melted chocolate, water, raisins, cherries and chocolate drops or chips, if using, and stir together.
2. Spoon the mixture into a 1 litre (1¾ pint) pudding basin and freeze overnight.
3. To serve, dip the basin into warm water for a few seconds and turn out on to a plate. Pour the melted chocolate over the ice cream. It will freeze instantly. Serve immediately or return to the freezer. If the bombe has been in the freezer for 24 hours, transfer to the refrigerator to soften slightly.

Brown Bread Ice Cream

100 g (4 oz) brown breadcrumbs
75 g (3 oz) caster sugar
75 g (3 oz) sugar
85 ml (3 fl oz) water
3 egg yolks, beaten well
3 egg whites, lightly whisked
300 ml (1/2 pint) double cream
150 ml (1/4 pint) single cream

Serves 6
Preparation time: *20 minutes, plus freezing*
Cooking time: *10 minutes*
Oven: *190°C, 375°F, Gas Mark 5*

1. Toss the breadcrumbs and caster sugar together and spread them out on a baking sheet. Bake them in a preheated oven for approximately 10 minutes until they are golden and crisp. Leave to cool.
2. Dissolve the sugar and water over a gentle heat. Boil until the syrup reaches the thread stage, 107°C, 225°F.
3. Pour the syrup over the egg yolks, whisking constantly until creamy.
4. Lightly whisk the creams together and add to the egg yolk mixture. Stir in the breadcrumbs and fold in the egg whites.
5. Pour the mixture into a 1.2 litre (2 pint) ice cream mould and freeze until solid.
6. Turn the ice cream out on to a plate 20 minutes before serving. Serve with a Fruit coulis (page 188) or sprinkle with finely chopped and toasted hazelnuts.

From the left: Pears with chocolate sauce; Chocolate chip bombe; Brown bread ice cream

Finishing Touches

Vanillekipferl

½ vanilla pod
50 g (2 oz) whole almonds
100 g (4 oz) unsalted butter
50 g (2 oz) caster sugar
110 g (generous 4 oz) plain flour
15 g (½ oz) cornflour
vanilla sugar, to decorate

Makes about 30
Preparation time: *15 minutes, plus resting*
Cooking time: *8–10 minutes*
Oven: *190°C, 375°F, Gas Mark 5*

1. Grind the vanilla pod and almonds to a powder in a grinder or food processor.
2. Cream the butter and caster sugar until light and fluffy, then mix in the flour, cornflour and almonds, divide into 2 equal portions and rest for 30 minutes.
3. Roll out each portion by hand to form a sausage about 30 cm (12 inches) long. Cut each sausage into 20 equal pieces. Roll out the pieces by hand to form small crescents.
4. Cover a baking sheet with non-stick silicone paper and arrange the vanillekipferl on it. Bake in a preheated oven for 8–10 minutes.
5. Sprinkle the vanilla sugar on to a shallow tray. Remove the crescents from the silicone paper while still warm and place in the tray. Shake lightly, turning the biscuits over so they are well-coated with the sugar.

Honey & Orange Flavoured Brandysnaps

100 g (4 oz) unsalted butter
100 g (4 oz) caster sugar
100 g (4 oz) clear honey
grated rind of 1 orange
1 tablespoon brandy
100 g (4 oz) plain flour

Makes about 12
Preparation time: *15 minutes*
Cooking time: *10 minutes*
Oven: *190°C, 375°F, Gas Mark 5*

1. Heat the butter, sugar, honey and orange rind in a pan over a low heat. When melted add the brandy. Away from the heat, stir in the flour and work to a smooth paste.
2. Cover 2 baking sheets with a sheet of non-stick silicone paper and place 1 heaped teaspoon of the mixture on to the sheet. Flatten into an oblong shape with a knife dipped in hot water. Repeat the procedure with the remaining mixture, leaving a good space between each one to allow for spreading. Bake in a preheated oven for 10 minutes.
3. Remove from the oven, then cool for 30 seconds. Lift a brandysnap off the silicone paper with a palette knife. Curl it around a thick-handled wooden spoon. If the brandysnaps harden before you can remove them from the sheet, return them to the oven for a few seconds to soften.

Variation:
Brandysnaps: Make as for Honey and orange flavoured brandysnaps replacing the honey with golden syrup, the grated orange rind with lemon rind, the brandy with 1 teaspoon cognac. Add 1 teaspoon ground ginger with the flour. Bake and roll in the same way.

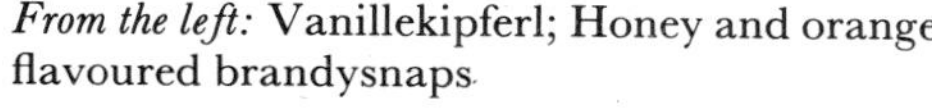
From the left: Vanillekipferl; Honey and orange flavoured brandysnaps

Chocolate Macaroons

125 g ($4\frac{1}{2}$ oz) whole almonds
2 egg whites
125 g ($4\frac{1}{2}$ oz) caster sugar
30 g (generous 1 oz) sweetened chocolate powder
2 sheets of rice paper
icing sugar

Makes 14–16
Preparation time: *15 minutes*
Cooking time: *18–20 minutes*
Oven: *200°C, 400°F, Gas Mark 6*

1. Drop the almonds into boiling water. Blanch for 30 seconds, then drain and remove the brown skins. Discard the skins and finely chop the nuts.
2. Place the nuts and 1 egg white in a mortar or small bowl and mix until smooth. Add half the sugar and half the chocolate powder and mix well. Add the remaining egg white, then the rest of the sugar and chocolate powder. The mixture should be quite stiff.
3. Cover a baking sheet with rice paper.
4. Fit a piping bag with a plain nozzle and fill with the mixture. Pipe 14–16 large dots on rice paper, leaving a good space between them. Dust generously with icing sugar and bake in a preheated oven for 18–20 minutes until set. Transfer to a wire rack to cool.

Shortbread

180 g (6 oz) plain flour
60 g (2 oz) ground rice or rice flour
60 g (2 oz) caster sugar
110 g (4 oz) unsalted butter,
cut into small pieces

Makes 8 pieces
Preparation time: *10 minutes*
Cooking time: *1 hour*
Oven: *160°C, 325°F, Gas Mark 3*

1. In a medium size bowl mix the flour, rice and sugar together. Add the butter and knead to a smooth paste.
2. Using the knuckles, spread the mixture evenly to line the base of a buttered 23 cm (9 inch) round baking tin. Using a kitchen knife divide into 8 wedges, cutting right through to the tin and prick all over with a fork.
3. Bake in a preheated oven for 1 hour.
4. Remove the biscuits from the tin and cool. Dust with caster sugar before serving.

Chocolate Fairy Fingers

2 egg whites
80 g (2½ oz) caster sugar
65 g (2½ oz) icing sugar, sifted
To decorate:
30 g (generous 1 oz) plain chocolate
15 g (½ oz) unsalted butter

Makes about 50
Preparation time: *15 minutes*
Cooking time: *45 minutes*
Oven: *120°C, 250°F, Gas Mark ½*

1. Line a baking sheet with non-stick silicone or lightly greased greaseproof paper.
2. Whisk the egg whites and 15 g (½ oz) of the caster sugar until very stiff. Combine the remaining caster sugar and icing sugar and fold into the whites.
3. Fit a piping bag with a 1 cm (½ inch) plain nozzle and fill with the meringue. Pipe 50 thin fingers on the baking sheet and bake in a preheated oven for 45 minutes. Lift off the paper and cool.
4. Place the chocolate and butter in a bowl standing over a pan of simmering water. Dip the ends of the fingers in chocolate and leave on a wire tray to set.

Variation:
Replace 25 g (1 oz) of the icing sugar with unsweetened cocoa powder, then bake the fingers for about 1 hour.

Langues de Chats

50 g (2 oz) vanilla sugar
60 g (2¼ oz) slightly salted butter, softened
2 egg whites
50 g (2 oz) plain flour

Makes about 20
Preparation time: *15 minutes*
Cooking time: *10 minutes*
Oven: *200°C, 400°F, Gas Mark 6*

1. Cream the sugar and butter in a mixing bowl until light. Beat in the whites one at a time, then fold in the flour.
2. Cover 2 large baking sheets with non-stick silicone paper. Fit a large piping bag with a 1 cm (½ inch) plain nozzle and fill with the mixture. Pipe 5 cm (2 inch) fingers on the paper, leaving enough space between them to allow for spreading.
3. Bake in a preheated oven for 10 minutes. Using a palette knife carefully lift the biscuits off the silicone paper and cool.

Almond and Ginger Tuiles

100 g (4 oz) flaked almonds
25 g (1 oz) preserved ginger, finely diced
20 g (¾ oz) flour
120 g (4½ oz) sugar
25 g (1 oz) butter, melted
2 egg whites
15 g (½ oz) flaked almonds, to decorate

Makes about 24
Preparation time: *15 minutes*
Cooking time: *12 minutes*
Oven: *200°C, 400°F, Gas Mark 6*

1. Mix the flaked almonds, ginger, flour and sugar in a bowl. Beat in the melted butter, then the egg whites. Do not be afraid of breaking up the flaked almonds.
2. Cover 2 large baking sheets with non-stick silicone paper. Arrange teaspoons of the mixture on the paper, about 12 to a sheet. Flatten each little pile with the back of a fork dipped in water and decorate each tuile with the flaked almonds. Bake in a preheated oven for 12 minutes.
3. Remove the baking sheet from the oven and cool for about 30 seconds. Lift the tuiles one by one with a palette knife and shape over a rolling pin until cool. (If the tuiles harden before they are removed from the sheet, return them to the oven to soften for a few seconds.)

Biscuits à la Cuiller

4 eggs, separated
160 g (5½ oz) caster sugar
120 g (4½ oz) plain flour
40 g (1½ oz) icing sugar

Makes about 40
Preparation time: *15 minutes*
Cooking time: *12 minutes*
Oven: *225°C, 425°F, Gas Mark 7*

1. Put the yolks and 140 g (5 oz) of the sugar into a heatproof bowl over a pan of simmering water. Whisk until thick and creamy.
2. Clean the whisk thoroughly, then whisk the egg whites with the remaining caster sugar until very stiff.
3. Remove the yolk and sugar mixture from the heat. Using a metal spoon, fold the flour and 1 tablespoon of the whites into the mixture. Delicately fold in the remaining egg whites.
4. Cover 4 baking sheets with non-stick silicone paper. Fit a large piping bag with a 2 cm (¾ inch) plain nozzle and fill with the mixture. Pipe ten 7.5 cm (3 inch) fingers on to each sheet. Dust with the icing sugar. Bake in a preheated oven for 12 minutes. Bake in two batches.
5. Carefully lift the biscuits from the paper using a palette knife and cool.

Below, top row: Almond and ginger tuiles; *bottom row:* Biscuits à la cuiller
Right, from the top: Hazelnut clusters; Chocolate truffles

Chocolate Truffles

100 g (4 oz) plain chocolate, broken into pieces
90 g ($3\frac{1}{2}$ oz) unsalted butter
20 g ($\frac{3}{4}$ oz) icing sugar
1 egg yolk
$1\frac{1}{2}$ tablespoons dark rum
40 g ($1\frac{1}{2}$ oz) cocoa powder

Makes about 25
Preparation time: *15 minutes, plus cooling*

1. Put the chocolate in a bowl placed over a pan of simmering water and leave the chocolate to melt.
2. Beat the butter, icing sugar, egg yolk and rum into the melted chocolate. Chill in the refrigerator.
3. Fit a piping bag with a 2 cm ($\frac{3}{4}$ inch) plain tube and fill it with the mixture.
4. Pipe 25 pieces of truffle mixture on to a baking sheet. Sprinkle cocoa powder on top and shake the tray until the truffles are well coated.
3. Shape the truffles roughly into balls. Shake them in cocoa powder again and chill until needed.

Hazelnut Clusters

100 g (4 oz) hazelnuts, shelled
50 g (2 oz) sugar
1 tablespoon water

Makes about 20 clusters
Preparation time: *20 minutes*
Cooking time: *7 minutes, plus cooling*
Oven: *190°C, 375°F, Gas Mark 5*

1. Put the hazelnuts on a baking sheet and bake in a preheated oven for 7 minutes. Rub off the skins while still warm.
2. Put the sugar in a pan and add the water. Bring to the boil, stirring until the sugar has dissolved, and boil for 3 minutes.
3. Take the pan off the heat and add the hazelnuts. Stir until a sugary crust forms around each nut.
4. Return the pan to a gentle heat. Continue stirring until the nuts are coated in a golden caramel.
5. Turn the nuts out on to a sheet of non-stick silicone paper.
6. Dip 2 teaspoons in a little salad oil. Working quickly, arrange the nuts in small clusters, with 3 nuts on the base in the form of a triangle and a fourth nut on top.
7. Serve within 8 hours, or the caramel may become sticky.

Chocolate Sauce

25 g (1 oz) unsalted butter
100 g (4 oz) plain chocolate, broken into squares
25 ml (1 fl oz) double cream

Preparation time: *15 minutes*

This sauce must be used immediately or kept warm over a very low heat.

1. Put the butter and chocolate in to a flameproof bowl over a pan of simmering water.
2. When the chocolate has melted, beat in the double cream.

Praline

50 g (2 oz) sugar
50 g (2 oz) whole almonds

Makes 100 g (4 oz)
Preparation time: *15 minutes, plus cooling*
Storage time: *keeps well in a dry sealed container*

1. Put the sugar in a heavy-based pan, moisten with water and boil for 3 minutes. Spoon a little of the sugar into a cup of cold water. It should form a soft ball, when pressed together with the fingers.
2. Add the almonds and remove from the heat. Stir with a wooden spoon until the sugar forms a crust round each nut.
3. Return to the heat. Stirring constantly, cook until the sugar has melted and caramelized. Pour on to an oiled plate or work surface and cool for 30 minutes.
4. Break the praline into pieces and grind to a powder in a blender, grinder or food processor.

Fruit Coulis

juice of ½ lemon
300 g (10 oz) fresh raspberries
75 g (3 oz) caster sugar

Makes about 300 ml (10 fl oz)
Preparation time: *10 minutes*

Frozen fruit may be used, with an extra 25 g (1 oz) caster sugar. Defrost the fruit completely. Blackberries, loganberries and strawberries are also suitable. Blackcurrants, redcurrants and apricots should be stewed first.

1. Pour the lemon juice into a liquidizer. Add the raspberries and blend for 10 seconds only to make a purée.
2. Strain the purée through a sieve into a mixing bowl, leaving the seeds in the sieve.
3. Add the sugar, stirring until completely dissolved.

Butter Cream

4 egg yolks
50 ml (2 fl oz) water
125 g (4½ oz) sugar
pinch of cream of tartar
125 g (4½ oz) unsalted butter, cut into cubes

Preparation time: *15 minutes*
Cooking time: *3–5 minutes*

1. Whisk the yolks in a bowl until they become light and creamy.
2. Put the water, sugar and cream of tartar in a pan. Boil hard for 3 minutes. Spoon a little boiling sugar into a cup of cold water. It should form a soft ball when pressed together with the fingers.
3. Whisk the yolks again, at the same time pouring the sugar into them in a steady stream. Whisk for a further 5 minutes.
4. Beat in the butter a few cubes at a time, and continue beating until the mixture becomes smooth and creamy.

Variations:
Flavour the cream by adding a few drops of essence of your choice, alcohol (e.g. rum, kirsch, whisky) to taste, a tablespoon of coffee dissolved in a little hot water, or 75 g (3 oz) plain chocolate, melted.

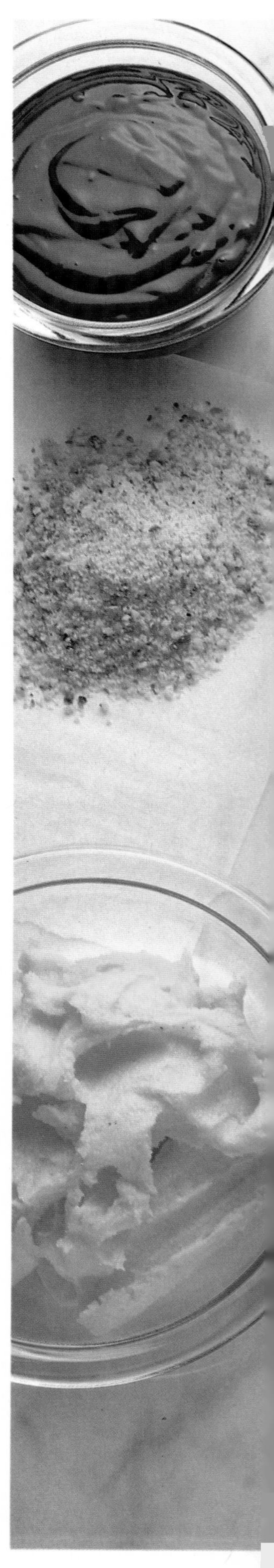

From the top left, clockwise: Chocolate sauce; Fruit coulis; Crème chantilly; Crème anglaise; Crème patissière; Butter cream; Praline

Crème Chantilly

150 ml (5 fl oz) double cream
25 ml (1 fl oz) egg white
25 g (1 oz) caster or vanilla sugar

Preparation time: 10 minutes

1. Put the cream in a mixing bowl, add the egg white and whisk until the cream begins to hold its shape on the whisk.
2. Add the sugar. Whisk until the cream is smooth and holds its shape.

Crème Anglaise

500 ml (17 fl oz) full cream milk
6 egg yolks
125 g (4½ oz) vanilla sugar

Preparation time: *15 minutes*

1. In a bowl, whisk the yolks and sugar until creamy. Gently heat the milk in a saucepan to simmering point, then pour the hot milk over the egg yolk mixture.
2. Pour into the rinsed pan. Heat gently, stirring continuously, until the sauce coats the back of a wooden spoon. The custard will curdle if boiled.
3. Pour into a clean bowl, cover and cool. This custard will keep for 2–3 days.

Crème Pâtissière

2 eggs
75 g (3 oz) vanilla sugar
25 g (1 oz) cornflour
250 ml (8 fl oz) milk

Preparation time: *15 minutes*
Storage time: *5 days in the refrigerator*

1. Whisk the eggs and sugar in a mixing bowl until light and creamy then whisk in the cornflour.
2. Heat the milk to simmering point, then pour over the sugar, egg and flour mixture. Stir well.
3. Return the mixture to the rinsed pan. Stirring constantly, heat until the sauce thickens.
4. Pour into a clean bowl and whisk briefly, then cool. To store, rub the surface with a lump of butter while still hot as this prevents a crust forming. Cover with an airtight lid or clingfilm.

Index

Q

R

S

T

V

W

Y

Z

ACKNOWLEDGEMENTS

Photography: Phillip Dowell; Laurie Evans; Roger Phillips; Charlie Stebbings.
Photographic styling: Liz Allen-Eslor; Antonia Gaunt; Maggi Heinz; Lesley Richardson.
Preparation of food for photography: Elaine Bastable; Emma Codrington; Lisa Collard; Caroline Ellwood; Clare Ferguson; Carol Hockin; Heather Lambert; Stella Murphy; Wendy Sweetser.
The publishers would also like to thank the following companies for the loan of props for photography: Elizabeth David, 46 Bourne Street, London SW1; Divertimenti, 68/72 Marylebone Lane, London W1; Leon Jaeggi & Sons Ltd, 232 Tottenham Court Road, London W1; David Mellor, 4 Sloane Square, London SW1; The Reject Shop, 209 Tottenham Court Road, London W1.